The New Forest: An Ecological History

THE NEW FOREST:

An Ecological History

by

COLIN R. TUBBS

DAVID & CHARLES : NEWTON ABBOT

7153 4383 1

Printed in Great Britain by
Clarke Doble & Brendon Limited Plymouth
for David & Charles (Publishers) Limited
Newton Abbot Devon

Contents

List of Illustrations

All photographs taken by Brian Rozzell

List of Illustrations

FIGURE 1. *Distribution of Iron Age Forts and Romano-British Potteries* (map)

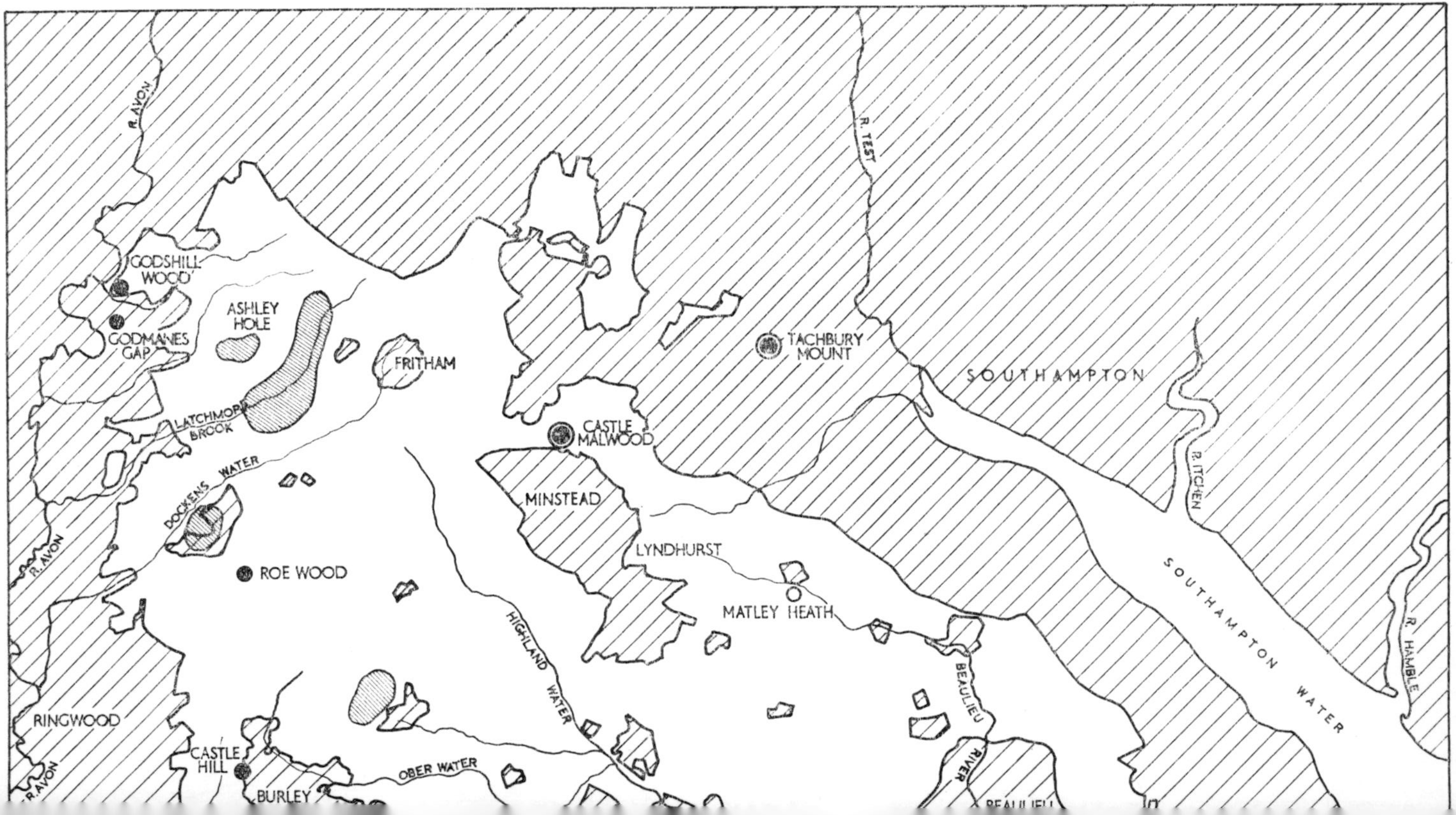

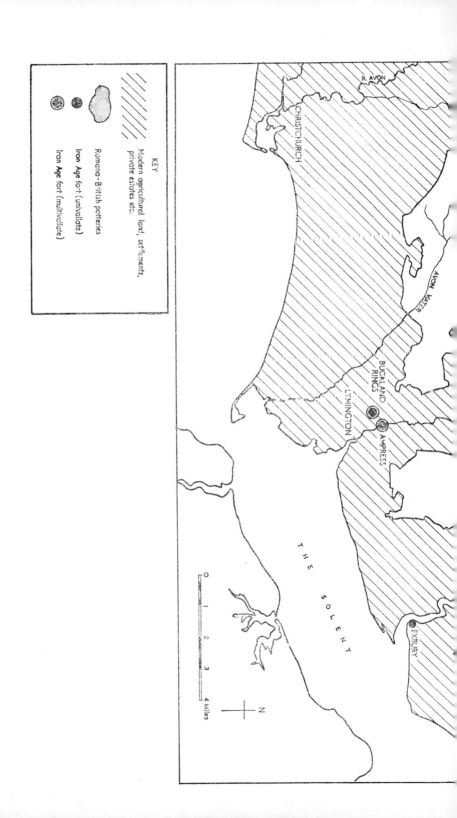

KEY

Modern agricultural land, settlements,
private estates etc.

Romano-British potteries

Iron Age fort (univallate)

Iron Age fort (multivallate)

R. AVON

CHRISTCHURCH

AVON WATER

BUCKLAND RINGS

LYMINGTON

AMPRESS

THE SOLENT

EXBURY

0 1 2 3 4 Miles

N

Introduction

IT is perhaps a matter for surprise that the New Forest, with its
peculiar institutions and agriculture, its outstanding biological
interest and its ease of access, has escaped the close attention of
little more than a handful of historians and field scientists in recent
years. Despite its ready accessibility it has comparatively seldom
been used as a teaching arena. Its unenclosed woodlands and heathlands, however, today comprise the largest single unit of 'semi-
natural' or 'unsown' vegetation remaining in the Lowland zone of
Britain, and for this reason it is unlikely that the neglect of the past
will be long perpetuated. As urban and industrial development and
agricultural reclamation continue to reduce and fragment the ground
available elsewhere for biological, archaeological and other field
studies, so attention is likely to become focused more closely on
the Forest. Such a trend is already discernible.

Although the area has long been recognised as something very
special, the local literature in most fields of study remains thin and
more often than not plagiaristic, 'folksy', or both. The first purpose
of this book, therefore, is to provide an accurate historical and
ecological backcloth to future research, and to present it in a manner
which will also be found acceptable to the layman.

The hypothesis that the landscape of Britain has arisen largely
from Nature's responses to human activity would scarcely be
seriously questioned. It would appear, therefore, that the history
of human land use, management and exploitation, and the economic
factors governing them, forms a coherent framework within which
to describe the development of the range of habitats which comprise
the landscape; for arriving at conclusions about the parts currently
played by biotic and anthropogenic factors in the dynamics of
habitats; for focusing the closest attention on the economic structure of agricultural and other practices from which such factors
arise; and for arriving at conclusions about the history, present
status and future of individual species of our fauna and flora.
Habitats are usually in the process of change, even though such

11

changes may be exceedingly slow and not readily demonstrable visually. The previous history of change is thus important in discerning what processes are at work at the present time, and in deciding precisely how to manage or control them. The first assumption of this book, therefore, is that most of the archaeological, historical and biological information relating to the Forest can be most usefully organised under the heading of ecological history.

I am only too conscious that this account of the Forest's ecological history tends on close examination to reveal almost as many cracks as there is wall. This is perhaps inevitable when so broad a framework is chosen for the study of so comparatively small an area. I can only hope that sufficient attention has been drawn to the cracks to prompt further exploration.

ONE

Man and the Physical Background

IN Britain, and indeed over much if not most of the world, the present vegetation and soils have developed from the interaction of geological and geomorphological factors, climate and the activities of man. In considering the ecological history of the New Forest—and indeed that of any part of this country—it is apparent that man has been the most potent force in the development of the present scene. Since Mesolithic times he has striven with increasing vigour to adapt his environment to his progressively more complex and sophisticated social and economic life. His activities have, at the same time, been constrained by the physical limitations of his environment and thus, his attempts to adapt Nature to his purpose have not always met with conspicuous success. In areas like the New Forest the base-poor quality of the parent materials from which the soils are derived proved a severe restraint to prolonged and intensive agriculture in early times. Man's early activities were largely responsible for further deterioration in soil potential and the onset of widespread heathland conditions. In later times, the peculiar legal status of the area as Royal Forest precluded the more intensive use which would otherwise have been possible with successive agricultural innovations. The purpose in this first chapter is to elaborate upon the physical background of the Forest area and to then outline the interactions between physical elements and the activities of man.

I

Geologically, the New Forest occupies a central position on the Eocene and Oligocene strata lying in the downfold of the chalk known as the Hampshire Basin. These strata—mainly soft sands and clays—are of sedimentary origin and were laid down in a

13

series of cycles of sedimentation during the Tertiary Era. The geological record of this period is complex but, in outline, alternate risings and sinkings in the land surface appear to have taken place during which series of marine, estuarine and fluvatile deposits were left as the sea first invaded the land and later retracted, leaving the work of deposition and re-distribution to rivers and their estuaries or deltas. Each phase of deposition left different types of sediment, the marine, estuarine or fluvatile origins of which may be most readily determined from their associated fossil remains of contemporary forms of life. The present site of the Hampshire Basin during this long period of geographical flux formed part of an extensive area of deposition known as the Anglo-Franco-Belgian Basin. Subsequent folding of the earth's surface, together with widespread denudation, however, have left only relics of the consolidated Tertiary formations, mainly in hollows represented in Britain today by the Hampshire Basin and Thames Basin. Because of the dip in the strata produced by folding, the older deposits are now exposed at the margins of the Basins, whilst the exposures become progressively younger towards their centres. In the New Forest sector of the Hampshire Basin, the sequence runs more simply from the oldest in the north to the youngest in the south.

Of the two earliest Eocene formations, the Reading Beds were mainly of freshwater origin and the immediately overlying London Clays appear to be entirely of marine origin. Both strata are now exposed as narrow belts (the London Clay about twice the width of the Reading Beds) at the margin of the chalk. Neither are now represented in the New Forest, although they outcrop immediately to its north. Next follow the Bagshot Beds, exposed in the extreme north of the New Forest as poor sands of fluvatile origin; and then the Bracklesham Beds, partly of marine and partly of fluvatile origin, the former yielding some fossil-rich and relatively bas-enriched glauconitic clays. The Barton Sands and Barton Clays follow next in the sequence, and are largely of marine origin. The Bracklesham and Barton Beds are exposed over a broad, central belt of the Forest.

Overlying the Eocene deposits are those of the succeeding Oligocene period. Of the four divisions recognised—the Headon, Osborne, Bembridge and Hamstead Beds—only the Headon Beds are represented in the New Forest. The Headon Beds exhibit great variety of texture and origin and appear to be the relics of very

14

varied contemporary conditions—freshwater lakes, brackish lagoons, estuaries and shallow seas. They occur mainly as loams, clays and clay marls—the last formerly of great agricultural importance in the area in historical times—and extend across the south of the Forest, although large tracts are covered by spreads of gravel deposited long after the Tertiary Era.

Superficial deposits of gravel, consisting of subangular flints and flint pebble, overlay large areas of the solid formations in the New Forest, forming caps of irregular but comparatively inconsiderable thickness over plateaux at heights varying from around 400 ft to less than 100 ft. The higher of these Plateau Gravels pre-date the lower-lying spreads (such as those overlying the Headon Beds), and the latter, like the Valley Gravels which occur as terraces along existing river valleys (such as those of the Test and Avon) were probably derived from the destruction of the higher series. Thus the higher level gravels in the New Forest have a fragmentary distribution along ridges between which erosion has re-exposed the solid strata to produce wide valleys. The Plateau Gravels almost certainly date from the Pleistocene, during which much of Britain was undergoing glaciation, and the rivers which produced them must have been of immensely greater volume than those of today.

Both Plateau and Valley Gravels are today of considerable economic significance. The latter are typically of a quality suitable for washing (Valley Gravels 'work wet') and grading to produce concreting aggregates. The Plateau Gravels usually contain a good deal of clay and also 'work dry', and, in the absence of water for washing, are used for the sub-base layers of roads and for drives, footpaths and similar purposes. The Plateau Gravels of the New Forest were worked more or less casually in the nineteenth century and probably before. Recent decades, however, have witnessed an almost phenomenal increase in demand for gravel throughout the country and a number of excavations have been opened on the plateau of the western fringe of the Forest, notably on the privately owned heaths of Rockford Common, Ibsley Common and Gorley Hill. Although the depth of the gravels rarely exceeds about thirty feet and is more often much less, excavation often involves the barbaric mutilation of open heathland scenery, which inevitably brings into conflict the requirements of industry and amenity and poses difficult problems of restoration.

Although no sheet-ice extended as far south as the New Forest during the Glacial period, clearly it was subject to periglacial conditions. Many soil profiles, particularly on the Plateau Gravels, exhibit a distribution of material in great whirls and loops, evidently an effect of solifluction. In the working face of a gravel excavation on Rockford Common, on the western edge of the Forest, these features extended to a depth of fifteen or twenty ft and give some idea of the grip which the ice must at times have had on the land. At other sites on the lower terraces in the south of the Forest, a rippled effect over the ground surface is visible and this, though not yet closely investigated, may have at least a superficial similarity for, for example, the 'stone stripes' of Breckland, which originated in the lateral sorting of clay and flints under periglacial conditions.[1] The Breckland features, like those of the Forest, at first sight closely resemble the ridge-and-furrow of early ploughing, the ridges being colonised by heather and the furrows by grasses.

The movement of material since deposition has not been confined to re-distribution in the profile associated with the action of ice. There has clearly also been a good deal of surface movement on slopes which may be as slight as about three degrees, and considerable infilling of valley floors. Thus a soil is not necessarily derived entirely from the solid formation beneath it but may be, as it were, 'two-storied'. The transported material is usually sand or loam, often with an admixture of gravel, and where it overlies clay it gives rise to a distinctive profile, the impervious sub-soil resulting in a 'perched' water table and the upper horizons being mottled by gleying and generally extremely acid.

From the ecological standpoint the geological history of the New Forest is not so important as the texture of the parent materials. This may vary considerably from area to area in what may be stratigraphically the same deposit, and would seem to be the most important single factor in determining relative soil fertility. The coarser the material the more prone it is to the degrading effects of leaching. Taken by and large, the parent materials of marine origin offer the better soils but the whole series, with the exception of the clay marls of the Headon Beds, tend to develop intrinsically base-poor soils. A further generalisation can be made about the actual distribution of the better soils. Owing to the later deposition of the more base-enriched material and the steeper dip in the strata as compared to the gradient of the land surface from north to south, there is an overall tendency for the environment as a whole to

Page 17: The open forest looking west across self-sown Scots pine in Alderhill Bot om (NGR SU20/13)

Page 18: The dissected plateau, extreme north of Forest, Long Bottom (NGR SU19/14) in foreground. 'Slumping' at junction of permeable and impermeable material on right

become progressively more base-deficient as one proceeds north-ward. This has, among other things, resulted in a tendency for past agricultural reclamations to be concentrated in the south of the Forest, and is reflected also in the greater diversity of the flora of the southern heaths and bogs.

A further general ecological feature of the New Forest may be appropriately introduced at this stage—the mildness of its modern climate. Only a very small proportion of the total pre-cipitation falls as snow and daily maximum temperatures from December to February normally average around 40 degrees Fahrenheit. Summers are warm and there is a tendency for the annual average of 30–35 in of rainfall to be well distributed over the year. The heathland areas of Dorset, which are really a west-ward extension of the New Forest, are subject to an even milder, though rather wetter winter, which is reflected in the better repre-sentation of 'mediterranean' and 'oceanic' elements in their flora and fauna—for example the Dorset heath (*Erica ciliaris*). The Dorset heathlands deserve further comparison in that their soils are, as a whole, considerably more impoverished than those of the New Forest, with acid tolerant heather dominant over most of their extent—a reflection of the acutely impoverished nature of the Bagshot Sands on which they largely lie.

II

Geomorphologically, the New Forest consists of a series of eroded benches or plateaux, at their greatest height in the extreme north, where they reach a maximum of 418 ft above Ordnance datum at Telegraph Post, and least high in the extreme south where they are less than 200 ft above Ordnance datum. In the north, stream erosion has left little more than a series of high ridges separated by wide, fairly steep-sided and almost U-shaped valleys. In the south and east of the Forest, where the plateaux are mostly at elevations of 50–150 ft, with a gentle slope towards the Solent, they are less fragmented by their drainage systems and generally form expansive, undulating plains. Many of the valleys here carry deep accumula-tions of peat. Between the northern, higher ridges, and the wide plains of the south, the Lymington River drains an extensive shallow basin into which project ridges from the higher ground. Over the greater part of the Forest the drainage is southward into

19

the Solent from three main catchment areas, the main streams of each of which are the Beaulieu River, the Lymington River (or Highland Water as its upper reaches are known) and the Avon Water. In the north and west of the Forest a series of more or less parallel streams drain south-west into the River Avon; and the north-east side of the Forest is drained eastward into the River Test by the Cadnam River and Bartley Water. These three drainage areas are separated by a high dog-leg watershed capped with gravel.

The catchment area of the Lymington River, together with the higher ground which separates it from that of the Beaulieu River, today carries the most extensive tract of woodland in the New Forest. Two hundred years ago this woodland area, which occupies a roughly central position in the Forest, could have been described as a mosaic of deciduous woodland, irregular glades and extensive 'lawns' (as the areas of sweet grasses are known locally). Subsequent enclosure and planting, initially mainly of oak (*Quercus spp.*), latterly partly of conifer, has obscured much of this picture, although it is still discernible in places today—notably in a zone extending along the Highland Water. The entire woodland area is for the most part closely circumscribed by the limits of the Headon Beds and Barton Clays, although it is true that in places it overlaps on to the adjacent Barton Sands, and occasionally on to the Plateau Gravels.

The Plains to the south and south-west of the central woodlands are now for the most part treeless. These today exhibit a complex mosaic of vegetation. The loams and clays of the Headon Beds usually carry grassland, dominated by bristle bent (*Agrostis setacea*) and colonised by bracken (*Pteridium aquilinum*) and gorse (*Ulex europaeus*), whilst the more impoverished soils—sands, gravels and base-poor clays—are dominated by heather (*Calluna vulgaris*).

To the north of the central woodlands, the Highland Water and its two main tributaries, Ober Water and Bratley Water, thrust deep, wide valleys into the high ground of the main Forest watershed. Here, the succeeding changes in parent material and soil, modified by the 'flush' effects in the valley bottoms, are reflected in clearly discernible changes in vegetation; from heather moor on the leached soils of the plateaux and the Barton Sands exposed immediately below them; through acid grassland associated with bracken and gorse on the Barton Clays of the lower valley slopes; to bog or, where alluvium has accumulated, to streamside lawn, in the valley floor. Much of this area—both plateaux and valley slope—can be shown to have carried woodland in comparatively recent times. Scattered hollys (*Ilex aquifolium*) and oaks and the remains of woodland flora on the heaths, further testify to the previously more wooded nature of the area, whilst there remain a few stands of big timber—notably Ridley and Bratley Woods.

The Beaulieu River drains a complex of heathlands, mainly on Barton Sands, lying to the east of the central woodlands. Gravels overlay the higher heathlands, whilst there are gravel deposits in the shallow valley of the Beaulieu River itself. In general both the plateau gravels and the Barton Sands are strongly leached and dominated by heather. Most of the small scattered areas of woodland—for example Pig Bush, King's Hat Inclosure, Foxhunting Inclosure and Crab Hat Inclosure—occur on isolated exposures of the Headon Beds. The extensive valley bogs in the area carry deep accumulations of peat, all of which have been worked extensively in the historically recent past. Peat workings show clearly on aerial photographs. The Beaulieu River has left a wide deposit of alluvial material along its valley, which is characterised by a stream-side belt of deciduous woodland, alternating with extensive 'lawns' which show up as bright green ribbons against the darker heather of the adjacent heathland. Matley Bog, Denny Bog, and three short lateral bogs draining into the Beaulieu River off Matley Heath, exhibit classic alder carr development with flanking zones of bog and wet heath.

The Avon Water drains an area in the extreme south-west of the Forest. Running throughout its course on Headon Beds, it receives notably more base-rich water than most Forest streams, and probably for this reason its valley bogs and flanking grasslands are characterised by a notably rich flora. Again, the aerial photographs show the remains of formerly extensive peat workings in the valley.

The expanse of Forest drained by the Millersford Brook, Black Gutter, the Latchmore Brook, the Dockens Water and the Linford Brook—the northernmost of the water courses draining west into the River Avon—embraces the largest area of the Forest undissected by main roads or lanes; at the same time it has a spaciousness in many respects comparable to that of the higher moorlands of Exmoor and Dartmoor. The streams today are of no great

volume, but their forerunners have bitten deeply into the Bracklesham and Bagshot Beds underlying the Plateau Gravels. The
northernmost of the streams—Millersford Brook and Black Gutter
—run in valleys lying between ridges which remain consistently
above 300 ft Ordnance datum, the valley bottoms lying 100–150 ft
below. Working south, the Latchmore Brook and Dockens Water
valleys are comparatively wide—at Latchmore Bottom, about a
mile from ridge to ridge—and the intervening plateau has in parts
been reduced to low, undulating heathland; Barton Clays and
Bracklesham Beds are successively exposed along the flanks of both
valleys. Further south still, the valleys of the Linford Brook and
Foulford Bottom are occupied by exposures of Barton Clay, with
Barton Sands outcropping on the extreme upper slopes immediately
below the Plateau Gravel.

Except where plantations have obscured the patterns of the
vegetation, the valley slopes of these streams present a mosaic of
wet heath, acid grassland—usually associated with bracken and
gorse—and relict woodland, whilst the plateaux are dominated
uniformly by heather. Almost all the valley slopes exhibit in some
degree the sudden breaks in slope caused by seepage at the junction
of permeable with impermeable material—often the junction of the
plateau gravels with clay—below which wet heath and bog conditions appear to have encouraged the 'slumping' of the valley slope.
Streamside lawns on alluvial deposits are a recurring feature of the
valley floors in their lower reaches, whilst in the upper reaches
bog, associated with an inconsiderable depth of peat, is more usual.

It seems probable, and in many cases it can be demonstrated,
that the little-leached soils of the valley slopes have in the not
very distant past carried more extensive woodland. Indeed, such
sites were chosen for the re-establishment of woodland by planting
during the past 250 years. Pitts Wood Inclosure, in a tributary
valley of Black Gutter; Sloden, Alder Hill, Amberwood, and Islands
Thorns Inclosures, in the Latchmore Brook valley; South and North
Bentley, Holly Hatch, and Broomy Inclosures, on the south slopes
of the Dockens Water valley; and Great and Little Linford, Roe
Wood, and Milkham Inclosures, in the Linford Brook valley, all
occupy valley slope sites. Probably a reasonable idea of the kind
of woodland which may have occupied the valley slopes before
enclosure is given by the existing unenclosed woodland on the
slopes of the Latchmore Brook and Dockens Water valleys above

the present limits of the statutory Inclosures, and by the woodland on the slopes of the valley above Pitts Wood Inclosure. At the latter site, 'holms' of holly, whitebeam (*Sorbus aria*), and oak, with some admixture of yew (*Taxus baccata*) and other species, occur on patches of better drained soil among wet heath a little below the break in slope at the junction of the gravels with clay. At the former sites, extensive woodlands of holly, whitebeam, hawthorn (*Crataegus monogyna*), rowan (*Sorbus aucuparia*), yew and oak extend along the valley slopes, mainly occupying a zone along which the Barton Clay outcrops, but also extending up on to the plateau gravels and down the slope on to the Brackleshams. At some points—Anses Wood and High Corner Wood, on the slopes of the Dockens Water valley, Fritham Wood, Eyeworth Wood, and Studley Wood in the Latchmore valley—beech (*Fagus sylvatica*), and oak woodland replaces the mixed 'holms', but there is some possibility that the species structure of these particular sites has origins in silvicultural management.

The relics of formerly more extensive woodland on the plateau gravels occur in several localities, all of which can be shown to have been more heavily wooded as recently as the late eighteenth century. Other areas exhibit recent colonisation by holly, both on the clays of the valley slopes and the leached soils of the plateaux. It is, further, of interest that in the north and west of the Forest, cultivation has advanced on to the Forest along the valley slopes—on the better soils—leaving the plateaux to the wilderness.

The drainage systems of Vales and Cranes Moor, the southern-most of those which lead into the River Avon, exhibit some physical differences from the more northerly valleys. The uppermost stretch of the system does indeed have similar characteristics, but the well-defined valley falls into a wide, low-lying basin, dominated by heather moor on very impoverished Barton Sand and exhibiting widespread colonisation by scots pine (*Pinus sylvestris*). The water-courses contain extensive peat deposits, which, like most others in the Forest, have been exploited in recent centuries. The area is reputedly exceptionally poor as grazing. It carries neither areas of grassland, nor, in contrast to most other districts of the Forest, is there any evidence for the relatively recent presence of deciduous woodland.

The catchment area of the streams which find their way into the River Test, which lies to the east of the Forest, comprise a pre-

Years	Climate	Human Cultures	Vegetation
1000 AD	Sub-Atlantic (cool and wet)	'Historical'	woodland clearance by man
BC 500	Rapid deterioration	Romano-British	
		Iron Age	spread of heathland
1000	Sub-Boreal (warm and dry)	Bronze Age	
2000			general reduction in species—diversity of woodland
3000		Neolithic	
4000	Atlantic (warm and damp)		maximum woodland cover (oak, alder, hazel, lime, elm)
5000		Mesolithic	
6000	Boreal (ameliorating)		pine-birch woodland; hazel and oak becoming prominent towards end of period
7000	Pre-Boreal (Sub-Arctic)		
8000			spread of birch woodland

TABLE I. *Generalised Post-Glacial Chronology in England and Wales*

dominantly wooded zone extending in a broad belt across the north-east of the Forest, together with the nearby National Trust commons added to the Forest by the New Forest Act 1964. The tract of woodland here lies almost entirely on Barton Clays, although sections of woodland occur also on the glauconitic clays of the Bracklesham Beds. The unenclosed woodland is largely of beech and oak fringed by areas of holly, whitebeam, rowan and hawthorn, and interspersed with clearings and glades which in some cases have been colonised by birch (*Betula spp.*). A belt of agricultural holdings, comprising the scattered villages of the Bramshaw area, separates these woodlands from the heaths of the National Trust commons, which lie almost entirely on poor Bagshot Sands.

The distribution of the lands in the Forest which have been brought into cultivation and have remained in cultivation to the present day, understandably appears to be largely governed by the distribution of the intrinsically better, that is the least base-deficient, parent materials, and possibly also to some extent by the relative proximity of the clay marls of the Headon Beds used for treating the land. Thus, in the south of the Forest, extensive areas of the plains lying on the Headon Beds have in the course of the centuries come into cultivation—the estates of the Cistercian monks at Beaulieu lay entirely on Headons. Similarly the manors of Brockenhurst and Lyndhurst—the latter the administrative 'capital' of the Forest for some centuries and today the headquarters of the Forestry Commission—lay at least partly on Headon outcrops, Minstead and Bramshaw on Barton clays. An examination in detail of the distribution of the enclosed agricultural lands shows that, with a few exceptions of limited areas, the base-poor, permeable sands were avoided: often an isolated smallholding will be found to sit neatly on a small exposure of Barton or Headon clay on the geological map.

III

Impoverished soils carrying heather and acid-tolerant grassland are today a major feature of the New Forest. It is apparent, however, that these are not primary conditions. The presence of widespread relics of former agriculture on the heaths alone suggests that they were once more productive than now. Analyses of the stratified pollen preserved in the peat accumulated in bogs on heathland in Britain and elsewhere have shown that the heaths arose as a secondary condition to an early woodland cover. Soil pollen analyses from New Forest sites (discussed in chapter three) have offered local confirmation of this. It has been convincingly demonstrated[2] that the vegetative succession has been accompanied by considerable soil degradation, and that man was the motivating force in the whole process.

With the retreat of the ice from northern Europe some 8,000 years ago, an ameliorating climate was accompanied by the spread of woodland. Contemporary man, represented by the Mesolithic cultures, lived in what was essentially an afforested environment. The evidence for his impact on the woodland is at best fragmentary and inferential. Mesolithic man was a hunter and food-gatherer, and the only way in which the small human population would have been likely to cause widespread modification of the environment would have been through the use of fire, perhaps to drive game. If some deforestation took place during Mesolithic times—and there is some suggestion of this, for example on Dartmoor[3]—it commenced in earnest during the succeeding Neolithic period (c 3200–1800 BC in Britain), which saw the advent of more or less settled forms of agriculture. By the time of the last Neolithic cultures, agricultural systems based on cereal cultivation, domesticated livestock, or both, were widespread throughout Europe. During the succeeding Bronze Age (c 1800–500 BC in Britain) and Iron Age (500 BC–AD 43) and during the Roman occupation (AD 43–c 410), farming methods in this country became progressively more sophisticated and the human population increased in size. Agriculture, albeit often a shifting form of agriculture, required the clearance of the woodland, whether for growing crops or rearing livestock. In many cases pastoral land uses would follow naturally on arable production. Land cleared and cropped persistently by the primitive techniques available would lose nutrient status to the point where cultivation was no longer worthwhile. It would then be used as grazing grounds. On much of the more base-deficient soils of northern Europe woodland clearance, and the subsequent failure to compensate adequately the soil for the decline in base status due to leaching and agricultural exploitation, led to the development of heathland and moorland conditions.

In Upland Britain the clearance of the woodland appears to have been widespread in Neolithic times. In the New Forest, in common with most other areas in Lowland Britain where heathland developed, the first significant woodland clearances seem to have occurred somewhat later, during the Bronze Age. There is, indeed, little evidence to show that Neolithic man settled in the area.

Efforts to relate the reduction in the woodland and the onset of soil deterioration with changes in climate—and particularly with the climate deterioration which occurred about 500 BC, when conditions became markedly cooler and wetter—are generally unsatisfactory. It is, however, conceivable that increased rainfall accelerated leaching in soils already cleared of their tree cover and thus contributed to their impoverishment.

In the New Forest, the progressive reduction of the woodland area and the extension of heathland has continued into modern times, although the process was retarded after the eleventh century, when the area became subject to the restrictions and controls over land use which designation as a Royal Forest implied. The later vegetation history is intimately associated with its legal status and management as Royal Forest. This at the same time severely limited reclamation: much more of the unenclosed commons would undoubtedly otherwise have been enclosed for agriculture as the techniques for reclaiming the poor soils improved in recent centuries. Today (and indeed since the early nineteenth century), it is technically feasible to reclaim even the most impoverished of the heathland soils.

In amplification of the broad outlines traced here, it is intended in chapter two to describe what is known or can be inferred of the periodicity and distribution of human settlement and land use; and in the succeeding chapter to elaborate upon its ecological consequences. In succeeding chapters attention is focused in more detail on the complex ecological history of the Forest during the recent centuries for which documentary evidence is available to lend weight to field investigation and archaeological evidence.

References

1 see A. S. Watt, 'Stone Stripes in Breckland, Norfolk', *Geological Magazine*, XCII, 2, 1955.
2 see esp G. W. Dimbleby, 'The development of British Heathlands and their soils', *Oxford Forestry Memoir, No 23*, 1962.
3 I. G. Simmons, 'An Ecological History of Dartmoor', *Dartmoor Essays*, Devonshire Soc for the Advancement of Science, Literature and Art, 1964, pp 191-215.

TWO

The Pattern of Settlement

DOMESDAY BOOK provides the earliest evidence from which it is possible to reconstruct a reasonably accurate picture of the size, distribution and land uses of the human population of the Forest area at a particular time. The evidence for man's activities in earlier periods is derived mainly from the earthworks and other traces which he left on the ground. Until recently, most archaeologists who devoted any attention to the New Forest were preoccupied mainly with the investigation of its more readily recognisable and datable features such as barrows and kiln sites and, valuable though such research has been, it has tended to divert attention from the broader picture of land use. In particular, the possibility of early farming activity received little attention, perhaps because of a belief that the poor soils of the area could never have supported primitive agriculture. Certainly Heywood Sumner, the Forest archaeologist of the twenties and thirties, suggested this and, in an unconvincing attempt to reconcile the presence of numerous Bronze Age barrows on the southern heaths with the poor quality of the soil, hypothesised that since the land was then higher in relation to the sea, farming was practised on the dry bed of the Solent and the heaths reserved for the burial of the dead.[1] Apart from the doubts which might be cast on the agricultural potential of the Solent, it is now clear that considerable soil degradation has taken place on the heathland areas since Bronze Age times.

Heywood Sumner's work deserves more than a passing reference. Sumner lived at Gorley on the fringe of the Forest, and besides carrying out a number of valuable excavations of Bronze Age barrows and Romano-British pottery kilns, he spent much of his time walking the Forest and recording with painstaking accuracy the earthworks which he found, most of them hitherto unknown. His books,[2] illustrated by his own distinctive and precise hand, are classics of their kind. They record, perhaps, the first serious excursion into what has since become known as field archaeology.

During the two decades before the 1960s, little was added to Sumner's work. Indeed, apart from the excavation of a number of barrows due to be destroyed during airfield construction during the Second World War,[3] and the excavation of another barrow in the late 1950s,[4] the Forest would seem archaeologically to have been virtually untrodden ground. During the period between 1961 and 1966, however, renewed field investigation, mainly by A. H. Pasmore, E. L. Jones and myself, revealed a large number of abandoned enclosures and systems of fields, none of which had previously been recorded, at least in print. These included many small fields on the fringe of the Crown lands, which were subsequently shown to be encroachments made and abandoned early in the nineteenth century. Of the remainder, many are almost certainly medieval, whilst others can be shown to be of much earlier origin. Few, however, exhibit readily discernible common features from which it might be possible to deduce their origin; and habitation sites—which might repay excavation—have not so far been satisfactorily identified. The composition of the pollen preserved in soils buried beneath an earthwork can be used to deduce its approximate age (see chapter three) and, in the absence of adequate archaeological or documentary dating evidence, soil pollen analysis has been a useful instrument of investigation.[5]

The intention in this chapter is first to attempt to deduce the pattern of human settlement and land use before the eleventh century, in so far as this is allowed by the archaeological evidence; and second to trace the development of the land use pattern which arose within the Royal Forest of medieval and recent times.

I

If the known relics of post-glacial human occupation of the areas which are now heathland in Lowland Britain are plotted on maps, they reveal a recurring pattern.

Mesolithic sites on heathland areas are widespread and it must be remembered that because Mesolithic man left few obvious traces on the ground—he built no barrows nor did he cultivate land—his relics would probably be under-represented. Evidence suggesting Neolithic settlement on heathland in Britain is, on the other hand, exceedingly rare, though the not infrequent finds of Neolithic arrowheads does suggest that such areas were hunted, perhaps on a fairly large scale, when one considers the weight of chance against isolated finds of this sort coming to light. In contrast, there is abundant evidence for the occupation of the heathland areas in the Middle and Late Bronze Age, and pollen analysis of soils buried beneath Bronze Age round barrows on the Lowland Heaths suggests that cultivation, perhaps a form of shifting cultivation, was practised—although how extensively is not clear, since the analyses relate only to the sites of the barrows and their immediate environs.

The archaeological evidence for Iron Age occupation of the heaths is sparse compared with that for the Middle and Late Bronze Age. The signs of Bronze Age occupation and the subsequent desertion of these areas in itself suggests the introduction of some factor inhibiting agriculture and it seems likely that the scant evidence of Iron Age occupation reflects the general abandonment of the heaths because their fertility had dropped to a point where cultivation was no longer possible by the techniques available. It seems unlikely that cultivation alone had been widespread enough to have brought about unaided a decline in fertility over such extensive areas. The root cause was more probably the progressive destruction of the primary woodland cover—which almost certainly commenced well before the Bronze Age. Neolithic man may not have settled on the heaths, but he probably hunted them and his influence may have been greater than the direct evidence allows. It has been suggested that the North American Indian increased the buffalo herds by increasing the area of grazing ground[6] and in much the same way Neolithic (and probably Mesolithic) man may have increased his game supply by forest clearance, probably using fire. Large scale forest clearance by fire was not unknown in historic times in this country. Clearance of the woodland would itself lead to soil deterioration which would ultimately render the heaths unsuitable for other than pastoral uses. Thus, the Bronze Age peoples probably settled in areas at least partially cleared of their woodland, on sites whose soils were already starting to deteriorate.

After Iron Age times and until comparatively recently, heathland areas in general have been regarded as the waste, suitable for free-range pastoral uses but only cultivable under great economic incentive. By no means all of the New Forest lies on impoverished heathland soils, and the modern pattern of settlement probably had its origins in the establishment of communities on the better sites in Saxon times and before, leaving the greater part of the area to be exploited for its limited grazing, its remaining timber and its other natural resources: peat turf for fuel, bracken for bedding and litter. Only within the past two centuries have the techniques been available and the economic incentives strong enough to prompt the widespread reclamation of heathlands and this, in the Forest, has been largely precluded by the peculiar legal position.

The pattern of early settlement in the New Forest and its environs conforms broadly with that described for the Lowland Heaths as a whole. Mesolithic finds have been widespread, but not suggestive of any large concentration of population. There is no evidence of Neolithic settlement, though periodic finds of isolated axeheads support the suggestion that the area was hunted. Hengistbury Head, on the south side of Christchurch Harbour, the estuary of the rivers Stour and Avon, would first seem to have achieved prominence as a port during the Neolithic period, but the route inland from there to the centres of population on the Wessex chalk apparently avoided the Forest: the river valleys themselves may have formed a natural link with the hinterland.

The most conspicuous and widespread relics of prehistoric man in the New Forest and elsewhere on the Tertiary deposits of the Hampshire Basin are the burial mounds, or barrows, left by the Bronze Age cultures. Some 176 round barrows have been recorded in the Forest by the Archaeology Division, Ordnance Survey, and this list is by no means exhaustive. Heywood Sumner, in the late 1930s recorded a further 133 on the heaths around Bournemouth,[1] whilst until fairly recently there was a comparable number on the heathlands surrounding Poole Harbour. Large numbers of these, however, have now been destroyed by the expanding zone of urban development and light industry round Bournemouth and Poole. Of the 176 barrows recorded in the Forest by the Ordnance Survey, no less than 102 had been mutilated in some way. A large number were opened by nineteenth century excavators who either left an inadequate record of their work or, more often, failed to leave a record at all. Most of those barrows which have been dated by excavation, have been assigned to the later Bronze Age cultures, when cremation was the more usual rite. Only two of the fifteen excavated in 1941-42 contained mortuary chambers suggesting an early Bronze Age origin.

Whilst the barrows themselves can yield comparatively little evidence of prevailing land use, analysis of the pollen preserved in the soil surfaces buried beneath them can provide some useful indications. Only one such analysis is available from the New Forest. Pollen analysis of the soil buried beneath a barrow near Berry Wood (su212052) which was excavated in the late 1950s and yielded cremation urns of the Late Bronze Age, suggested that the structure was erected on or very close to agricultural land, possibly recently abandoned.[7]

This conforms well with similar evidence from heathlands elsewhere. Some further suggestion of prehistoric land use may be sought from features other than barrows. Fieldwork since 1961, based partly on a study of aerial photographs, has revealed some twenty-five comparatively extensive banked and ditched fields, or systems of fields, and a further twenty small isolated enclosures or pounds. The twenty-five more extensive fields or systems of fields exhibit no recurring pattern in their layout and though at least three may be comparable to the more familiar 'Celtic' fields of the Wessex chalk and elsewhere, others suggest either extensive pastoral enclosures or a series of large arable fields. At most sites the layout of the system is now incomplete, and many sections of bank are missing. Many sites are probably—and in some cases can be shown to be—of medieval origin. Others, however, date from earlier periods. For one site, an extensive enclosure on Beaulieu Heath (su414054) there is archaeological evidence to suggest a prehistoric date. In 1963, when the site was being sub-soiled prior to planting by the Forestry Commission, small pieces of Bronze Age or early Iron Age pottery were recovered from its ditch.

The assignment of prehistoric dates to the other three sites depends on pollen analyses of the soils buried beneath their banks. In 1964 pollen analyses of buried soils from six of the total of forty-five sites were carried out by Professor G. W. Dimbleby. Three sites were assigned a probably medieval date. A small enclosure on Hatchet Moor (sz355994), however, was estimated to be of Bronze Age date, whilst two others were assigned a probable Iron Age origin. Of these two latter sites, one (near Pilley, sz344994) comprised a number of small fields not unlike a 'Celtic' field system; the bank sampled at the other was one of a number of much wasted fragments forming the now incomplete enclosure of an extensive tract of heathland in the south-west corner of the Forest (sz208998).

These results suggest that the relicts of prehistoric agriculture—whether arable or pastoral—in the Forest may be more widespread than has hitherto been assumed. The assignment, however tentative, of Iron Age dates to two of the sites is especially interesting in view of the paucity of the Iron Age record in this kind of environment.

Leaving aside the possibility of more conclusively assigning enclosures and field systems in the Forest to the Iron Age, the only monuments of the period in the area would appear to be a number of hill forts, a single small barrow on Hatchet Moor and what was described by Sumner[2] as a pastoral enclosure on Gorley Hill (SU165112). Sumner excavated the last site and dated it from pottery as Late Iron Age. The site has now unfortunately been destroyed by gravel extraction. The Hatchet Moor Barrow was excavated in 1941–42. Barrow burial was exceptional in the Iron Age, and the Hatchet Moor barrow is of particular archaeological interest in having yielded the remains of what appeared to be the first Iron Age cart burial recorded in this country. Of the hill forts, four (Castle Hill, Burley, SU198040; Roe Wood, SU199089; Malwood Castle, SU279120; and Tachbury Mount, SU330145) occupy positions on the main Forest watersheds. Two (Godmanscap, SU168152 and Goshill Wood, SU166161) commanded the Avon valley; two more (Buckland Rings, SZ315968 and Ampress, SZ324968) commanded the upper estuary of the Lymington River; and another at Exbury (SZ419987) commanded the estuary of the Beaulieu River. A circular earthwork, resembling a small univallate Iron Age fort, built on Matley Heath beside the Beaulieu River (SU336086)—not a readily defendable position—has also been tentatively assigned to the Iron Age.

Hill forts appear mainly to have served the defensive requirements of local populations and their size and distribution may perhaps form some rough guide to the pattern of larger settlements in the four or five centuries before the Claudian invasion of AD 43/5. With the exception of Buckland Rings, the forts of the Forest area are small and thinly distributed compared to those of the Wessex chalk. Only four occupy positions in the hinterland of the Forest, and of these, three are univallate, connoting an early date. Their distribution (see figure 1) may reflect the consolidation of the main centres of population on the better soils after the more widespread settlement—albeit perhaps a shifting settlement based on pastoralism—of the Bronze Age.

One further group of archaeological features offer evidence of prehistoric man. In recent years some thirty 'boiling mounds' have come to light, widely distributed about the Forest. These are normally small crescent or kidney shaped mounds of calcined, fractured flints, invariably situated beside a stream or other natural water supply. Boiling mounds are now widely accepted as the sites of cooking hearths, the food evidently being placed in containers of water, the temperature of which was raised and maintained by casting in fire-heated flints. The fracture patterns and colour of the flints comprising the mounds is consistent with heating followed by rapid cooling by immersion in water and the shape of the mounds is suggestive of distribution around a hearth. The practicability of cooking by this method has apparently been satisfactorily confirmed by experiment. A boiling mound in Millersford Bottom (SU208173), excavated by the New Forest Section of the Hampshire Field Club in 1967, yielded Bronze Age pottery[8] and it is possible that the distribution of boiling mounds in the Forest provides some further indication of the widespread nature of land use in Bronze Age times.

Known traces of settlement in the Forest during the Romano-British period are confined to an extensive pottery industry, the location and extent of which is indicated approximately in figure 1. The industry may have been served by a road leading ultimately to Winchester, but both this and a second 'road' taking a line parallel to Southampton Water from Totton to Lepe are of doubtful authenticity. The pottery industry prospered mainly in the valleys of the Latchmore Brook, Dockens Water and in Ashley Hole, in the north of the Forest, with an outlier near the present settlement of Burley. Probably less than thirty kilns or groups of kilns have been identified, but the quantity of pottery occurring on the surface in the valleys upon which the industry was centred suggest that many more remain to be found. A number of excavations of kiln sites were carried out by Heywood Sumner in the early decades of this century.[9] More recently, three kilns were excavated by Miss E. M. Collinson in 1955,[10] and a further two by Mrs V. Swann on behalf of the Ministry of Works in 1966. The potteries were probably in production mainly during the third and fourth centuries AD, although in the absence of a more systematic study precise dating of their products is difficult. There is no real indication of the size of the industry at any one time and it may well have been smaller

Page 35: Denny Bog (NGR SU34/05)—valley bog with central willow carr associated with accumulation of peat in a wide, shallow basin

Page 36: Streamside lawn on alluvium, Latchmore Bottom (NGR SU184125)

than the number of known kilns at first suggests, if only because of the limitations imposed by the quantity of wood fuel required to sustain it over a long period of time. Fresh research, directed perhaps at assessing the size and potential output of the industry, and its impact on the woodland resources of the area, would be of considerable interest both archaeologically and biologically.

It is significant that there is a complete absence of Roman villa sites in the Forest area, although there is abundant evidence for occupation of the nearby chalk during the Romano-British period and to the west, Clausentum, now part of the County Borough of Southampton, developed as a small town. One is left with the impression that the Forest area, and indeed the tertiary deposits of the Hampshire Basin in Dorset to the west, was left as an enclave of land largely regarded as uncultivable, or at least not economically cultivable compared with the better soils elsewhere, and in which exploitation was concentrated mainly in the pottery industry. Extensive enclosure banks associated with the main centres of the industry and usually assigned a contemporaneous date, suggest the possibility of subsidiary agricultural activities, most likely of a pastoral nature.

With the disintegration of the Roman administration the potteries fade into obscurity. Indeed, the whole record of the ensuing centuries until the Conquest is obscure. The *Anglo-Saxon Chronicle* refers briefly to fighting between the British and invading Saxons in the late fifth and early sixth centuries, relating the story of a landing at Cerdicesora by Cerdic and his son, and their subsequent movement inland from the coast to defeat the Britons at Cerdicsford, identified as Downton, just north of the Forest. By general concensus, Cedricesora seems to have been somewhere at the head of Southampton Water, though various historians have attributed the landing to other sites on the New Forest coastline. The pattern of Saxon and Jute invasion is by no means clear, but it seems sufficient to record here that the place names of the Forest area appear to be largely Germanic in origin and it is likely that the centuries following invasion saw the stabilisation of settlement on the more fertile sites, forming the nuclei of the present pattern of permanent agricultural occupation in the Forest, recorded first in Domesday. It is quite conceivable that some of the anomalous enclosure sites recorded recently on the Forest heaths may be of Saxon origin. It is unfortunate that from pollen analysis of buried soil surfaces it is difficult to distinguish between a Dark Age and

C

Medieval date because the changes in the species composition of the pollen are insufficiently dramatic.

Thus, the foregoing is a brief survey of the fragmentary evidence relating to human settlement in the Forest area prior to the Conquest. With the Conquest, the land use pattern assumes peculiar characteristics arising from the status of the area as Royal Forest, and man's activities become governed and conditioned by an individual and complicated administration. To a large extent it would also be true to say that one passes from the quicksands of inference to the firmer ground of the written word. It is clear, however, that the extent of human settlement in early times, even in such a district as this, where population and productivity have generally assumed to have been small, presents a wide field for research—indeed, that the quicksands remain largely un-negotiated.

II

Domesday mentions a number of Forests, but only in the case of the New Forest does it supply any volume of detail. The main account forms a special section in the Hampshire folios and is entitled, *In Nova Foresta et Circa Ea*, 'In the New Forest and around it'. It refers to a total of 102 holdings in seventy-five named and seven un-named places. Of these, forty-six holdings in thirty-two named and five un-named places are recorded as completely or almost completely 'in the Forest' and their sizes and values are given retrospectively, the implication being that depopulation had taken place on afforestation. Fifty-six holdings in forty-three named and two un-named places are recorded as having been only partly afforested, and it would seem that here only the outlying woods and wastes had been affected by afforestation. A number of other sites are mentioned, which appear to have been unaffected by afforestation. In so far as the names can be identified, the distribution of settlements mentioned in Domesday is shown in figure 2. With a few exceptions, the fifty-six land holdings mentioned as being partially afforested formed a zone peripheral to the area known today as the New Forest. Most lay on the valley terrace soils of the Avon valley and on the comparatively fertile land between Christchurch and Lymington, with a group around the head of Southampton Water and a thin scatter down the west side of the Water.

Of the forty-six holdings completely or almost completely afforested, all of those which have been identified lay in the hinterland of the Forest or on a coastal belt extending on either side of the Beaulieu River. These were recorded as having possessed a total of 110 plough teams, although for eleven, no plough teams were recorded at all and one of these was described as waste. Finn[11] calculated that their total population was likely to be something in excess of 2,000 people. After afforestation, that is at the time of the Domesday survey, they were reduced to nothing in value except at twenty-one sites in fourteen named and three un named places where a total of 95½ acres of meadow—little more than a collection of tiny paddocks—remained, apparently unaffected by afforestation.

That details of land use and tax assessment were recorded for the thirty-seven afforested villages is an anomaly which has never been satisfactorily explained. If they no longer existed—had in fact been the victims of the Conqueror's traditional depopulation—for what reason were their former values required? Who provided the information? It is tempting to conclude that they were depopulated on paper alone; that afforestation merely put them beyond the scope of the survey. Of the thirty-two named sites, twenty-two have been identified with a reasonable degree of certainty and all but five of these have been settlements on private freehold land since at latest the close of the medieval period and probably before. It thus seems uncertain whether depopulation at the 'making' of the Forest, some time between 1066 and 1086, was followed at a later date by re-occupation, or whether occupation has been continuous. As Dr Finn comments, however, inclusion 'in the Forest' and subjection to the Forest Law must at any rate have seriously damaged the local economy, which is suggested by the very fact that of the thirty-two named places a large proportion remain unidentified, and by the fact that others are represented today by the names of farms and localities and not of settlements or parishes. Two of the supposedly depopulated villages—Slacham, interpreted as Sloden (SU210130); and Juare, now the site of Eyeworth Lodge (SU225145)—are of special interest because, assuming their identification is correct, they occupied the sites of former Romano-British potteries. The pottery industry itself does not seem to have persisted after the fourth century, but it is conceivable that the two villages had a more prolonged history of occupation. Their sites would certainly bear further investigation.

In sum, the Domesday evidence shows that by the eleventh century the area afforested by the Conqueror carried a scatter of villages distributed on the intrinsically better soils. None were large and the area was but thinly populated with, according to Dr Finn's calculations, less than one-tenth of a plough team and less than one-third persons per square mile. Whether they were depopulated or not, the locations of the settlements appear, as figure 2 suggests, to have formed the basis of the modern pattern of enclosed agricultural land.

Afforestation did not necessarily mean that the land afforested became the property of the Crown. The Norman Kings exercised the prerogative of subjecting other men's lands to the Forest Law, which though not implying any change in ownership meant that they could neither be enclosed nor cultivated and that free range pastoral uses became subject to a variety of odious restrictions. Domesday Book is not specific on the matter, but it seems likely that much of the land afforested at the making of the Forest remained in the ownership of subjects. The extension of enclosure and settlement thus required either disafforestation or some modification in the Forest Law. Both were achieved in the thirteenth century. Henry II, Richard I and John, having by then greatly extended the Royal Forests, the conflict between the increasing land requirements of a growing population and the sterilisation of great tracts by afforestation was bound to find expression in pressure for reform from the landowning nobility. The *Charta de Foresta* of 1217, the year after John's death, conceded extensive disafforestations and also made legal the enclosure and cultivation of private lands in Forests under licence from the Crown. By 1279 a firm perambulation, or legal boundary, was established for the New Forest, which placed the peripheral belts of holdings partly afforested by the Conqueror unarguably outside the Forest and the Forest Law. This perambulation remained substantially the same until modified by the recent New Forest Act 1964.

Thus, the way lay open for the development of the modern pattern of enclosure. This is not to say that the disafforested lands were all immediately available for cultivation, though they could now be grazed without the restrictions imposed by Forest Law. Apart from the question of common rights, large tracts remained unsuitable for cultivation until improved techniques of reclaiming base-deficient soils became available in the eighteenth and nineteenth centuries. Much was then enclosed after Enclosure Awards;[12] some remained unreclaimed until very recent years.

Within the Forest the present pattern of agricultural holdings arose over the centuries from a combination of grants of land by the Crown, enclosure of private freehold under licence (and very often without it), and sheer encroachment. All three methods became sources of revenue to the Crown in later medieval times, the first two by way of direct payments and the last by way of fines imposed by the Forest courts (see chapter four). The progressive extension of the area of enclosed land appears to have come to an end in the seventeenth century, by which time most of the areas of intrinsically better soils had been reclaimed. There is evidence to suggest that many other areas were enclosed during the medieval period and subsequently abandoned to the heath, perhaps because their site fertility proved too low to make permanent enclosure economic, perhaps because they offended the whims of the Forest administration of the time. Of the six field systems investigated by soil pollen analysis, a medieval date was suggested for three. The most extensive of these sites, the 'Crockford complex' (SU357992) extends over upwards of 200 acres of Hatchet Moor, and consists of a series of regular shaped embanked fields. The layout suggests large estate management rather than the site of a village and the proximity of the site to Beaulieu at first suggested a monastical enclosure: certainly the Abbey at Beaulieu would have had the resources to enclose such an extensive area and Cistercian sheep husbandry is suggested by the place name 'Shipton Holms' which occurs within the site. Documentary evidence to confirm or refute its monastical origins, however, is so far lacking.

For another site there is more positive evidence of a medieval date. This is an enclosure of about twenty-five acres, with banks and ditches in a similar state of preservation today as those at Crockford. It can be identified in the Forest perambulation of 1301 as, 'the land . . . of John of Fandon' and in that of 1670 as, 'a place called John of Farringdon's Close . . . where there are yet to be seen (banks) where the ancient enclosure was.' It is conceivable that this and other sites, perhaps including Crockford, were enclosed during the land-hungry thirteenth and fourteenth centuries and abandoned at the Black Death or during the ensuing period when livestock husbandry—which in the New Forest would be

41

based on the open Forest grazings—became more profitable than arable farming. To the ecological historian the existence of abandoned medieval enclosures is of interest in itself. Many of these are today on extremely base-deficient soils, and it is difficult to believe that prior to the technical innovations of the eighteenth century they would have been enclosed for agriculture had they been in their present state. They are thus a further indication of the degrading process at work in the Forest environment.

Reference has been made in general terms both in this and the previous chapter to the woodland depletion and soil degradation which has accompanied man's exploitation of the base-poor soils of areas such as the New Forest. Precisely what processes have been responsible for the depletion of the soil nutrient capital? What evidence is there to associate these processes with human activity? The main purpose of chapter three is to examine questions such as these and to paint in a more detailed picture of long term vegetational change and pedogenesis than has so far been attempted.

References

1 Heywood Sumner, *Local Papers*, London, 1931.
2 see esp *Ancient Earthworks of the New Forest*, London, 1917.
3 C. M. Piggot, 'Excavation of fifteen barrows in the New Forest 1941–2', *Proc Prehist Soc*, 9, 1943.
4 R. McGregor, 'A Late Bronze Age barrow at Berry Wood, near Burley, New Forest, Hampshire', *Proc Hampshire Field Club & Arch Soc*, XXII, 1962.
5 C. R. Tubbs & G. W. Dimbleby, 'Early Agriculture in the New Forest', *Advancement of Science*, June 1965.
6 F. G. Roe, *The North American Buffalo: a Critical Study of the Species in its Wild State*, Toronto, 1951.
7 G. W. Dimbleby, *The Development of British Heathlands and their Soils*, Oxford Forestry Memoir No 23, 1962.
8 *Proc Hampshire Field Club & Arch Soc* (in press).
9 Heywood Sumner, *Excavations in New Forest Roman Pottery Sites*, London, 1927.
   Heywood Sumner, *A Descriptive Account of Roman Pottery Sites at Black Heath Meadow, Linwood and Sloden, New Forest*, London, 1921.
   Heywood Sumner, *A Descriptive Account of the Roman Pottery made at Ashley Rails, New Forest*, London, 1919.
10 Barry Cunliffe, 'Report on the excavation of three pottery kilns in the New Forest, 1955', *Proc Hampshire Field Club & Arch Soc*, XXIII, 1965.

11 R. Welldon Finn, 'Hampshire' in *The Domesday Geography of South East England*, ed H. C. Darby & E. M. J. Campbell, Cambridge, 1962.

12 see eg, the Rev James Willis' account of the enclosure and reclamation of some 7,000 acres of heathland in Christchurch Parish, 'On Waste Land', *Communications to the Board of Agriculture*, VI, 1808.

FIGURE 2. *Distribution of settlements recorded in Domesday Book (map)*

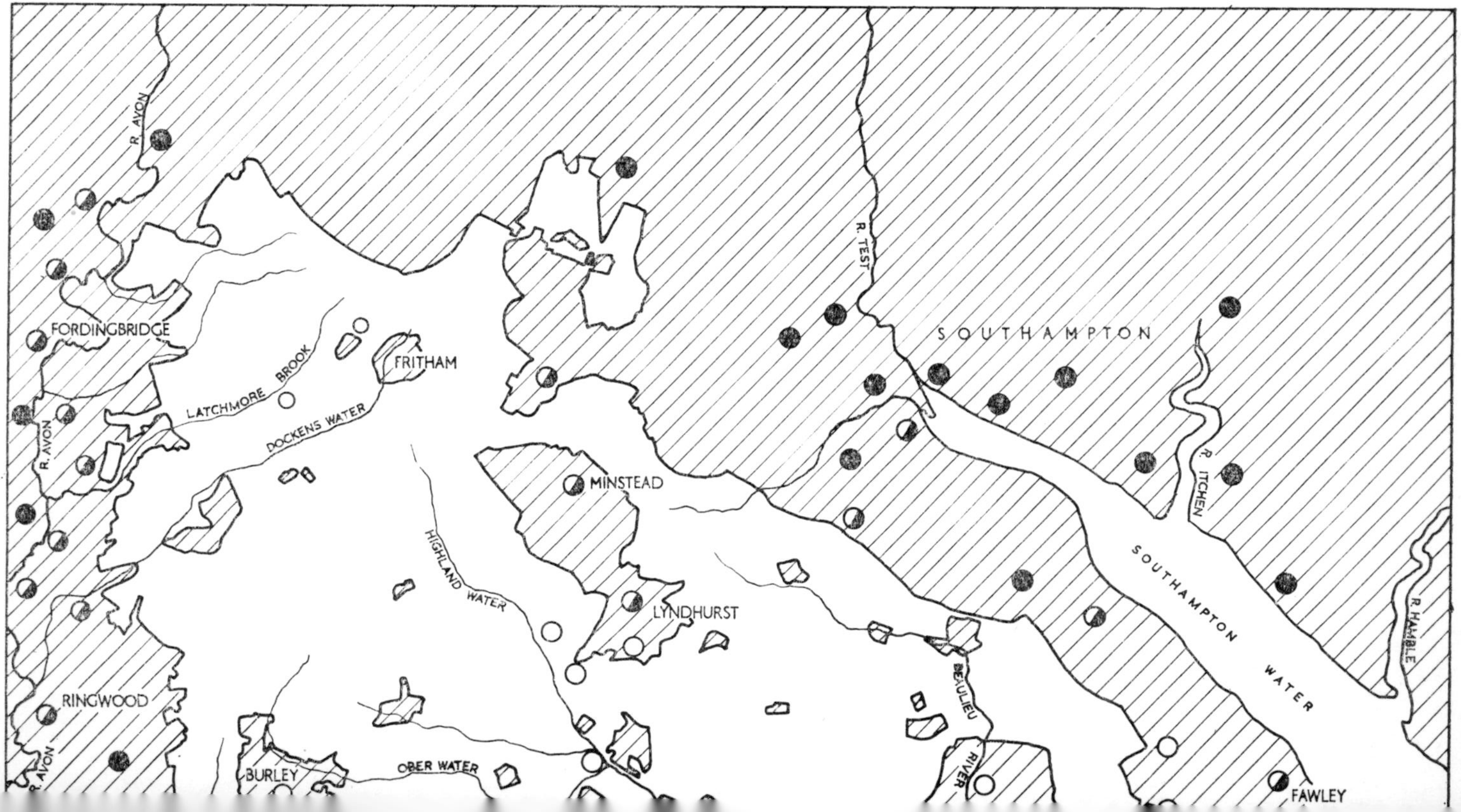

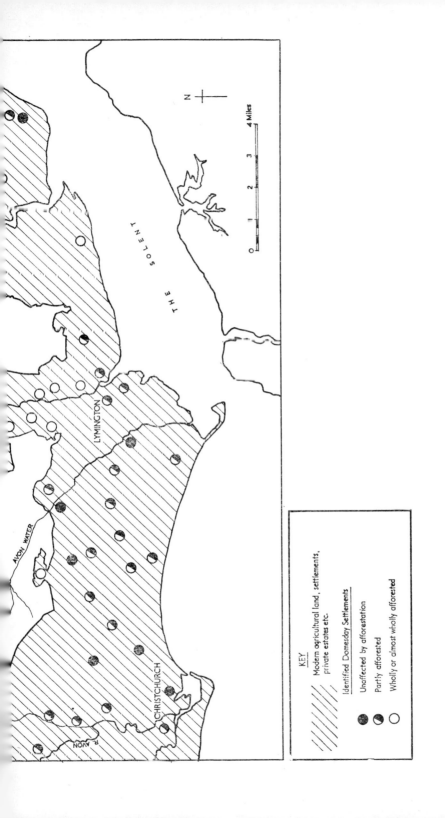

THREE

Man, Soils and Vegetation

THE function of the ecological historian is to synthesise information derived from many different, though often allied, fields of research. Thus, the archaeologist may establish much about man's early activities and from this a good deal may often be inferred about his ecological setting. To establish more precisely the nature of this setting, the changes which have taken place in it and the part man has played in them, however, the archaeological data needs to be related to the physical background and to the information provided by the soil scientist and pollen analyst. This is the main purpose in this chapter.

It is appropriate here, first to examine the processes of soil degradation which are likely to have accompanied or followed the removal of the early tree cover; to outline briefly the use of soil pollen analysis in revealing past vegetative change and to consider in what manner the biological data may be related to the archaeological record.

I

In a mature woodland soil, the base status of the upper horizons is maintained by the removal of nutrients through the root systems of the trees and their return to the soil surface in the litter. The maintenance of a woodland cover would thus appear to be the most efficient way of countering the general tendency for soluble mineral salts to be leached down through the soil horizon through the action of rainwater, although it is true that leaching can take place under some tree species, notably beech, where they are growing on particularly base-deficient parent material.

There is no doubt that the removal of the tree cover would in itself tend to encourage leaching. Alway and McMiller[1] showed that the burning of deciduous woodland can cause a decrease in

46

soil base status and nitrogen status and a corresponding increase in acidity. It would appear that the less calcareous the parent material, the more likely it is that the secondary vegetation will be acid tolerant and will thus fail to contribute sufficiently to the upper horizons of the soil to offset the effects of leaching. This is especially true of heather, whose litter forms a raw, acid humus; whose vegetative nature and close cover of the ground makes it susceptible to frequent fire, with consequent damage to soil structure; and which offers intense competition to other species more likely to have an upgrading effect on the soil. With the establishment of ling as the dominant feature of the vegetation it would seem that a vicious circle is likely in which a progressive trend towards acid tolerant vegetation and away from the primary woodland is inevitable.

The actual, physical removal of the tree cover apart, it is apparent that most forms of human exploitation of the soil must result in a decline in fertility and potential productivity. Shallow ploughing, by exposing the soil surface to the weather, would also be likely to aggravate leaching. The primitive techniques used by early man would almost certainly have been inadequate to turn the soil sufficiently to reach a base reserve which would serve to counteract this. The removal of crops, either in the form of arable produce or in the carcasses of livestock reared on the ground, and such practices such as the cutting of bracken for bedding and litter and turf for fuel, would all contribute to the depletion of the soil fertility. In the absence of some adequate system of replacing the lost nutrients it seems inevitable that human activities must in general lead to soil degradation, which would be most pronounced on the parent materials poorest in bases and usually coarsest in texture.

In such materials, leaching has frequently resulted in the formation of podzol soil profiles. Here, under a vegetation usually dominated by ling and under a surface layer of acid humus and humus stained mineral soil (A_0 and A_1 horizons), there is a pale bleached zone (A_2) from which almost all the available bases—and especially lime and iron—together with the finer particles of clay and the humus colloids, have been removed by leaching. These have accumulated at a lower level as a dark brown layer of humus-pan (B_1) and, immediately below that, a red-brown or orange-brown precipitate of iron compounds which frequently forms a hard, rocklike layer—the iron pan (B_2). Beneath the pan there is the little altered parent material. The exact processes involved in the formation of a podzol remain largely anomalous: it seems uncertain, for example, whether the downward movement of iron and humus are necessarily separate processes—certainly profiles exist in which either the humus or iron pan appears to be absent. It should be borne in mind, too, that podzol soil profiles do not in every case indicate extremely acid conditions. Iron leached soils may have a relatively high fertility, whilst certain soils of the brown earth type, exhibiting little or no visual leaching, may be relatively acid. There is no doubt, however, that podzolisation results in a decrease in soil fertility and an increase in acidity, and that the pan itself is a considerable barrier to root penetration and to water. Podzols are therefore liable to extreme drought in summer and by contrast, to waterlogging after heavy rain; in Upland Britain, under a heavy rainfall, the pan has contributed to the spread of blanket bog.

Between the acutely impoverished podzols and their forerunners, the brown forest soils, are a range of soil types which can be conveniently classified together as acid brown earths, in which it is often not possible to distinguish visually the degree to which leaching has proceeded. In the New Forest such soils usually carry grass-heath, often with some vestiges of a former woodland cover; in the absence of grazing, browsing and burning they are readily colonised by trees, so long as the grass does not form a mat too dense to allow the establishment of seedlings.

Over the greater part of the Lowland Heaths the condition of the soil, however leached it may appear to be, does not seem to be the most important factor in a vegetational succession from heathland back to woodland. Certain areas excepted—notably some of the Dorset heaths which are extremely nutrient deficient—the heaths are readily colonised by acid tolerant species such as birch and scots pine. In the New Forest, holly, oak, hawthorn and other species appear capable of colonising all but the most impoverished soils providing a nearby seed-source is available. Many of the heaths of Berkshire and Surrey have virtually succeeded to birch wood. In the Forest there is little doubt that the major factors inhibiting a succession to woodland over much if not most of the heathland areas, are browsing and grazing by deer and by commonable stock, and a regime of controlled heath burning, an object of which is in fact to maintain the open nature of the ground. It is to be doubted whether in the long term such a regime is desirable from the standpoint of soil conservation.

The process of podzolisation has accompanied the change from deciduous woodland to heather moor. A more intimate picture of this broad vegetative change, and its absolute correlation with the periodicity of human activity has been provided very largely by soil pollen analysis, and has perhaps been most ably expounded by Professor G. W. Dimbleby.[2]

In acid soils pollen grains may be preserved for exceedingly long periods of time, often many thousands of years. The pollen grains are gradually washed down through the soil profile, so that their vertical distribution indicates their relative age and thus the changes which have taken place in the vegetation of the site from which the samples were taken over the period covered by the pollen record. Interpretation is complicated by such factors as differing rates of decomposition of the pollen of the various species represented, by the varying abundance with which different species produce pollen and differentials in the rates at which pollen of different species passes down the soil profile. The interpretation depends basically upon an evaluation of the dominant species at any stage in the profile and of the degree of representation of light-demanding herbs and shrubs which are unable to flourish under a tree cover. The changes down the soil profile in the relative frequencies and percentages of the pollen of the various species represented provides data from which a picture of environmental change over the period covered by the pollen record may be constructed.[3] The method has now been applied by various workers on the heathland soils of Europe and Britain and their results have shown a generally consistent picture of vegetational change, although the assignment of dates to specific stages in the pollen record remains somewhat problematical and interpretation can only be in general terms. Nevertheless, this is generally sufficient to demonstrate the major changes which have taken place in the passage of time.

The outstanding recurrent feature shown by soil pollen analyses from British sites carrying heath vegetation today may very broadly be described as the transition from woodland to heather moor with a transitory phase of grass heath. The analyses also reflect the changes in the species composition of the tree and shrub flora which have occurred in postglacial times. These have in turn been related by various methods to successive changes in the climate since the Atlantic period, and thus the representation of the tree and shrub species in an analysis may be used to approximately deduce the span of time covered by a pollen record. Within any given area, ideally comparison should be made with analyses of pollen stratified in local peat deposits: it is unfortunate that for the Hampshire Basin such analyses as have been carried out do not extend later than the Atlantic period, the profiles presumably having been truncated by peat-cutting.[4]

In Britain both lime (*Tilia*) and elm (*Ulnus*) were components of the early woodland of the Atlantic period, although the latter, being calcicolous is scarcely represented in pollen analyses from acid soils. Both species became reduced in abundance in the Sub-Boreal and had generally disapppeared by the beginning of the Sub-Atlantic, around 500 BC. Pine (*Pinus*) probably persisted locally until the Iron Age (the early Sub-Atlantic), but the poor representation and frequent absence of the species from the pre-Iron Age pollen record in southern England suggests that the species had no prominent place in the ecosystem until historically recent times, that is following its reintroduction in the eighteenth century. Beech, which is today a major component of the tree flora of the New Forest, appears to have been but poorly represented prior to the Iron Age. Dimbleby and Gill[5] have shown that on some New Forest woodland sites it has made only a relatively recent appearance and that it has largely supplanted oak as a dominant. They concluded that the evidence suggested that beech had followed oak only within the last few centuries, and suggest that Anderson's argument[6] that the species is spread avificially explains its appearance in the Forest woodlands. Holly, too, seems to have become abundant only since the late Bronze Age, at least in the New Forest, and it is possible that it did not assume its present position as the dominant understory species until recent centuries. Hazel, (*Corylus*) once the most prominent shrub species, has, since the Iron Age, become drastically reduced in its representation on acid soils.

Seagrief's analyses of the peat deposit of Cranesmoor bog in the New Forest,[4] though not extending beyond the Atlantic, are useful in indicating the local composition of the early woodland. The pollen record reveals a sequence in which pine forest, dominant at the start of the record in the Boreal period, was replaced by deciduous woodland in the Atlantic, the latter at first being dominated by oak, hazel and elm and subsequently exhibiting an intrusion of lime and alder (*Alnus*), with birch giving rising values towards the end of the record. The proportion of non-tree pollen to tree pollen was high throughout the profile and there was no suggestion that heathland existed in the area during the period covered by the pollen sequence.

The absolute correlation between the vegetation of a given site and a specific period in the past may be obtained from the pollen preserved in soils buried beneath, and hence 'fossilised' by, earthworks for which there is archaeological dating evidence—such as barrows, hill forts and enclosure banks. The pollen of the buried soil surface will give a picture of the vegetation at the time of the construction of the earthwork and successive samples down the buried soil profile will provide a picture of earlier vegetative change. Analysis of samples continued upwards through the mound will also provide some information on changes in vegetation subsequent to its construction, although interpretation is generally more complex because of the pollen which may already have been preserved in the mound material. At the same time, the buried soil type itself will be available for comparison with the active soil of the land surface nearby.

Pollen analysis of a buried soil may itself be used to estimate the age of earthworks for which there is no archaeological or documentary evidence.[7] The species composition of the pollen in the buried soil surface, coupled with the degree to which the analyses indicate that the early woodland had been opened up, will provide some indication of the age of the earthwork, although over the long periods of time involved, the weight given to the various criteria must inevitably be somewhat arbitrary and the resultant dating bracket within which the earthwork was constructed must be regarded as wide and tentative.

II

Eighteen pollen analyses from New Forest soils are now available. All were carried out by Professor G. W. Dimbleby and all have been published in detail elsewhere.[8] It is thus proposed to confine attention to a more or less general discussion rather than to consider each in detail, drawing upon the considerable volume of data from pollen analyses of soils from the British heaths as a

Man, Soils and Vegetation

whole—both those of the Upland and the Lowland zones—for comparison.

Of the Forest analyses, eight relate to soils which carry woodland at the present time—Pondhead Inclosure, Matley Wood, Berry Wood and the five small deciduous woods on the open Forest investigated by Dimbleby and Gill.[5] Of the remaining ten analyses, all from sites which are now heathland, two refer to active soils. The remainder are of soils buried beneath archaeological features and in some cases also of the profiles of the features themselves; further information is summarised in the following table.

Site	Archaeological/ documentary dating evidence	Dating suggested by analysis
1 Barrow near Burley, su212052	Late Bronze Age[9]	
2 Lyndhurst Old Park Bank, su314077	First documentary reference AD 1291	
3 Enclosure bank, Setley Plain, sz303994		Medieval
4 Enclosure bank, Crockford, sz357992		Medieval
5 Enclosure bank, Hincheslea, su265009		Medieval
6 Enclosure bank, Holmsley, sz208998		Iron Age
7 Enclosure bank, Pilley, sz344984		Iron Age (?)
8 Enclosure bank, Crockford, sz355994		Bronze Age

Site numbers correspond to those in the text of this chapter.

Page 53: Re-seeded area, Matley Heath (NGR su34/07). Reclaimed 1946, cropped 1947-50, ley undersown with final oat crop. Fences removed 1951. Alder carr of Matley Bog beyond

Page 54: (above) *Molinia/Eriophorum* bog, Shatterford Bottom (NGR SU34/06); (below) Gorse and heather—breeding habitat of Dartford Warbler and Stonechat

Of the two analyses from active surface soils, one is worth describing very briefly, since although it exhibits complexities it nevertheless demonstrates the transformation from woodland to heathland conditions. The soil from the second site proved to be surprisingly poor in pollen.

The site sampled was on *Calluna-Molinia* dominated heathland to the north of Burley. The parent material was Barton Sand with a clay fraction in the subsoil and the soil type was a humus-gley podzol. Samples were taken from the soil surface to a depth of 18 in. The pollen in the lowest 4 in clearly indicated woodland conditions, with lime, alder and hazel as major species. In the next 6 in the pollen stratification appears to have been severely modified, probably due to solifluction, but the upper 8 in show the development of the present vegetation on the site from a period when hazel scrub was dominant. Cereal pollen occurred in the last phase and possibly indicates that cultivation took place on or in the vicinity of the site. There is little indication of the span of time covered by the analysis, but the final heath-development phase may have taken place in prehistoric times, a hypothesis suggested mainly by the occurrence of lime, and less consistently, elm pollen throughout the profile: the record during the period when *Calluna* has been dominant would be absent owing to the recurrent destruction of the surface humus by fire and perhaps also by turf cutting.

Most of the British material relating to buried soils comes from barrows assigned to the Bronze Age, and it is possible to reconstruct a good deal of the picture of Bronze Age man's environment on those areas which are today characterized by heath. The periodicity of human occupation of the Lowland heaths, and in particular of the New Forest, has been outlined in chapter two. It appears likely that the impact of man on the vegetation would first have been widespread and appreciable in the Bronze Age. Earlier fire clearance may well already have modified the early woodland and brought into being extensive areas of open country; much of the woodland itself may have been re-growth after earlier clearance. Pollen analyses from soils buried beneath Bronze Age barrows on the Lowland Heaths indicate that the Bronze Age peoples inhabited a mosaic of grass-heath and open woodland, in which hazel was a prominent shrub, and oak the best represented tree species, and that this vegetation was secondary to a more complete woodland cover. In many cases, the barrows appear to have been built on abandoned agricultural land, which in some cases had recently succeeded or was in the process of succeeding to heath or bracken or, alternatively, to hazel scrub. How extensively arable cultivation was practised is not clear, since the analyses relate of course only to the immediate environs of the barrows. Most probably cereal cultivation would, in the late Bronze Age at least, tend to be secondary to livestock husbandry and the area of cultivated land would in any one instance be small.

It is unfortunate that the pollen spectra do not distinguish clearly between arable and pasture land. Early cereals were self-pollinated[10] and are in consequence poorly represented in the spectra. Farming may be indicated by the associated weed flora, but this would occur both on arable and pasture. Moreover, if the pasture were grazed intensively the pollen production of the grasses would be restricted and they would be under-represented in the analyses. Professor Dimbleby[2] summed up the evidence thus: 'The only reasonably certain evidence of arable farming is cereal pollen, and this occurs in such small quantities that it is difficult to be sure whether it applies to the site itself or to the near vicinity. However, the consistent occurrence of cereal grains in successive samples, combined with a variety of weed pollens, is highly suggestive of cultivation.' He considered that cereal production would have been patchwise rather than extensive. The mere fact that cereals could be grown by the primitive techniques available, however, clearly implies that the heathlands were then considerably more fertile than today.

In most instances soils which have been recorded from beneath Bronze Age barrows on sites which are now heathland in Britain, exhibit podzol profiles, although these are normally immature or incipient, contrasting markedly with well developed podzols under the adjoining heath. On the Continent, soils recorded from beneath Neolithic structures on heathland have more often been of a brown earth type, whilst Bronze Age soils have generally shown some degree of podzolization. It is unfortunate that Neolithic sites on heathland in this country are not available for comparison.

Podzolization in the Bronze Age soils had clearly often commenced under grass-heath. Such a development would appear to be taking place today in some Forest sites, for example on Rockford Common, one of the manorial wastes within the perambulation. Here slight bleaching below which there is some appearance of iron deposition can be seen in the soil profile of an enclosure which has been ploughed, probably in the nineteenth century, and which today carries bristle bent and bracken. This degrading brown earth is formed on a gravelly loam. Similar visually obvious soil degradation would seem to be a widespread feature of soils carrying acid grassland and bracken in the Forest. At a number of sites where *Calluna* has replaced woodland within the past hundred years, probably with an intervening though short-lived grassland phase, incipient podzolization is now apparent in the soil profile. Such sites clearly deserve further attention. It is perhaps significant that they are invariably on the intrinsically base-poor Barton Sands or on gravels. It seems clear, however, that although the establishment of *Calluna* is likely to accelerate leaching, *Calluna* cannot itself always be regarded as the instigator of the process.

It is unfortunate that only two pollen analyses from the New Forest refer to Bronze Age soils, one from beneath a Late Bronze Age barrow (site 1) and the other from beneath the bank enclosing a small field. The pollen from the buried soil of the former showed that by the time the barrow was constructed the vegetation had succeeded from hazel scrub to heather and bracken, the last species being the more important in the sample from the actual buried surface. The buried soil exhibited the A horizon of a podzol, with a well marked bleach zone, but the B horizon had scarcely developed. In contrast the soil profiles of the adjacent heathland exhibited a strongly developed B horizon. That of the mound itself showed—surprisingly—only slight signs of podzolization, although the material appeared to be old subsoil, which is often apparently less prone to podzolize. A more frequent feature of the soil profiles of barrow mounds on heathland sites is the development of a well defined podzol, indicative of continued soil degradation subsequent to the building of the barrow.

The second Bronze Age soil (dated by its pollen) is from beneath a small enclosure which lies today on an extensive tract of treeless heathland whose vegetation comprises a mosaic of acid grassland, with gorse and heather (site 8). The site sampled lies on heather moor, the soil profile beneath which is a gley-podzol; the bank itself also exhibited a podzol profile. The pollen spectrum of the buried soil suggested that the enclosure itself was in a clearing in a relatively well wooded area. The woodland comprised hazel and oak; alder was abundant and both lime and elm are represented. This flora, together with the absence of beech and hornbeam from all stages of the profile indicated a Sub-Boreal date. The buried soil was a gley-podzol, and such a woodland community would scarcely exist on the degraded buried soil, yet must have been near enough to have influenced the pollen rain so markedly; thus a woodland clearing is suggested for the small enclosure. The non-tree pollen is dominated by grasses and heather with some suggestion of an increase in bracken immediately prior to the building of the bank : such was probably the vegetation of the clearing. In the span of time since the building of the bank the woodland has completely disappeared and widespread degradation would appear to have taken place in the soils of the area.

III

It has frequently been observed that the evidence for Iron Age occupation of heathlands is exceedingly limited, and as was suggested earlier, this may be linked with a general deterioration in the potential productivity of the environment, due either directly or indirectly to human activity. From the fragmentary evidence which has emerged from recent studies of the New Forest and to which reference was made in chapter two, it is conceivable that in this area human occupation was more widespread than has generally been assumed. The spectra from the enclosure bank at site 6 (Holmsley) strongly suggested an Iron Age date. The buried soil was a humus-iron podzol and at the time of the construction of the bank, bracken was dominant, although heather was beginning to appear. This vegetation had gradually replaced woodland of Sub-Boreal type. Pollen analysis of the profile of the bank itself showed the gradual replacement of the bracken by heather. A podzol had formed in the bank itself with the B horizon formed around the old land surface, but whether this had commenced under the bracken or under the heather is impossible to say.

The second analysis, from Pilley, noted earlier in the table as indicating an Iron Age (?) date (site 7) exhibited anomalies which are not readily explained. In the buried soil, surface beech was well represented and there were traces of hornbeam, both of which connote a Sub-Atlantic date. The non-tree pollen : tree pollen ratio was high, indicating extensive woodland clearance in the vicinity. On the other hand, the lime percentage was high, suggesting a date in the

Sub-Boreal. It only seems possible to reconcile these factors by assuming a date at or near the Sub-Boreal/Sub-Atlantic transition, that is, the Iron Age or just possibly the Romano-British period. The pollen sequence in the buried soil illustrates once again the transition from woodland to grass-heath, grasses and heather being co-dominant on the site when the bank was built; the buried soil was an immature humus-iron podzol.

The remaining four enclosure banks whose buried soils have been studied were all of much later construction. One is closely datable and was the enclosing bank of Lyndhurst Old Park (site 2), the first documentary reference to which occurs in 1291. The remaining three are also almost certainly medieval. The buried soil of Lyndhurst Old Park bank showed the replacement of hazel scrub, with some alder, by heather. The buried soil was a massive humus-iron podzol little different from the soil of the surrounding *Calluna* dominated heathland today. The vegetation and soils of the site have clearly changed little since the bank was built.

At the other three sites the banks were again all built in open country. The tree flora represented in the buried soils is clearly Sub-Atlantic, with in at least one case (site 4, Crockford) the strong suggestion of a relatively late date.

At Crockford the bank, part of a system of enclosures, was erected on an unleached brown earth dominated by grasses and completely open. The vegetation and soil profile in the vicinity has remained unchanged since the construction of the bank. The site had previously been under cereal production. The development of open ground from a woodland or scrub phase is not represented in the analyses, although samples were only taken to a depth of 6 in. At the other two sites, by way of contrast, the banks were erected on considerably more degraded soils. At Hincheslea (site 5), the buried soil was a deep podzol. The site had been cultivated and after the abandonment of the arable, bracken had taken over dominance, a sequence of events most probably closely associated with the degraded condition of the soil. Bracken was dominant at the time the bank was built, although heather was becoming prominent. The pollen sequence from the bank itself showed that, subsequent to the building of the bank, heather gradually replaced the bracken. It remains dominant on the site today. The reason for the construction of the bank on the abandoned arable is not clear. At Hincheslea one sees a sequence of events similar to that which occurred at Holmsley but which took place at a much later date. A similar sequence is discernible in the analysis from Setley (site 3). Here grass-heath dominated the site when the bank was built; the soil was a well developed podzol. Only three samples were taken, at the buried surface, merely to date the bank, and the sequence of events subsequent to its construction is indicated by the present vegetation—heather. These examples serve to illustrate the relative recency of heather in many parts of the New Forest. At neither Hincheslea or Setley is an early woodland or scrub phase represented in the analyses, in the latter case certainly and in the former case probably, because sampling was carried to an insufficient depth.

IV

The preceding examples serve to demonstrate the general directions of vegetative change and soil development on those areas which are today heathland in the New Forest. Reduced to its simplest form, the direction of vegetative change may be expressed thus:

1   2   3

woodland — hazel/grassland/grass-heath — heather

In the New Forest (and elsewhere) a period of bracken domination frequently intervenes between the second and third phases. It has been shown that during the second phase farming has taken place on sites on heathland for which pollen analyses are available, or at least has taken place in their vicinity, and that this is associated with the early stages of soil degradation. The ultimate dominance of the acid-tolerant heather after the abandonment of these areas has probably accelerated the process. It is not to be assumed, however, that the hazel/grass-heath phase has necessarily always been followed by further habitat deterioration or that heathland vegetation has necessarily always persisted on any given site once it has become established. In the New Forest, the brown earth status of the soil has been maintained over extensive areas, often on the sands and gravels normally most conducive to podzolization. Such areas today carry grassland (*Agrostis setacea, Molinia* and locally *Agrostis tenuis* and *Festuca ovina*) often associated with

bracken and gorse (*Ulex europaeus*). That this is not necessarily
a 'flush effect' is demonstrated by the wide distribution of such
a community on level plains and plateaux. This vegetation type is on
many sites associated with a thin scatter of trees and shrubs—
oak, hawthorn and holly—suggestive of relic woodland. Indeed,
there is evidence to show that many such sites have succeeded from
woodland to grassland in very recent times, as will be demonstrated
in later chapters. A considerable area of the unenclosed Forest has
retained a woodland cover, although whether any given site has
had a continuous history of woodland domination is usually problematical.

Several woods in the New Forest have been investigated by soil
pollen analysis. Dimbleby and Gill[5] showed that at two of six
small woods studied by them, oakwood had become established
on former heathland. At the remainder, woodland conditions had
been continuous over the period covered by the pollen record, but
sampling was taken to no great depth and would not appear to
cover any very long period of time.

Three other sites have been studied by Professor Dimbleby.[2]
A pollen analysis from Berry Wood revealed what appears to have
been a long period in which the site was a mosaic of woodland
and grass-heath. This gave way to oakwood, oak gradually achiev-
ing the supreme dominance which it maintains at the present time.
The pollen record would appear to fall into the Sub-Atlantic period.
The soil here was an acid brown forest soil, practically unleached.
A second analysis, from Matley Wood, is even more interesting. At
the start of the pollen record the site was in cultivation, although
there seems to have been a certain amount of hazel scrub in the
vicinity. This phase is succeeded by one in which bracken appears,
accompanied by a little woodland re-growth, and finally becomes
dominant. This must obviously have followed the abandonment
of the arable. Lastly, this is in turn succeeded by oakwood. The
trees on the site are around 200–250 years old. That at least a
part of Matley Wood was under silvicultural management, probably in medieval times, is suggested by enclosure banks typical of
medieval 'encoppicements' and it may be that the present woodland
had its origin in deliberate planting. Again, the soil may be regarded
as being of the acid brown forest soil type. Professor Dimbleby
considered that the earliest pollen was almost certainly post Bronze
Age and possibly a good deal later, and it is conceivable that the

site was a pre-Conquest village, one of those depopulated by the Conqueror and whose site has not been identified. It would seem to have been farmed for some considerable time.

The third woodland site was Pondhead Inclosure. Here, it is known that the present oak–chestnut stand was planted on farmland in 1810 and the main feature of Professor Dimbleby's investigation was the soil type itself. This was clearly a regenerating podzol. A deep layer of mull humus overlaid the bleached A_2 horizon of the podzol and this serves to demonstrate that under certain conditions the trend towards soil degradation may be reversed. In this instance, as with other examples of regenerating soils, it is impossible to say whether the regeneration commenced whilst the site was under agricultural use—apparently grazing land —or since the establishment of a tree cover. The crux of the matter lies largely in the ability of the introduced vegetation to reach the base reserves of the subsoil. Soil profiles not dissimilar to that at Pondhead Inclosure were described by Dimbleby and Gill on sites where oak would appear to be colonising heather moor in the wake of an initial colonisation by holly.

V

In most of the relevant local literature[11] the conviction is expressed that much, if not most, of the heather-dominated lands of the New Forest, and especially those on the markedly leached gravels, could never have carried woodland, even in very early times. Even without direct or inferential evidence to the contrary, however, it is highly unlikely that the New Forest was an exception to the general sequence of events which have been demonstrated for the British heathlands as a whole. The soil pollen analyses from the Forest provide local confirmation of this, although if they are taken in isolation they might not, in view of their limited nature, provide firm evidence that the whole of the Forest conformed to the pattern of change which they show. Soil pollen analysis apart, however, it can be shown that even the most degraded soils of the plateau gravels and Barton and Bagshot sands are not necessarily always inhibitive to the establishment of trees.

In sum, it would be fair to say that human activity in post-glacial times has been closely associated with the gradual reduction of the deciduous woodland; that on the areas of Lowland Britain which are today heathland the reduction of the woodland, together with agricultural exploitation, has been accompanied by soil deterioration which has on the whole inhibited land uses other than those of a purely pastoral nature; and that such pastoral land uses have probably contributed further to the depletion of the woodland area in historic times. Pearsall[12] has shown that in Upland Britain the disappearance of the woodland since medieval times has been closely associated with pastoral economies and in some cases with policies of deliberate destruction. In the New Forest (as in other Royal Forests) the maintenance of large populations of deer has been an additional factor.

In the New Forest, the visible tendency for the heaths to revert to woodland in the absence of grazing, browsing and burning, and the evidence already quoted for the re-establishment of woodland on heathland sites, suggests that there has been a constant and gradual fluctuation in the relative areas of woodland and open ground, depending on the relative activity of the anthropogenic and biotic influences at work, with the general emphasis on woodland depletion. This certainly seems to have been the overall pattern during the centuries for which written records are available. Young[11] suggested that the relative areas of woodland and heathland had altered little since Norman times, but from the evidence available it might be inferred that the New Forest of the Conqueror was in fact more wooded than the Forest of today. One imagines the whole process of the wood-heath transition as the gradual fragmentation of the oak/hazel dominated woodland and scrub into ever-widening clearings, and the equally gradual fusion of the clearings until the woodland took on the conformation of its medieval and later limits. Today the hazel, so much a feature of the pollen analyses, has virtually disappeared, a process which it is tempting to correlate with the progressive decalcification of the soils. Timber planting in the past two or three centuries has obscured much of the pattern of vegetative change in recent times, but there is some weight of evidence, considered in later chapters, to show that the process of overall woodland depletion continued into historically recent times.

References

1 F. J. Alway & P. R. McMiller, 'Interrelationships of soil and forest cover on Star Island, Minnesota', *Soil Science*, 36, 1933.

2   G. W. Dimbleby, 'The development of British heathlands and their soils', *Oxford Forestry Memoir No 23*, 1962.

3   For detailed account see G. W. Dimbleby, 'Soil Pollen Analysis', *J Soil Science*, 12, 1961.

4   S. C. Seagrief, 'Pollen diagrams from Southern England: Wareham, Dorset, and Nursling, Hampshire', *New Phytologist*, 58, 1959.
    S. C. Seagrief, 'Pollen diagrams from Southern England: Cranes Moor, Hampshire', *New Phytologist*, 59, 1960.

5   G. W. Dimbleby & J. M. Gill, 'The occurrence of podzols under deciduous woodland in the New Forest', *Forestry*, XXVIII, 2, 1955.

6   M. L. Anderson, 'Avificial woods arising from the dissemination of seeds by birds', *Sylva*, 30, 1949.

7   see: G. W. Dimbleby, 'Pollen analysis as an aid to the dating of prehistoric monuments', *Proc Prehist Soc*, 20, 1954.

8   Dimbleby, 'The development of British heathlands and their soils', *Oxford Forestry Memoir No 23*, 1962; Dimbleby & Gill, *loc cit*; C. R. Tubbs & G. W. Dimbleby, 'Early Agriculture in the New Forest', *Advancement of Science*, June 1965.

9   The archaeological report on this barrow is given in: R. McGregor, 'A late Bronze Age barrow at Berry Wood, near Burley, New Forest, Hampshire', *Proc Hants Field Club & Arch Soc*, XXII, 1962.

10 J. Iversen, 'The influence of prehistoric man on vegetation', *Danm Geol Unters*, 4, No 6, 1949.

11 eg F. E. Kenchington, *The Commoners' New Forest*, London, 1944; D. W. Young, 'The New Forest', *Forestry*, 9, 1935; as was noted in chapter two, Sumner, *Local Papers*, London, 1931, took a similar view.

12 W. H. Pearsall, *Mountains and Moorlands*, London, 1950.

FOUR

The Royal Forest

ONE major pragmatic consideration has governed man's exploitation of the greater part of the area within the present perambulation of the New Forest since the eleventh century, and possibly before. The appropriation of the area by the Crown, and its subsequent peculiar legal status as Royal Forest, prevented the reclamation and cultivation of some 67,000 acres of land, even though the technical difficulties of reclaiming even the most infertile soils were largely overcome during the eighteenth century and despite the land hunger in Lowland Britain during the past two hundred years. Within this 67,000 acres of Crown lands, successive Acts of Parliament since 1698 provided for the enclosure of land by the Crown for the growth of timber, and there are today about 19,600 acres of statutory silvicultural enclosures, of which not more than 17,600 acres may be behind fences at any one time. Apart from roughly 2,300 acres which are absolute freeholds of the Crown, the remainder of the Crown lands, about 44,500 acres, are common grazings embracing a mosaic of heathland, bog and woodland.

The agricultural economy arising from the use of the common lands by bordering smallholders has played an essential role both in the preservation of the Forest as a unit of administration and land use, and in its history of vegetative change. The intentions of this chapter are to trace the successive changes in the management of the Forest and to describe the manner in which the land use interests of the Crown and of the commoners ensured its retention as an administrative and economic unit—to provide, in fact, the framework within which to describe its more recent ecological history.

I

In early Saxon times the wilder, more infertile tracts of country were regarded as common hunting grounds, available to all, but

65

with the gradual emergence of the concept of an aristocracy, these free rights of the chase appear to have been usurped and to have eventually become the prerogative of the overlord. The later Saxon kings claimed as part of their prerogative the right to reserve to themselves the chase, at least of the deer, over any part of their kingdom which they might define. These Royal hunting grounds, as well as the demesne lands of the Crown, were gradually formed from what had formerly been the folkland, common to all. The restrictions on the use of the Royal hunting grounds, other than by the Crown or its nominees, became progressively more restrictive until they assumed the rigorous nature of the Norman Forest Laws.

It has commonly been asserted that much of the New Forest was Royal Forest before the Conquest. Satisfactory evidence in support of this is lacking, however. All that can be said is that the area had been afforested by 1086, the date of the Domesday compilation, and that much, if not all of the afforestation can be attributed to William I.

The act of afforestation and the subsequent management of a Forest were directed mainly towards the conservation of deer for the chase and—probably more important—as a reservoir of meat 'on the hoof', and of hides, which could be tapped as and when required. A Forest did not necessarily imply a tree covering, nor did it preclude the continued holding of private lands within it, but might be best described as an area subject to Forest Law in contradistinction to Common Law. Forest Law provided for the regulation and control of all activities which could conceivably be contrary to the purpose of the Forest and laid down various penalties for infringement. It is well known that in Norman England these penalties were extreme—a man might lose his life for the killing of a stag—but later, successive modifications introduced a degree of leniency towards Forest offences which, together with the various privileges which eventually became known as rights of common, formed a considerable compensation for the restrictions on economic expansion which Forest Law implied.

Afforestation was based on the prerogative enjoyed by the sovereign that all wild animals were in his possession. Forests generally —and medieval documentary evidence shows that this was the case in the New Forest—included the lands of subjects besides those of the Crown. Before the Charta de Foresta of 1217, such lands could not—in theory at any rate—be enclosed, nor could timber be felled on them, cultivation take place or game be killed: subsequently it was allowed under licence from the Crown. Their major value, therefore, lay in their grazings. Clearly it would have been unreasonable to prohibit fencing and at the same time to enforce restrictions on the roaming of stock on to the Crown land, and as a matter of practical management the right of free range of stock appears to have gained mutual acceptance and to have been the origin of many later rights of grazing.

Although the first consideration in the management of a Forest was the deer, it is known that pre-existing pastoral land uses and other exploitation of the soil were allowed to continue, but that such exploitation was subject to close control and definition.

Before afforestation, the common wastes would have been freely grazed. Pigs would have been turned out on the mast in the autumn —the Domesday valuation of woodland turns on its capacity to maintain swine—timber, turves and peat taken for fuel, bracken cut for bedding and litter, and to some extent at least, game killed, as necessities to the survival of the communities. Under Forest Law the exploitation of these natural resources became controlled for the benefit of the deer and, with the passing of time, became rights of common exercised by immemorial prescription under privilege of the Crown, eventually in the New Forest becoming defined and limited and recognised by statute in the late seventeenth century.

Medieval Forest Law provided for the removal of cattle from the Forest during the midsummer fence month (20 June–20 July), when the hinds and does were dropping their calves and fawns respectively, and during the winter heyning (22 November–4 May), the period of the year when keep was shortest. Together these periods covered more than six months of the year, but there is evidence to show that in the spacious conditions of the New Forest the winter heyning, at least, was not customarily observed, certainly by later medieval times. The period during which pigs might be turned out was restricted to about two months in the autumn, when the mast fell. Here the interests of both Crown and commoners were served: green acorns, although perfectly good pig food, can, when eaten in excess and without a considerable bulk of fibrous food, cause death by poisoning in both cattle and deer. It was, therefore, in the interests of the Crown that pig should compete with deer for the green acorns until late November, by which time only brown, ripe acorns remained. The right to take wood and turf fuel became restricted to carefully defined and adjusted quantities. Such exploitations became regulated on manorial wastes in medieval and later times by the manor courts, but in this case the object was more nearly the conservation of natural resources for the benefit of the commoners.

The extent to which the provisions of Forest Law were observed or enforced in the New Forest varied over the centuries with the interest shown in the area by the Crown and with the vigilance, or alternatively the negligence and corruptness, of its officials. For long periods, particularly during and after the sixteenth century, it was openly flouted, and by the early seventeenth century its provisions and purposes and the functions of the courts which were supposed to administer it—and which by that time sat only irregularly—had become uncertain and nebulous. The standard work on Forest Law, Manwood's *Treatise and Discourse of the Laws of the Forest*, first published in 1598, was in fact written in an attempt to clarify the situation, and to define the rights of the Crown in the Royal Forests. This work, however, has been shown to contain a number of misconceptions. A more accurate account of early Forest Law and its administration is that of Turner in 1899.[1]

The documentary evidence relating to Forest administration prior to the thirteenth century is fragmentary, and after the thirteenth century the whole administrative structure became progressively decadent. Turner showed that during the thirteenth century Forest Law was administered by two courts, to which a wide range of officials were responsible. The lower court, the Court of Attachment, known in some Forests as the Court of Swainmote and in later centuries in the New Forest as the Court of Swainmote and Attachment, was presided over by the Verderers and held proceedings which were in the nature of preliminaries. Its function was to enrol presentments made by Forest Officers as to Forest offences and to issue attachments for the attendance of offenders at the higher court. In certain minor cases it appears also to have had the authority to determine offences. In most cases, however, it was unable to impose fines or other punishments. The final judgement and the imposition of penalties was left to the higher court, the Justice in Eyre, which was originally intended to sit in each Forest every three years. After the thirteenth century, however, the regularity with which this court was held came to vary considerably.

By the sixteenth century it was held only intermittently in all but one or two Forests. In the seventeenth century only two courts were held in the New Forest, the second in 1670, being the last in forestal history. The appointment of Chief Justice in Eyre was finally abolished early in the nineteenth century.

Clearly, without the supreme court, the lower court was to a large extent powerless. By the sixteenth century it had come to function more in the manner of a manorial court than a Forest court. It dispensed the privileges of the Forest and controlled the exploitation of the wastes as much or more for the benefit of the commoner than the Crown. At the same time, Forest Law had become so weakened in the absence of the supreme court that infringement proceeded without redress. The Law itself had been softened by successive charters from the original savagery of Norman times to the point where its game laws were less rigorous than those of the nineteenth century at Common Law. Hammersley[2] has commented, however, that,

> the laws were known and observed in principle at least; now they served through the lower forest courts, to regularise the exploitation of traditional forest privileges, to prevent excess, and to exclude intruders. A law designed to establish a royal privilege now safeguarded the commoner's interests. They and the Crown, were by it precluded from more rational and more profitable husbandry.

In the case of the New Forest an alternative view would be that they made secure an agricultural economy based on the exercise of common rights which was well adapted to the exploitation of marginal land.

Attempts were made to strengthen the powers of the Court of Swainmote and Attachment in the New Forest in enactments of 1698 and 1800, but it was not until the New Forest Act of 1877 that the powers of the court received close definition. Then the Verderers became a statutory body responsible not for safeguarding the interests of the Crown, as the Forest courts had officially been, but for safeguarding and managing matters relating to the interests of the commoners.

The executive officer in charge of a Forest or group of Forests was the Warden, or Lord Warden, a post which could be hereditary or which could be held by appointment by letters patent during the king's pleasure. The Verderers, four in number in the New Forest before the 1877 Act, were elected by the county. The ordinary work of the Forest, such as gamekeeping, was carried out by Foresters and other lesser officials, many of whose posts became honorific positions held by the local squirearchy who in turn employed others to carry out the actual work. The Regarders—originally twelve knights of the county—were responsible for examining the Forest perambulations and reporting on its general state in answer to a set of interrogatories known in medieval times as the Chapter of the Regard. In the sixteenth, seventeenth and eighteenth centuries one of their main functions came to be the inspection of the woods and the marking of timber for felling.

By the early eighteenth century, the range of Forest appointments in the New Forest seems to have multiplied considerably. At the top end of the scale, appointed by letters patent, was the Lord Warden, a post which carried occupation of the King's (or Queen's) House, Lyndhurst—today the local headquarters of the Forestry Commission—and of the Manor of Lyndhurst, together with numerous perquisites which probably amounted to a considerable cash sum annually. Also appointed by letters patent were the Riding Forester, with an annual salary of about £500, and Woodward with a salary of about £200. Both posts had paid deputies and both were sinecures held by the local gentry.

Owing appointment to the Lord Warden were almost innumerable lesser honorific posts, again mostly held by the local gentry, who in turn employed the keepers who actually carried out the work of preventing Forest offences and presenting offences to the Court of Swainmote and Attachment. The keepers received no salary, but were paid in kind.

Both Verderers and Regarders were elected by the free-holders of the county. Again, although no salary was attached to these posts, there were various perquisites and the duties required of these officers were far from being entirely onerous. Finally, representing the rising star of silviculture, was the Deputy Surveyor, responsible for silvicultural management operations in the Forest, and answering to the Surveyor General.

II

Whilst initially the purpose of the Forest courts was the enforcement of Forest Law for the benefit of the deer, the Justice in Eyre became, during and after the thirteenth century, a source of revenue

Page 71. (above) Stock grazing *Agrostis setacea/Molinia* grassland from which bracken has been eradicated, Latchmore Bottom (NGR SU18/12) Hasley Inclosure in background; (below) The *Agrostis setacea* and *Molinia* sward. The *Molinia* has been bitten down by stock in preference to the *Agrostis*

Page 72: (above) Cattle drift, September 1968, Ocknell Plain; (below) Holly colonisation of heathland, Boldrewood (NGR SU236089)

to the Crown. As the penalties for Forest offences became more lenient the majority of its convictions took the shape of fines, and the value of a Forest to the Crown turned largely from its capacity to carry a large head of deer to its capacity to show a substantial monetary return in the shape of fines inflicted by the Justice Seat—often regarded as forms of 'licensing' rather than fines—and payments in respect of grants of land and privileges within and over the Forest. It was by way of grant from the sovereign that a considerable proportion of the private land within the present perambulation of the New Forest found its way into private ownership.

It is difficult to come to conclusions about the size of the Conqueror's Royal Forest. No perambulation of that period has come to light and one is left only with the distribution of the afforested and partially afforested villages recorded in Domesday. These fall into an area within the natural boundaries of the River Avon, the edge of the chalk, the Solent and Southampton Water, and from this one can only conclude that these were the recognised limits of his Forest. These natural limits enclose an area of about 220 square miles. The area within the present perambulation is approximately 144 square miles, of which more than a third is private land in agricultural or residential use. Most of the land outside the existing perambulation but within the limits of the Forest at Domesday, and also probably a large proportion of the existing private lands within the modern perambulation, had probably found its way out of the hands of the Crown by the middle of the fourteenth century.

At Domesday, shortly after the afforestation of the New Forest by the Conqueror, the total population of England and Wales was probably less than one and a half millions. It has been estimated that by 1348 this had increased to 3,750,000.[3] Such a marked increase in population gave rise—particularly in Lowland Britain where population was densest—to a considerable land hunger. The open field systems round existing villages expanded. Thousands of hamlets and farms managed in severalty came into being. Older towns increased in size and many new ones were created. Considerable areas of heathland and other traditional grazing lands were reclaimed in the course of these two centuries. At the same time the open field systems of the medieval manor, still predominant over a good deal of England late in the fourteenth century, did not allow for the extensive adoption of improved agricultural methods. Crop yields were low. With the extension of arable on to physically less productive land the average yield per acre declined steadily. For these and other reasons the demand for land was proportionately greater than during some later periods of agricultural expansion. The land hunger of the thirteenth century terminated with the Black Death. By 1374, the population had dropped to an estimated 2,250,000, and to about 2,100,000 between 1410 and 1430.[3]

Under these circumstances of increasing demands on land and increasing land values, it would have been surprising had the Crown managed to retain an unrelaxed hold on an untilled area the size of the New Forest, some of it, especially the river terrace soils of the Avon valley, of medium or above average quality. Most of the larger units of land—that which now comprises the ring of large estates which surrounds the Forest—seem to have been manœuvred into the hands of the nobility, some by grant or purchase, some by sheer appropriation backed up by a strenuous assertion of rights which the Crown often found inexpedient to deny. Not only the title of the Crown to such lands was disputed, but also its right to extend to them the Laws of the Forest: it would be denied that the land had ever been in the Forest. By the end of the thirteenth century the legal boundary within which the Forest Law applied— the perambulation—had been retracted to exclude from the Forest a wide peripheral belt which included the manors of the Avon valley, much of the better soils of the Headon Beds on the southern coastal zone, and a good deal of land on the north and north-east sides of the Forest. From then until the New Forest Act 1964, the perambulation remained little altered.

Many of the inroads made on the Forest at this period are poorly documented, the exceptions usually being lands which passed into private ownership by grant of the Crown. Among these is a grant of 10,000 acres at Beaulieu, to the Cistercian Order in 1204. This was followed, between 1236 and 1324, by the enclosure of a further 791 acres of 'waste' and 'heath' in the Forest by the Abbey of Beaulieu. Various other ecclesiastical establishments held lands by grant in the Forest and at least one, Netley Abbey, another Cistercian House, encroached upwards of 300 acres of the Forest in 1252 and 1331.[4] These examples serve to emphasise the demands on land of poor or at least below average quality. On a smaller scale, numbers of vaccaries were enclosed from the Forest by the Crown as early as the beginning of the thirteenth century, and later passed into private ownership by grant to become small farms.[5]

Side by side with such major encroachments, the small scale enclosure of plots of land for dwellings and smallholdings appears to have progressed over the centuries, leaving few documentary traces until creeping encroachment from the boundaries of the Crown land received official attention during the late eighteenth and early nineteenth centuries and was finally checked by successive enactments providing means of prosecuting offenders without recourse to a non-existent Justice Seat.[6]

III

It will be seen that the early purpose of the Crown in the New Forest was the preservation of deer, and that the Forest, in common with other Royal Forests, also came to represent a considerable source of income in the form of fines for Forest offences and grants of land and privileges. Silviculture—to avoid confusion the term will be used in preference to forestry throughout—first emerges as a major form of management during the fifteenth century, and appears first to have gained some statutory recognition in an enactment of 1483—Forest Law was by then interpreted to mean that neither the Crown nor the subject could enclose land in a Forest. From the fifteenth century the interest of the Crown underwent a gradual change from deer preservation to timber production, prompted by concern for the diminishing timber resources in England and by the realisation that timber was, therefore, gaining in market value. It must be emphasised that the change in management interest was exceedingly gradual. It, in fact, occupied about three centuries. The fifteenth century saw the expansion of the export of woollen goods, and the building of the first ships designed specifically as ships-of-war as necessary adjuncts to the protection of overseas trade. The following century saw the development of England as a maritime country. It has often been too readily assumed that the demand for timber increased sharply whilst timber resources throughout the country declined. Cunningham[7] drew attention to the apparent concern for the decline in timber resources during the sixteenth and seventeenth centuries and other writers have considered that the late sixteenth or early seventeenth centuries saw a critical point in the decline of timber reserves.[8] Ham-

75

mersley, however, gives figures and material supporting the view that the Crown woods produced no substantial income from their timber during the period 1540–1640, that the sales of wood were curiously casual, that no central, single administration evolved to deal with revenue from the woods (suggesting that such revenue was regarded as comparatively unimportant), and that revenue varied considerably from area to area without any relation to the comparative areas of woodland, all of which implied that no major crisis in timber reserves occurred.[9] It is probable that such a crisis did not occur until the second half of the seventeenth century, and that even then it was not so much a crisis of declining volume of timber available, but of a decline in the volume of timber easily accessible to shipyards and of the quality and odd shapes required by the shipwrights—ship timber necessarily included limbs and stems of special shapes and sizes, some of which could only be grown by accident. The crisis is probably reflected in the tonnage of shipping built in the seventeenth century. During the reigns of James I and Charles I, less than 30,000 tons were built in forty-four years. During the Commonwealth, more than 36,000 tons were built in ten years. Shortly after, in the 1670s, the first strenuous efforts at timber conservation were made in the New Forest.

The New Forest, largest of the Royal Forests, together with the Weald of Kent and Sussex, contained the largest reserves of timber in Lowland Britain within easy reach of coastal sites suitable for development as shipyards. In the Weald, suitable shipbuilding timber had probably suffered considerable depletion by the double drain of shipbuilding and the ironworking industry by the late fifteenth century, although it would appear that timber supplies suitable for the ironworking industry were probably nowhere near exhaustion by the Civil War.[9] Industrial consumption of timber from the New Forest, however, seems to have been negligible, and it was on the nearby waters of the Hampshire coast that the early navy of Henry VII was very largely built.

Early silvicultural practices will be returned to in a later chapter, but it is relevant to record briefly that the medieval and seventeenth century enclosures were managed on a basis similar to that usually known as coppice-with-standards, the coppice being leased out for fuel wood, charcoal and various forms of domestic consumption, whilst the timber trees were reserved to the Crown. The neglect to which the coppices can be shown to have been subject by their tenants reflects the consistently low market prices for coppice produce within economically transportable distance of the New Forest, although one would have thought that there would have been a fairly good market on the relatively treeless downland close at hand. In a timber survey of 1608, the surveyor went so far as to suggest the introduction of ironworks to use the surplus fuel.[10]

Silviculture demanded the enclosure of land against browsing and grazing by deer and commonable stock. The greater the area so enclosed the smaller that which was available to the commoner for grazing. In the early small enclosures of the fifteenth, sixteenth and seventeenth centuries lay the seeds of conflict between Crown and commoners. The documentary evidence of the seventeenth, eighteenth and nineteenth centuries show that a vigorous pastoral economy based on the use of the common grazings had developed in the Forest. The conflict of interests, that of the Crown in the enclosure of land for silviculture, and that of the commoners in the retention of the open grazings and in other resources of the open Forest, culminated, after enclosure Acts of 1698 and 1808, in the New Forest Deer Removal Act of 1851, by which the Crown surrendered its right to keep deer in the New Forest, and in lieu of which took powers for silvicultural enclosure on a hitherto unprecedented scale; and then in the New Forest Act of 1877, by which the powers of the Crown to enclose land received close regulation and control and which assigned to the commoners a statutory area of about 45,000 acres over which they might permanently exercise their rights.

The reports of various Enquiries during the reigns of Elizabeth I, James I and Charles II[11] show clearly that the early silvicultural enclosures were inadequate for the purpose of timber conservation. They were too small, they depended mainly on natural regeneration as against deliberate planting for replenishment, and the dual system of management, by which both Crown and tenant had an interest in the produce, lent itself to their depredation. Meanwhile the timber suitable for the shipbuilding industry underwent a steady depletion during the sixteenth and seventeenth centuries. A survey carried out in 1608 gave a total of 123,927 oaks fit for the navy;[11] a further survey of 1707 gave a return of only 12,476.[12] Clearly only large scale enclosure and planting of oaks could adequately meet the need for timber conservation. The first enclosure

Act was finally passed in 1698 and provided for the immediate enclosure and planting with oak of 2,000 acres of land and the subsequent enclosure of 200 acres annually for twenty years. The Act was poorly drafted and introduced the concept of a 'rolling power' of enclosure by the Crown which was never subsequently given a common interpretation by all parties concerned. The 'rolling power' implied that the Crown, whose power was delegated to the Office of the Surveyor-General of Woods as far as silviculture was concerned, could continue to enclose and plant *ad infinitum* so long as no more than 6,000 acres, the total specifically provided for by the Act, were behind fences and free of common rights at any one time. Theoretically this implied that if enclosure and planting proceeded to the limits imposed by soil conditions inhibiting the success of oak crops, all the better grazings in the Forest would disappear beneath trees and the value of the common rights would be much reduced. In fact, under the Act of 1698 only 3,296 acres were ever enclosed and planted—1,022 acres immediately following the Act, 230 acres in 1750 and 2,044 acres in 1776—and the dispute over the rolling power lay dormant until the following century.

The Act of 1698 contained the first legal recognition of rights of common over the New Forest, although claims to rights had already been registered at the Justice Seats in 1635 and 1670. The Act also provided that the enclosures which were to be made should be on such land as, 'could best be spared from the commons and highways.' The impression gained is that the Crown, whilst claiming its 'rolling power' of enclosure was not at that time prepared to challenge local interests too seriously. By the end of the eighteenth century, many of the enclosures which had been made had undergone considerable degeneration through lack of attention and the depredations of commoners and minor Crown officials alike. Three enclosures, Wilverley Inclosure, Aldridgehill Inclosure and Rhinefield Inclosure, totalling 735 acres had by the end of the century been converted into rabbit warrens by the keepers, to whom the sale of rabbits was a source of revenue.[12]

The *Fifth Report of Commissioners to Enquire into the Woods, Forests and Land Revenues of the Crown*, presented to Parliament in 1789, revealed fundamental defects in the administration and management of the Forest which, so long as they continued, would inevitably preclude successful silviculture. Such defects had already been made clear in the reports and returns made by various Commissions as early as the sixteenth century, but in no such straightforward and forcible a manner as they were now presented. The Report of 1789 revealed the strange anomaly of an administrative structure originally designed for, and a management which continued to perpetuate, the preservation of large numbers of deer from which virtually no revenue had accrued for well over a hundred years, in which no sovereign since Charles II had showed the slightest personal interest, and which severely restricted the development of silviculture, potentially the main source of income.

'The only object of great consequence . . .', states the Report, 'is the increase and preservation of Timber: how far that object is regarded in the present management of this Forest will appear on a slight attention to the nature of its . . . (administration).' It points out that those responsible for the enclosure, planting, felling and marketing of timber had no control over the various grades of Forest official whose functions had originally been connected with deer management but whose posts had by then become honorific appointments carrying perquisites ranging from the right to take timber to moneys from the sale of rabbits and deer. At the same time, 'the perquisites of the Surveyor General' and his deputies, who were responsible for silvicultural management, 'also hold out strong inducements to promote the profuse felling of timber, but none for its increase and preservation.' Indeed, many officials responsible for the plantations at the same time held honorific positions in the hierarchy of the old deer Forest which were quite incompatible with their duties as regards timber management and conservation. The Report enlarges on the anachronism of deer preservation as follows:

> The only article of produce from this Forest, besides . . . (the timber) is the deer. From the information of the keepers it appears that the number killed annually is about 76 brace of Bucks and about 17 brace of does. The greater number of these are Fee Deer, supplied to the various Forest officers, and deer given to the proprietors of neighbouring estates by way of compensation for the damage sustained by them . . . (from the deer).

It emerges from the Report that the day-to-day care of the plantation depended on the under-keepers. This is enlarged upon in the following passage:

> In this situation the greatest care should have been taken to allow no perquisites to those men, that they should make it for

their interest to do anything that might be prejudicial to the Forest, or lead them to counteract the great public object of increasing and preserving the timber and woods. But if a keeper should perform his duty in every particular necessary to promoting this object, he would lose the greater part of his present emoluments, which depend on the increase and encouragement of what is destructive to the wood and timber. For it appears that . . . (their incomes) . . . are derived chiefly from Fees for Deer (ie they received a fee for each of a specified number of deer they killed), Profits by Sale of Wood, and by the Breed of Rabbits and Swine. . . . The mode of paying those who have care of this valuable Forest is certainly such as no man would adopt in the management of his own property.

In enumerating the causes of the general failure of silviculture since its inception in the New Forest, the degeneration of the Forest woodlands as a whole during the previous two hundred years or more, and particularly, the degeneration of the Inclosure made following the Act of 1698, the Report points out that the Forest was so over-stocked with deer that, 'many die yearly, of want, in winter'; that, 'great waste and destruction is made of the hollies and thorns, which afford the best nursery for young trees, and much wood of a larger size is cut by the keepers' under the guise of cutting browse for winter feed for the deer 'to increase their own profits'; that rabbits, far from being controlled, were encouraged by the keepers as a source of income; that many of the keepers made a considerable living from pigs, which were allowed in the Forest, both within and outside the Inclosures, throughout the year; and that the Inclosure fences were everywhere in such a state 'as to keep out neither deer, horses, cattle or swine.' The Report adds further that neither the fence month nor the winter heyning had been observed; that excessive quantities of timber were taken for re-sale under the pretence of the exercise of rights to fuel wood (*estovers*); and that 'fern, heath and furze' was cut on a widespread scale 'with the certain effect of destroying whatever young shoots are coming through them.'

It is clear that the Forest was then, and had been since the Forest courts had fallen into disuse, exploited to the hilt, that deer preservation was an anachronism and contrary to the sound management of the timber, and that for a very long period of time the whole antiquated administrative structure had been riddled with opportunities for 'pickings', perquisites and general exploitation of the grazings and woods. As Cobbett remarked, the Forest 'had been crawled upon by favourites.'

The Report of 1789 recommended the disafforestation of the New Forest. The area which the Crown was to retain was to be devoted to the single purpose of silviculture and the remainder was to be partitioned among those who could prove that they had rights of common over it. These recommendations were never implimented, but various enactments made during the early years of the ninetoonth century made some rather ineffectual attempts to tighten up the administration and management. The most important of these was an Act of 1808, providing for further silvicultural enclosure.

IV

The enclosure Act of 1808 confirmed the existing 2,247 acres of enclosures made under the Act of 1698, and provided for further enclosure up to a total of 6,000 acres which could be behind fences at any one time. There was subsequently some dispute as to whether the wording of the Act was intended to mean that more than a total of 12,000 acres should ever be enclosed. The Crown continued to claim its right to a 'rolling power' of enclosure but there appears to have been no major protest from the main body of the commoners such as that which followed the later Act of 1851, although greater advantage was taken of the opportunity provided for silviculture than following the 1698 Act, and the Office of Woods appears to have maintained a much better control over the management and care of the Inclosures made, largely perhaps because its own administration had been greatly improved. Between 1808 and 1817, 5,557 acres were enclosed and planted, and between 1830 and 1848 a further 1,147 acres were similarly treated.

The Report of the Commissioners of 1789 had clearly demonstrated that deer preservation was an outdated and expensive survival of medieval England. Most Royal Forests had long been more of a liability than an asset to the Crown and many were disafforested and partitioned between the Crown and those freeholders with common rights over them, early in the nineteenth century. In 1848, a Select Committee of the House of Commons was appointed to investigate what changes were essential in the management of the Forests which remained. In evidence before this Committee it was shown beyond doubt that every buck killed in the New Forest cost the Crown £100 or more; that about 120 bucks were killed annually; and that these went mainly to neighbouring landowners as compensation for damage done by the deer on their estates. Some evidence was also given on behalf of the commoners to the effect that the deer competed with their stock for keep. The view of a subsequent Commission, the Royal New and Waltham Forests Commission, which sat in 1849, was that the deer should be 'removed' and that the Crown should receive compensation for the relinquishment of its interests in deer preservation in the shape of an allotment of land for silviculture, over and above that already enclosed. The original provision of the ensuing Bill was for the enclosure of an additional 14,000 acres. It would appear that the Bill was pushed through Parliament before opposition among the commoners could be organised, but the last minute representations of a number of local landowners to the Office of Woods did succeed in obtaining a reduction from 14,000 acres to 10,000 acres.

Looking back from a distance of a hundred years or so, it seems strange logic that the Crown should receive compensation for relinquishing a self-imposed liability, but then it seems equally strange that the liability had been self-inflicted for such a space of time as two hundred years or more: one can only conclude that the Forest had, indeed, been 'crawled upon by favourites' and that corruption and exploitation, once firmly entrenched, were not easy to dislodge in the atmosphere of seventeenth and eighteenth century intrigue.

By the provisions of the New Forest Deer Removal Act, 1851, the Crown finally and firmly established its purpose in the New Forest as the growth of timber. The Act took powers for the enclosure of 10,000 acres in addition to that which had already been enclosed in pursuance of the Acts of 1698 and 1808, and was worded in such a manner that the Crown, or Office of Woods, was able to continue to assert its right to a 'rolling power' of enclosure, provided always that the total area of land behind fences at any one time did not exceed 16,000 acres. Its other major provisions were for the removal of the deer within three years of the passing of the Act, and for the compilation of a Register of Claims to Common Rights.

The decimation of the deer—their complete removal, as might have been expected in so large an area, proved impossible—following the Act of 1851, resulted in profound ecological and economic changes which will be enlarged upon in later chapters. The provisions as to enclosure, the claimed rolling power, and attempts by the Office of Woods to enforce the fence month and winter heyning —for the Crown still claimed its old Forestal rights, despite the 'removal' of the deer—were the subject of widespread agitation and alarm among the commoners. The arbitrary choice of sites for enclosures, taking in much of the grazings without providing the commoners with opportunities for expressing their views, and the alleged misappropriation by the Office of Woods of some of the moneys from the sale of small parcels of land to cover the cost of compiling the Register of Claims to Common Rights and from the sale of land for the Southampton–Dorchester railway, were further sources of complaint. Perhaps the commoners saw in the Act of 1851, above all, the culmination of the threat to their rights which had been implied by the rolling power claimed under the previous Acts of 1698 and 1808. Protest found a coherent voice with the formation of the New Forest Commoners' Defence Association and the New Forest Association. Petitions to the House of Lords resulted in the appointment of a Select Committee to consider the commoners' causes of complaint. The Committee, which sat in 1868, concluded that there must inevitably be a perpetual state of conflict between Crown and Commoners, and recommended disafforestation and partition between the two bodies. A Bill to disafforest the New Forest was, in fact, introduced in 1871 by the Secretary of the Treasury, but was subsequently withdrawn and a resolution passed in the House of Commons that, 'no felling of timber in the New Forest should take place except for the thinning of the young plantations, and no fresh enclosures should be made pending legislation on the New Forest.'

A Select Committee of the House of Commons sat in 1875 to reconsider the commoners' case which was by this time backed up by a growing public interest in the amenities of the area, represented chiefly by the Commons and Footpaths Preservation Society, which wielded considerable influence. This time, in a decidedly more liberal atmosphere, recommendations were made which were to form the basis for legislation directed towards the much closer definition of the respective rights of Crown and commoners, and which were intended as a basis for reconciliation between them.

The resulting New Forest Act of 1877 restricted the enclosure of land for silviculture to those lands which had been enclosed pursuant to the Acts of 1698, 1808 and 1851—about 18,000 acres—and finally denied the Crown the right to a rolling power of enclosure. Only 16,000 acres were to be behind fences at any one time. The remainder of the Forest—nearly 45,000 acres—was to be permanently available for the exercise of common rights.

The Act released the commoners from the possibility of the enforcement of obsolete restrictions such as the winter heyning and the fence month, and completely re-constituted the old court of Swainmote and Attachment. Compounded as it had been of outdated Forest Laws with a few additional duties conferred by various Acts since 1698, the function of the Court of Swainmote and Attachment was nebulous and ill-defined. The oath of the Verderers, who presided over the Court, was to protect the Crown's rights in all respects and to do justice in disputes between commoner and commoner over their respective rights. The actual enforcement of Forest Law had lain with the Lord Warden, the supreme officer of the Crown, a post which had become redundant with the passing of the Deer Removal Act and whose duties had passed to the Office of Woods.

The Act of 1877 abolished the oath to the Crown, increased the number of Verderers from four to six, one of whom was to be the 'Official Verderer' appointed by the Crown and the remainder of whom were to be elected by commoners and parliamentary voters of parishes within the Forest. They were to become a Body Corporate in perpetual succession, with powers to sue and be sued; to hold land as requisite to their functions; to employ officers as required for the control and management of commonable stock; to defray costs by levying dues—'marking fees'—on the commoners for each animal turned out on the Forest; to make Bye-Laws for the control of stock on the Forest and for the benefit of the health of the commoners' animals; to maintain the Register of Claims to Common Rights made in pursuance of the 1851 Act; and to dispose of the moneys from the sale of land for the Southampton–Dorchester railway for the benefit of the commoners. Every Verderer was given the powers of a Justice of the Peace for Forest matters and the Court of Swainmote and Attachment became a Court of Petty Sessions. In short they were to be responsible for the management of all matters relating to the running of stock on the Forest. In practice they became also the voice of the commoners.

The Act was a major triumph for the commoners. Unfortunately, reconciliation between Crown and commoners—or between Office of Woods and Verderers—was to be frustrated for many years to come. For more than thirty years there seems to have been constant friction between the officers of the Crown and the Verderers. Most accounts of the nineteenth and twentieth century history of the Forest, including that of Lascelles,[13] who was Deputy surveyor from 1880 to 1915, are inclined to lay much of the blame at the door of the Verderers, whom it is stated, pursued their newly-imposed function of protecting the rights of the commoners to the point of attempting to establish that all such land which had been assigned to the exercise of common rights by the Act of 1877 was the property of the commoners and that the sole right of the Crown in the Forest was that of limited silvicultural Inclosure. In pursuing this course, it is pointed out, the Verderers would appear to have conveniently overlooked section 12 of the 1877 Act, which reserved to the Crown all rights in the Forest other than those expressly diminished by the Act. It is certainly true that the Verderers challenged the right of the Crown over matters such as the granting of wayleaves and easements.

The most oft-quoted case is that of the Verderers' challenge to the right of the Office of Woods to allow sawmills on the open Forest on the grounds that the grazings were thereby restricted, a case which was taken to the High Court in 1894.[14] Reading the correspondence which passed between the two bodies during this period, and reading the transcript of the High Court case, however, it becomes clear that the Verderers were by no means indulging in the deliberate obstruction and irresponsibility usually attributed to them, but were attempting to establish finally and precisely the respective limits of the rights of Crown and commoner. The Crown officers, on the other hand, appear to have been distinctly uncooperative—some of Lascelles' letters seem deliberately provoking. The sawmill case was settled out of court—it was agreed to move the mill from Holmsley Lawn to a less important grazing area— and neither this point at issue nor others such as the definition of responsibility for drainage and clearance of scrub on the open Forest was finally setttled.

It has further been alleged[15] that after the 1877 Act the officials of the Office of Woods took the mistaken view that the provisions of the Act, and especially that relating to their limited right of enclosure, made successful silviculture a dead letter, and that not until 1913 does it appear to have been appreciated that the Act had left the Office of Woods ample scope. It is certainly true that over the greater part of the period from 1877 to 1913, a large proportion of the Inclosures were either without fences or were fenced poorly and that big falls of timber were rare: but then a large proportion of the plantations had only come into being in the 1850s and 1860s, as a result of the 1851 Act—the period was one of timber conservation rather than production and also, by the latter years of the century, fences would have been largely superfluous since protection against stock was not by that time universally necessary. Moreover, neither Lascelles nor other contemporary observers leave the impression that silviculture became neglected—inded, the contrary seems the case. It would seem that progressively distorted local tradition, repeatedly plagiarised in print, has produced a picture of the period following the Act of 1877 which is some way from the truth. To re-adjust the picture here is not merely of intrinsic historical interest but serves to illustrate the caution with which many accounts of local affairs must be taken.

V

The management of the New Forest passed to the Forestry Commission under the Forestry (Transfer of Woods) Act 1923. The statutory Inclosures were by that time in a poor state. Most of the fences were down and, according to local accounts, the commoners strongly resisted attempts to remove their stock from the Inclosures. Heavy wartime fellings had taken place and there was need for a large scale programme of replanting. At the same time public interest in the amenities of the Forest was growing rapidly—had indeed, been focusing increasingly on the Forest since the 1870s—and there was considerable criticism of the alleged intention of the Forestry Commission to manage the Inclosures purely from an economic point of view and to steadily convert the hardwood stands to more profitable conifer crops. Criticism was finally met by a statement made by Lord Clinton, then Chairman of the Commission, in the House of Lords in 1928, to the effect that the Forestry Commission were aware of the amenity value of the area and

regarded its amenities as being of first importance. In the following year an Advisory Committee was appointed to make recommendations on the selection and treatment of outstandingly
picturesque areas within the statutory Inclosures. This Committee
met regularly until the 1939–45 war, and consisted of representatives of the Verderers, the National Trust, the New Forest Association and the Commons & Footpaths Preservation Society. Its
formation marked the real beginning of increasingly friendly relations between the Verderers and the Forestry Commission.

After the war of 1939–45 it became clear that the New Forest
Act of 1877 had been left in a somewhat anomalous position by
more recent, general legislation, and that changes in the administration of the Forest had become necessary in order to bring it into
line with modern conditions, whilst respecting the various rights
over it. In 1946 the Minister of Agriculture appointed a committee
to investigate and report on the administration and management of
the Forest, and to make recommendations for adjusting it to modern
conditions, having due regard to the rights of the commoners and
the general interest of the public in amenity. *The Report of the
New Forest Committee* (The Baker Report), was laid before Parliament in September 1947. It exceeded even the forthrightness of
the Report of 1789 in clarity, commonsense and a clear perception
of the relative importance of the interests involved. When, however,
a new Bill was drafted, many of the recommendations of the Committee were omitted. Petitions were heard in 1949 by a Select Committee of the House of Lords, and the amendments subsequently
made in the Bill far exceeded the hopes of the local petitioners.
The resulting Act, the New Forest Act 1949, embodied most—but
by no means all—of the original recommendations of the New
Forest Committee. The Act, together with the recent New Forest
Act 1964, which is fundamentally a further effort to keep abreast
of rapidly changing conditions, largely govern the administration
of the Forest today.

The modern administration of the New Forest is unique. It is
also complex and all too often inadequately understood, even by
many whose activities are in one way or another affected by it.
For this reason, the following chapter is devoted to a fairly detailed
description of the present administration and the respective roles
of the two statutory bodies, the Forestry Commission and the
Verderers of the New Forest.

References

1 G. J. Turner, *Select Pleas of the Forest*, London, 1901.
2 George Hammersley, 'The revival of the Forest Laws under Charles I', *History*, XLV, 1960, p 87.
3 J. C. Russell, *British Medieval Populations*, 1949.
4 R. A. Donkin, 'The Cistercian Settlement and the English Royal Forests, *Citeaux*, XI, 1960.
5 W. J. C. Moens, 'The New Forest, its afforestation. . . .', *Arch J*, 60, 1963.
6 C. R. Tubbs and G. W. Dimbleby, 'Early Agriculture in the New Forest', *Advancement of Science*, June 1965.
7 W. Cunningham, *The Growth of English Industry. . . .*, Camb, 1938.
8 eg R. G. Albion, *Forests and Sea Power*, Camb, Mass, 1926.
9 G. Hammersley, 'The Crown Woods and their exploitation in the sixteenth and seventeenth centuries', *Bull Inst Hist Res*, XXX, 1957.
10 Public Record Office, SP 14/42.
11 Public Record Office, E/178.
12 *Fifth Report of Commissioners to Enquire into the Woods, Forests and Land Revenues of the Crown*, 1789.
13 Hon G. W. Lascelles, *Thirty-Five Years in the New Forest*, London, 1915.
14 *Attorney General v Verderers of the New Forest*, High Court, Queens Bench Division, 10 December 1894.
15 eg by F. E. Kenchington, *The Commoners' New Forest*, London, 1944.

Page 89: (above) Nineteenth-century gravel working recolonised by heather, Matley Heath (NGR SU345068); (below) Oak clump on Hampton Ridge (NGR SU204143): a relict of a formerly extensive wood

Page 90: Pony grazing along woodland edge

FIVE

Modern Administration

THE New Forest Act 1949 reconstituted the Verderers for the second time, and further extended their powers. Their number was increased to ten: the Official Verderer, nominated by the Crown; five Verderers elected by persons occupying an acre or more of land to which common rights attached; and four Verderers appointed respectively by the Minister of Agriculture, the Forestry Commission, the Local Planning Authority, and the Council for the Preservation of Rural England. The qualifications for an elective Verderer was henceforth to be the occupation of not less than an acre of land to which common rights attached, instead of the seventy-five required by the 1877 Act. Electoral procedure was modernised; the powers of the Verderers to make bye-laws for maintaining the health of commonable stock were increased; and additional powers were conferred which enabled the Verderers to have a measure of control over additional silvicultural Inclosure of the open Forest, the improvement of the grazings and other matters affecting the common land of the Forest.

The Act resolved two problems which had arisen persistently since the passing of the 1877 Act, and went some way to providing for a solution to a third which was beginning to emerge. In the first place it answered the prickly question of who was responsible for drainage and the clearance of scrub from the grazings of the open Forest by assigning these duties to the Forestry Commission. In the second it placed on the Forestry Commission the duty of preparing plans upon which all the lands for which common rights had been acknowledged in the 1858 Register were to be marked: the 1858 Register had merely defined the lands by reference to their numbers on the tithe maps and the establishment of rights had subsequently become a somewhat complicated and cumbersome business. The Atlas of Claims made pursuant to the 1949 Act is probably unique in Britain. The third problem, that of the increasing numbers of road accidents between animals and motor vehicles, had assumed little more than an embryo form at the time of the Act's passage through Parliament. Today it may be said to have matured. *The Report of the New Forest Committee* 1947, had recognised the problem but—understandably—had not foreseen its future magnitude. It took note that a large proportion of the accidents took place outside the Forest and were caused by straying animals—many of them habitual 'lane-crawlers'—and recommended that the Forest should be contained by road-grids. It recommended, too, that when the main A31 trunk road through the Forest came to be modernised, stock should be denied access to it by means of a 'ha-ha' wall. The Report did not, however, place such main emphasis on the problem of road accidents that a Report of, say, ten years later would certainly have done. Section 16 of the 1949 Act embodied, *inter alia*, provision for implementing the recommendation regarding the exclusion of stock from the A31, but went no further in ensuring the prevention of accidents between stock and vehicles. It was to be another fifteen years before the problem was tackled more adequately.

The 1949 Act made three further main provisions. It empowered the Verderers to consent to the enclosure by the Forestry Commission of a further 5,000 acres of the open Forest for silviculture; it provided for the temporary enclosure of land on the open Forest for carrying out improvements in the grazings; and it provided for the active management of the 'Ancient and Ornamental' woodlands of the open Forest, management which had hitherto been precluded by the 1877 Act, and which was now needed in many places as the old timber fell and regeneration was prevented by the browsing of commonable stock and deer. During the later war years and immediately afterwards, some thousand acres of the open Forest had been cropped and reseeded, although the operation had strictly speaking been illegal under the then existing legislation. The reseeded sites made a valuable contribution to the Forest grazings, and the Act now sought to place possible future operations on a legal footing. Advantage has since been taken both of this provision and that relating to silvicultural enclosure. In 1958, the Verderers consented to the enclosure by the Forestry Commission of 2,000 acres of the open Forest, gaining not only monetary compensation, but some useful grazing land in the form of reseeded strips round the perimeter of the new Inclosures; the strips serving not only as grazing land but also effective firebreaks. Shortly after, three areas were enclosed and reseeded under the direction of the Verderers.

In the years which followed the 1949 Act, two main inter-related problems came sharply into focus. The phenomenal rise in the numbers of motor vehicles on the roads was reflected in a progressive increase in the numbers of accidents involving commoner's animals. By 1955 the annual total of accidents stood at 170—115 animals killed and 55 injured—representing about 5 per cent of the total head of stock depastured on the Forest. In 1963 the figure stood at 349 accidents—289 animals killed and 60 injured—representing 8.2 per cent of the total depastured. Of the total for 1963, 104 accidents occurred outside the perambulation. Of those within the Forest, the two main trunk roads—the A31 and A35—had between them claimed 133 accidents. Clearly the situation had become intolerable both from the point of view of animal owners and motorists—quite apart from the suffering occasioned by the animals themselves. Not the least unhappy were the insurance companies.

The associated problem arose from the exercise of common rights over manorial wastes adjacent to, and often contiguous with, the commons of the Forest itself, but outside its legal boundary. A substantial head of ponies and cattle were depastured on the adjacent commons and by the custom of vicinage animals turned out on them could roam on to the Forest and *vice versa*—a situation which was in the very least highly unsatisfactory. It was indeed, fraught with anomalies. The depasturing of stock on the adjacent commons was subject to none of the controls imposed by the Verderers' Bye-Laws in the interests of animal health, nor did those who turned out stock on the adjacent commons pay marking fees to the Verderers. The presence within the Forest of animals not subject to the Bye-Laws constituted a recurring threat to the spread of contagious diseases. It made for difficulties in controlling pony breeding, since there was nothing to stop scrub stallions turned out on the adjacent commons from roaming on to the Forest.

At the same time, to some extent the commoners turning out stock on the adjacent commons were receiving—free—the benefit of the Verderers' and their servants' services. In some cases the situation had arisen whereby an animal owner possessed common rights over the New Forest and also claimed rights over the adjacent commons: if he cared to turn out stock on the Forest he was obliged to pay marking fees: if he turned out on the commons he had no such obligation, yet still received many of the services given in return for the marking fees. Clearly, the problems arising from the close proximity of controlled and uncontrolled commons needed to be resolved.

The solution had been suggested first by the 1947 Report, which had recommended that the adjacent commons should be brought under the dual control of the Forestry Commission, who should purchase or come to management agreements over the adjacent commons, and of the Verderers, whose Bye-Laws should be extended over the adjacent commons—in other words, that the commons should be brought within the perambulation of the Forest. The Report suggested that all claims to common rights over the adjacent commons should be investigated, the lands upon which such rights arose should be marked on the Atlas of Claims and the new commoners be included on the Electoral Roll of those entitled to vote in the elections of Verderers.

These recommendations of the 1947 Report were not adopted by the resultant Act of 1949. Later consideration of the problems arising from the adjacent commons and from the increasing animal accident rate, however, suggested that the answers to both lay largely in the concept of a single, controlled area of common land, its boundary gridded and fenced to prevent straying, and its stock under the single control of the New Forest Verderers. The gridding and fencing of the perambulation had become an obvious necessity by the late 1950s, the fencing of the A31 equally so. The former would not appear to have required specific legislation: the latter was provided for by the 1949 Act. The actual extension of the perambulation to include the adjacent commons within the Forest and the application of the Verderers' Bye-Laws to them, however, could not be effected without recourse to Parliament.

It is not proposed here to trace in detail the events which preceded the passing of the recent New Forest Act 1964. The gridding and fencing of the entire area—Forest and adjacent commons—and the fencing of the A31 was carried out in 1963 and 1964, but objection and procrastination arose once the proposal to bring the adjacent commons within the legal boundary was made known in the form of a Private Members Bill which was ultimately steered through Parliament by Sir Oliver Crosthwaite-Eyre, DL, MP. A cynic might observe that the objections raised by the commoners turning out stock on the adjacent commons were based on a reluctance to pay marking fees, which contrasted markedly with their readiness to accept the benefits provided by the grids and fencing—which were paid for by the New Forest commoners, via the Verderers, the County Councils involved, and by donation. It is, however, too soon after the event to pass opinion and comment on the rights and wrongs of the various petitions against the Bill: passion is still larger than life and the personalities and politics involved scarcely bear discussion so soon after the event. Beyond paying tribute to the unremitting efforts on behalf of the Forest by Sir Oliver Crosthwaite-Eyre—whose grandfather played so large a part in the prelude to the 1877 Act—it is intended to confine attention to the practical effects of the Bill and the new responsibilities it placed on the Forestry Commission and the Verderers.

The New Forest Act 1964 altered the perambulation of the Forest to include some 3,500 acres of adjacent commons—Rockford and Ibsley Commons, Gorley Hill and Hyde Common, lying contiguous with the Forest on its west side; Hale Purlieu, on its north side, and an extensive tract of commons, mainly owned by the National Trust, to the north-east. These added areas became subject to the Verderers' Bye-Laws and to the Bye-Laws of the Forestry Commissioners. The Act provided that the Forestry Commission should re-open the Atlas of Claims so that those persons claiming rights of common of pasture over the adjacent commons could register their right. Thus, in effect, they become commoners of the New Forest. An anomaly remains, in that rights of common of mast and other rights are not required to be registered, although the full implications of this do not yet seem clear. The Act provided for the maintenance of the perambulation fencing and gridding; for the erection of drift-fencing at particularly dangerous points on roads within the Forest; and for the fencing of the A35—carried out in 1967.

The Act makes a number of other, miscellaneous provisions. It alters the pannage season from 25 September to 22 November to any period of not less than sixty consecutive days as may be fixed by the Forestry Commission after consultation with the Verderers. It empowers the Verderers to make enclosures for containing stock in severe weather. It provides for the possible creation of new ornamental woods. It increases the size of the fines which may be imposed under the Verderers' and Forestry Commission Bye-Laws.

Perhaps more important, it contains the first statutory recognition of the needs of wildlife conservation in the Forest by placing on the Forestry Commission and the Verderers the obligation to have regard for the desirability of conserving 'flora, fauna and geological and physiographical features of special interest', in the performance of their duties under the New Forest Acts 1877–1964. The interests of amenity had been met in previous enactments, particularly in respect of the old woodlands of the open Forest, but here, for the first time, lies some recognition of the outstanding wildlife interest of the area—despite the confusion of terms illustrated by the marginal note to the conservation clause in the 1964 Act, which reads, 'Preservation of Amenity'.

It is, I think, desirable to crystallise this account of recent modifications in the administration of the Forest with a clear enumeration of the various responsibilities of the two statutory bodies largely involved and a precise statement of their position *vis à vis* one another.

FORESTRY COMMISSION

The Forestry Commission may be regarded as the agents for the owner of the soil of the Forest, and it is thus responsible for all matters of administration arising from ownership of the soil, irrespective of the limitations placed on its activities by law, such as the limitation of the right to enclose land for silviculture. The Deputy Surveyor administers the Forest, having as assistants two District Officers controlling the several beats into which the statutory Inclosures are divided, an Estate Officer for land agency and an Executive Officer and clerical staff for the administrative work. Some 200 forest workers are employed for the silvicultural work, and some seventeen keepers for the extemely varied work which comprises the job of a New Forest Keeper: this includes deer control, supervision of controlled burning of the open Forest, supervision of the New Forest Bye-Laws and control of campers and other visitors. Most of the Keepers are sworn in as Special Constables.

Except for the holders of turbary rights, and except for the statutory provision relating to reseeding areas of the Forest, the Forestry Commission alone have the right to touch the soil of the Forest, and such timber as grows upon it. They are thus responsible for the granting of wayleaves and easements connected with such works as pipelines, access paths and tracks to private residences, car parks, recreation grounds, golf courses and so on. In most cases such permissions are not granted without consultation with the Verderers.

The Forestry Commission Bye-Laws are intended for the regulation of the reasonable use of the Forest by the public, who have since time immemorial been permitted access over it, and for securing the preservation of its timber, flora and fauna. Camping, the deposition of waste materials, the erection of any structure of any description—such as advertisements—and any disturbance of the soil of the Forest is prohibited by the Bye-Laws save under permission of the Commission. To camp in the Forest, therefore, requires a permit. It is some measure of the popularity of the area that in 1966 roughly 300,000 camping permits were issued for over-night stays. In general, therefore, the Forestry Commission may be described as the custodian of the general amenities of the Forest, its wildlife, and also the sporting facilities it offers. The latter are rented to a number of carefully chosen shooting licencees. Wildlife conservation is the subject of a close and sympathetic liaison between the Forestry Commission and the Nature Conservancy. In an agreement signed in 1959 the Forestry Commission formally recognised the important nature reserve status of the Forest, and arrangements were made for the safeguarding of certain areas of special importance. On a wider basis the Conservancy are consulted over matters such as heather burning, drainage proposals and the management of the unenclosed woodlands.

In addition to these general administrative functions devolving on ownership of the soil, the Forestry Commission has a number of specific powers and functions within the Forest:

1 Silviculture

The Commission has the duty of managing the statutory Inclosures for silviculture, but with a very high regard for the interests of amenity. 'Amenity', when used in relation to the planting and production of timber, amounts largely to the maintenance of as large a proportion of hardwoods within the Inclosures as is practicable, and despite the much higher financial return from softwood production. It is, also, not the policy to clear fell extensive areas, but in so far as is possible, to maintain a 'patchwork' pattern of silvicultural management.

2 Management of 'Ancient and Ornamental' Woodland

The 'Ancient and Ornamental' woodlands of the Forest are those areas of woodland which are not subject to statutory Inclosure and form part of the open Forest. Under section 13 of the 1949 Act, the Commission has the duty of securing the regeneration of these woods under working plans approved by the Verderers, provided that no enclosure made shall exceed twenty acres in size and provided that it is thrown open when out of danger from damage by stock. Section 10 of the 1964 Act also provides that the Commission, if authorised by the Verderers, may enclose areas of up to a similar size, for the purpose of creating new 'ornamental' woods, but it seems unlikely that advantage will be taken of this, at least not on any scale.

3 Drainage and scrub clearance on the open Forest

Section 11 of the 1949 Act provides that it shall be the duty of the Forestry Commission to maintain bridges and culverts on the open Forest, for securing that the Forest shall be properly drained and that the grazings are kept 'sufficiently clear of coarse herbage, scrub and self-sown trees'. The New Forest is probably the only area in Britain where the Forestry Commission has an obligation to destroy potential timber!

4 Atlas of Claims to Common Rights

The Forestry Commission had the duty of compiling the Atlas of Claims pursuant to the 1949 Act and now has a similar duty in respect of the rights arising from the areas added to the Forest by the 1964 Act.

VERDERERS

Under the 1877 Act, the Verderers became responsible for the care and maintenance of the health of commoners' stock depastured on the open Forest, and for the regulation of rights of common. In order to carry out these functions they were empowered to draft Bye-Laws for submission to Quarter Sessions, whose confirmation was required to validate them, and to employ officers—the Agisters—to look after stock on the Forest and enforce the Bye-Laws. Their duties also include today the collection of marking fees, which are the main source of the Verderers' income. The 1949 and 1964 Acts considerably enlarged the powers of the Verderers to include the following main powers and functions:

TABLE II

Present Day Land Use and Administration of the New Forest

Land Tenure	Area (acres)	Land Use	Administration and Management
1 Private Freehold	25,791		Subject to Local Authority jurisdiction. Bye-Laws of New Forest Verderers apply to the manorial wastes
(a) enclosed	c 22,300	Villages, farms, etc.	
(b) unenclosed	c 3,500	Manorial wastes subject to exercise of common rights	
2 Crown Land	67,024		
(a) Statutory Inclosures	19,656 (includes 2,010 acres planted under 1949 Act)	Devoted to timber production but with high regard for amenity and wildlife	Managed by Forestry Commission. Free of common rights whilst enclosed. Subject to Bye-Laws of Forestry Commissioners.
(b) Crown Freehold	2,376	Mainly plantation, agricultural and residential land	Owned and managed free of common rights by Forestry Commission
(c) Crown Leasehold	487	Plantations	Areas leased by Forestry Commission from estates bordering Crown lands proper and managed for timber production
(d) Open Forest	44,505 (includes c 9,000 acres of woodland)	Subject to exercise of rights of commoners	Forestry Commission are responsible for all matters arising from ownership of the soil (eg wayleaves, easements, etc), and for drainage, scrub clearance, etc, for benefit of commoners and amenity. Subject to both Forestry Commission and Verderers' Bye-Laws. Verderers responsible for supervising exercise of common rights and improving grazings. Forestry Commission and Verderers jointly responsible for safeguarding amenities and wildlife

1 subject to confirmation by the Minister of Agriculture, to widen the scope of their Bye-Laws dealing with the health of stock on the Forest and for the regulation of rights of common of pasture and mast; and to extend their Bye-Laws to the areas added to the Forest under the latter Act;

2 to authorise the Forestry Commission to enclose up to another 5,000 acres of the open Forest for silviculture;

3 to authorise the Forestry Commission to enclose parts of the Ancient and Ornamental woodlands for the purpose of regenerating them, and to authorise enclosure for the creation of new ornamental woods;

4 to authorise the enclosure of land for the purpose of improving the grazings, provided that the total area enclosed at any one time does not exceed 3,000 acres;

5 to agree to the transfer of land to the Minister of Transport or to a Highway Authority other than the Minister, for the purpose of road construction and improvement;

6 to agree to the exchange of parcels of intermixed lands;

7 to ensure that the fencing of the A31 and A35 is adequate; to ensure that the fences and grids containing the Forest shall be maintained; and where and if necessary, to erect fencing on the Forest in order to reduce the risk of accidents between vehicles and stock;

8 and jointly with the Forestry Commission, to preserve the amenities of the open Forest and to have regard to the conservation of wildlife.

The Verderers hold a bi-monthly Court in the Verderers' Hall, Lyndhurst, at which their Bye-Laws are prosecuted and at which any member of the public, whether a commoner or not, is able to make a presentment asking for the Court to consider any matter which he or she considers in need of attention. The Deputy Surveyor sits in court as an observer. On most occasions representatives of the three societies mainly concerned with the Forest—the New Forest Association, the New Forest Commoners' Defence Association, and the New Forest Pony Breeding and Cattle Society—are present, and if they have presentments to make they are presented in a competent, businesslike manner which serves to emphasise the resourcefulness which is the keynote of most of the Verderers' proceedings.

Finally, in this chapter it is perhaps convenient to summarise the administration of the Forest from the vantage point of the various categories of land use into which the district may be divided. For convenience of reference, these are, therefore, summarised in table II.

SIX

Agricultural Economy

MUCH of the periphery of the Forest, and most pockets of enclosed agricultural land within it, comprise small or comparatively small holdings to which are attached the various rights which may be exercised over the unenclosed commons. Most holdings are under about fifty acres, and the profitable management of many rests largely on the exercise of their common rights, particularly that of grazing. The economy of individual holdings varies greatly, but the long established basic system has been for the meadows to be shut up for hay and the stock run on the Forest until keep becomes short there. The holdings thus have the capacity to reduce both overheads in purchased food-stuffs and capital outlay in land. For several hundred years the agricultural economy has been based on the use of the common grazings.

Together with the deer, the exploitation of the Forest for grazing, fuel, marl and other purposes, as integral parts of the rural economy, have been significant modifying forces in the ecological history of the unenclosed lands. In particular, the 'grazing force' has set limits on woodland regeneration and has been a major factor in checking a succession to woodland on the open heaths. It is thus important to explore the history and structure of the agricultural economy and, specifically, to try to identify fluctuations in the number of stock turned out and the economic factors involved.

I

The importance of common rights and the extent to which they were exercised over the New Forest before the seventeenth century can be deduced only from their invariable inclusion in grants of land by the Crown; from presentments at the Forest Courts as to their abuse; and from the petitions of commoners alleging unreasonable restrictions of their rights. The fragmentary evidence from these sources suggests that in medieval times the area supported a vigorous pastoral economy, although it is not possible to construct a sensitive picture of its changing fortunes over the centuries. Certainly, from the thirteenth to the sixteenth centuries, cattle, ponies and to some extent, sheep, were grazed on the Forest, often —according to presentments to the Forest Courts—in numbers which were considered excessive. Some of the biggest graziers were evidently the various religious houses in the area—the Abbey at Beaulieu; the Priories at Christchurch and Braemore. At the same time it is clear that the commons were equally important to the occupiers of much smaller holdings, as is evidenced by the complaint of certain copyholders of the manor of Cadnam and Winsor, adjacent to the Forest, to the Court of Chancery in 1591.[1] The Lord of the Manor was attempting to enclose the manorial waste. The complainants deposed that they were, 'poore copieholders of the manor of Cadnam and Winsor, and their whole estates and livynge' depended on the use of the common, 'so that yf they should be abrydged of their annycent customes it would be their utter undoing'. The common remains unenclosed to this day, despite a further enclosure attempt during the nineteenth century—on which occasion the earlier decision of Chancery was produced as evidence by the copyholders of the manor.

If the pre-seventeenth century evidence is sparse, the New Forest is probably unique for its later successive Register of Claims to common rights—the first compiled in 1635—and for the volume of nineteenth- and twentieth-century material amplifying the importance of the rights in the local economy; little of which had previously been studied more than cursorily until recently.[2]

The first and second Registers, compiled by the Regarders on the occasion of the Justice Seats, or Forest Eyres, held in 1635 and 1670, are essentially similar, but the latter has the advantage of a good English translation from the original Latin.[3] The entries are long and detailed and give a good picture of the importance attached to rights of common and their place in the rural economy.

A total of 307 claims were registered, appertaining to about 65,000 acres of land lying within the limits of the Forest as they appear to have been at Domesday. The relatively small number of claims refers to many times that number of holdings because the Lord of each manor submitted a single claim in respect of all his tenants and copyholders, each separate holding, however, being described in the general claim. In the Register of Claims made pursuant to the New Forest Deer Removal Act, 1851,[4] some 1,200 separate claims are recorded, reflecting the passage of numerous parcels of the manorial estates into small freeholdings.

Most of the claims registered in 1670 refer to holdings of between one and fifty acres and to rights of common of pasture for commonable beasts (ie cattle, ponies, donkeys and mules); right of common of mast (the right to turn out pigs during the pannage season, ie from 25 September to 22 November); right of common of turbary (the right to take turf fuel); right of common of estovers (the right to take fuel wood); and right of common of marl (the right to take marl from recognised pits on the open Forest). Turbary often appears from the context to include the cutting of 'furze faggots' for fuel and 'fern' for bedding and litter, whilst many claims embody the right to take 'fern heath or furze' in addition to turbary. All but a very small number of claims are in respect of each right apart from that of grazing for sheep.

Sheep rights were claimed for the manors of Beaulieu and Cadland and for other lands formerly in the possession of the Cistercian houses at Beaulieu and Netley. It would be exceedingly interesting to establish the extent to which Cistercian sheep farming was adopted in the New Forest. Wherever the Cistercians settled they introduced their sheep, and the sheep rights appertaining to Beaulieu Abbey strongly suggest that the New Forest was no exception. That the rights were used is also certain from the Eyre Rolls: at the Forest Eyre for 1280, for example, the Abbot of Beaulieu was presented for surcharging the Forest with, 'a great amount of horses, mares, cattle, sheep and other animals . . . whereof they know not the number'. Later, in the seventeenth century, a considerable number of people were presented before the Swainmote and Justice Seats for depasturing sheep without possessing the right to do so. At the 1635 Eyre, five such cases were presented, involving a total of 270 sheep. Before a Swainmote in 1665, thirteen cases were presented, involving a total of 333 sheep.[5]

Whether large numbers were ever grazed on the open Forest, however, remains uncertain, but quite possible in view of the economic incentives to sheep husbandry from the fourteenth to the seventeenth centuries. Certainly, however, by the seventeenth century and perhaps earlier, sheep did not occupy a prominent position in the local pastoral industry. As Pearsall has shown,[6] sheep have probably been the greatest inhibitory factor in woodland perpetuation in upland Britain in historic times. Yet the returns of the Regarders of the New Forest to enquiries by the Exchequer in the sixteenth and seventeenth centuries never mention sheep damage when they enumerate causes of woodland degeneration, although damage by cattle, ponies and swine is constantly reiterated.[7]

It is noteworthy too, that the later *Fifth Report of Commissioners to Enquire into the Woods, Forests and Land Revenues of the Crown*, 1789, does not even refer in passing to sheep. Certainly by that time very few were depastured. The only contemporary writer who refers to them is Gilpin, who, more or less in an aside, notes that, 'The sheep does not frequent the Forest in any abundance. Here and there . . . a little flock on a dry, gravelly hill. . . .'[8]

In the Register of claims to common rights published in 1858, common of pasture for sheep was allowed for 5,696 acres of land at Beaulieu; 176 acres at Brockenhurst; the Manor of Cadland and certain adjacent property; and 540 acres of land in the parish of Fawley. The exercise of the rights, however, was closely restricted. One example will suffice. The right appertaining to the land at Brockenhurst is defined thus:

> Common of Pasture of and within the soil of our Lady the Queen's said Forest from a certain place called Sheepe Lane to Wilverley Cross, except the Lawns and woods in the plains and wastes of our Lady the Queen, for two hundred sheep as appertaining to his said lands.

Precise figures for the numbers of stock depastured on the Forest are available for the years 1875 and 1884–1893 and from 1910 onwards. In 1875, 438 sheep were depastured. Between 1884 and 1889 the number varied from 4 to 36 and lastly in 1893 a figure of 100 is given, which suggests a belated experiment in sheep husbandry on the open Forest.[9] Thereafter the references cease. It is persistently asserted today that sheep 'don't do well' on the Forest: yet the numerous place names such as 'Shappen', 'Shipton', 'Sheepwash' and so on, sprinkled across the southern parts of the Forest suggest that the rights were at one time used on some scale.

Most of the claims to pasture rights in the 1670 *Abstract* either state that the right is claimed 'for all times of the year except the fence month' or 'at all fit and proper times of the year according to the assize of the Forest'. The winter heyning, significantly, is never mentioned as such. Certain claims, notably those deriving from Letters Patent, specify the right of pasture to include the fence month. Similarly, claims to rights of common of mast are not always confined to the pannage season; some are claimed 'for all times of the year', usually 'except the fence month'. Most claims concede the old Forestal rule of *levancy* and *couchancy*—the limitation of the number of animals which might be turned out in spring and summer to that which could be maintained on the holding in winter.

Rights of common of estovers and turbary were in 1670 limited only to that amount of turf and wood fuel respectively which was 'reasonably necessary' to the claimant. Such rights were quite clearly not supposed to be exercised for profit by resale, and it was abuse of this stipulation which later led to the close definition of the quantities which might be taken in respect of individual rights.

The *Abstract* shows that there were three main classes of persons who might exercise rights of common over the New Forest in the seventeenth century: the Lords of the manors laying in or adjacent to the Forest, each with his Park or Manor Farm and one or two moderate sized farms out on lease; the very numerous tenants and copyholders of the manors, each with his cottage and piece of ground, or with a holding of a few acres; and a class of freeholders —frequently assuming the title of Yeoman in the claims—with holdings not usually exceeding fifty acres and more often of between fifteen and thirty acres, with many less than fifteen acres. This last class accounted for the largest number of claims, although they were a minority of the total number of holdings.

It is clear that communal manorial organisations of open fields had long been replaced by holdings managed in severalty, if indeed the more formal manor had ever existed in the area. Clearly, too, the majority of the holdings were too small in themselves to be self-supporting. From this and from the nature of the claims registered in 1670, it can be deduced that the economy was mainly one of stock-keeping based on the use of the common lands. The judicious exercise of rights of grazing and mast, supplemented by those of turbary, estovers and marl, the cutting of bracken for bedding and litter and gorse for fuel and fodder, enabled the small farmer to maintain himself in a state of independence impossible of attainment without the rights.

II

The Government Report of 1789 (quoted extensively in chapter four) was tendered to Parliament after two, and probably three, centuries of ineffectual application of the Forest laws. Stock was turned out with little respect for the customary restrictions of the Law and the keepers responsible for the day-to-day prevention of Forest offences were themselves making a comfortable living out of stock-keeping on the Forest.

The Report states,

> Some of the keepers deal largely in swine, which are suffered to remain on the Forest at all seasons . . . the Keeper of Rhinefield Walk alone had a stock of between 70 and 80 in November last. Fern, heath and furze,

the Report continues, were everywhere cut without restriction,

> And those who make a trade of cutting turf and peat, for sale, are becoming so daring as to threaten the burning of the Forest if they are interrupted.

With the revived interest of the Crown in the enclosure of land for silviculture which followed the 1789 Report, however, the rights of the commoners were to receive increasingly closer definition and the exercise of the rights increasingly closer supervision. Indeed, the very fate of the commons and of the livelihood of large numbers of the commoners was to hang in the balance with the enclosure acts of 1808 and 1851, the assertion of the Crown to a 'rolling power' of enclosure and the attempts at disafforestation and partition, before the commoners were finally to receive the protection of the New Forest Act, 1877.

The first Enclosure Act of 1698, as has already been described, was never fully implemented. It has not been possible to trace any contemporary record of petitions against the Bill by commoners, but G. E. B. Eyre, without stating his source, says that in one such petition the commoners, 'describe the Forest as immemorially "a great nursery for breeding cattle" and speak of "many thousands" as "dependent" on their rights of "pasture, turbary and pannage" in it.'[1] Probably it was as a result of the petition that the Act

Page 107: Unenclosed woodland. The margin of Bratley Wood (NGR SU22/08). The beeches are probably of late seventeenth-century origin and the wood exhibits only scattered subsequent regeneration

Page 108: Pollard beeches probably dating from seventeenth-century, Bratley Wood (NGR SU22/08). The slender trees in the background are mainly of early eighteenth-century origin. Note absence of understory

embodied the first statutory recognition of common rights and stipulated that the enclosures made should be of land which could 'best be spared from the commons and highways'.

The Enclosure Act of 1808 seems not to have been preceded by any similar petition. This is in marked contrast to the later, strenuous resistance to the Crown's efforts to obtain greater powers for itself. The resistance to enclosure and disafforestation in the second half of the nineteenth century, however, was organised and led by a nucleus of radical landowners (the people in fact who would have profited most by disafforestation in the long run) and professional men, not by Forest smallholders, as a reading of the evidence given before the various Select Committees will readily confirm. To men such as Mr G. E. B. Eyre, son of the squire of Bramshaw; Mr W. C. W. Esdaile, JP, a large landowner; and Mr C. Castleman, JP, solicitor and company director, must go much of the credit for upholding the rights of the commoners and for preserving the Forest as a unit. In 1808, with the war in full swing, it is unlikely that such an element—even if it then existed—would have been prepared to resist the fairly limited enclosure of land for the growth of ship-building timber. Later in the century they were to have a much stronger hand.

The evidence tendered by Messrs Castleman, Esdaile, Lovell, Compton, Eyre and others before the Select Committees of 1868 and 1875 show clearly the value of common rights, the extent to which those exercising such rights were dependent on them, and the overall depreciation in the value of the common rights resulting from silvicultural enclosure by the Crown. *The Register of Decision on Claims to Forest Rights*, published in 1858, Eyre's study of the smallholding economy in the Forest after the middle of the nineteenth century,[1] a few other printed sources and some MS material, are further contemporary sources which provide a picture of the smallholding economy of the New Forest during the middle and latter parts of the nineteenth century.

The resistance to disafforestation and silvicultural enclosure and the final success of the commoners in obtaining the safeguard of the New Forest Act, 1877, has been outlined in chapter four. The rolling power claimed by the Crown was clearly the greatest immediate threat to the rights and thus the livelihood of large numbers of the commoners. It was freely admitted by the Chief Commissioner of Woods, in evidence before the Select Committee of 1868, that the avowed intention of his department was to reduce the real value of rights of common by enclosing and planting as much of the best grazings as possible in order that the commoners' share in the Forest, in the event of disafforestation, should be as small as possible.[10] It was also clearly intended to obstruct the exercise of common rights to the limit to which this was legally possible. The attempts to enforce the fence month and winter heyning, after the Deer Removal Act—'for the purpose of protecting non-existent deer during the production of an imaginary progeny', as one writer referred to the fence month[11]—seem, however, to have been somewhat unsuccessful.[12]

The precise value of common rights over the New Forest was never legally determined. In evidence before the Select Committee on the Woods, Forests and Land Revenues of the Crown, 1848, it was estimated that in the event of disafforestation, the interests of the commoners was about one half the area of Crown lands. It was later suggested, before the Committees of 1868 and 1875, that it lay between one-half and two-thirds. In fact, as a result of the enclosure of much of the better grazings following the Act of 1851, the real value was considered to have considerably depreciated. It was estimated that if the Office of Woods exercised its claimed rolling power of enclosure to take in the remainder of the good grazing land, stated to be about 11,000 acres, the real value of the rights would be reduced to about one-sixth.

Precisely what rights were legally admitted, to which lands they were attached and to what extent the Crown was able to restrict their exercise is shown in the *Register of Decisions to Claims* published in 1858. The preamble to the register makes it clear that although the Crown had relinquished its interest in deer preservation in 1851, it reserved the right to enforce the fence month, winter heyning and pannage season. The former two bones of contention between Crown and commoners were finally removed by the New Forest Act, 1877. Turbary rights were limited by the Register to specified numbers of turves in respect of each right allowed. This right, and those of estovers and marl were to be exercised only, 'by the view and allowance of the Foresters'—in practice the keepers employed by the Office of Woods.

The Commissioners responsible for the register considered 1,311 claims, almost every one of them for rights of common of grazing, turbary, estovers and mast, many also for marl, and a few for rights of common of grazing for sheep. Approximately 1,200 claims were allowed, but in no case were they allowed for all the rights claimed. The intention seems to have been to 'tighten up' on the use of the open Forest.

III

In evidence before the Select Committee of 1875, Mr W. C. D. Esdaile, JP, analysed the *Register* as follows:

I find that the smaller commoners come out . . .
207 own 1 acre,
200 own 1-4 acres,
126 own 4-10 acres,
51 own 10-20 acres,
44 own 20-30 acres,
beyond which I have taken them to be larger holders.[13]

These figures referred to freeholders only. Of the 'larger holders' —ie the 571 claims allowed by the Commissioners which make up the difference between the 629 claims above, and the total of 1,200 the majority of claims are in respect of freehold holdings of less than eighty acres: a number are for the larger estates, each of which submitted single claims for up to about 150 tenants with common rights, each occupying holdings of less than fifty acres, the vast majority of less than twenty acres.

It is worth comparing these figures with those of Kenchington in 1944.[14] He gives the total number of agricultural holdings in New Forest parishes as 1995, sub-divided as follows: 731 under five acres; 316 between five and ten acres; 274 between ten and twenty acres; 287 between twenty and fifty acres; 178 between fifty and 100 acres; and 218 over 100 acres. Not all these holdings had common rights attached to them, but a short Act of 1879 empowered the Verderers to issue licences for the depasturing of stock by non-commoners. Of the total, Kenchington estimated that approximately two-thirds of the holdings represented the main source of livelihood to their occupiers. He states that

holdings smaller than 50 acres . . . account for approximately 23 per cent of the total area of agricultural land;

but that they represented 81 per cent of the total number of holdings. His description of these smaller holdings may broadly be considered to hold good today:

111

Many of these tiny holdings were equipped and stocked not as smallholdings proper but as miniature farms. Most engage in cattle keeping, either as cowkeepers or as rearers of young horned stock, using the holdings as a source of winter forage and pasturage, and a winter base for stock running on the Forest.

A further account of Forest smallholdings which it is worthwhile considering, is that of Jebb, in 1907.[15] Jebb seems to have obtained most of his information from G. E. B. Eyre, and there is an interesting account of Mr Eyre's estate at Bramshaw. The 2,700 acre estate had sixty-eight holdings in 1907, the largest of which was eighty-three acres and the smallest one acre. A more detailed analysis is given as follows:

18 holdings of 6   acres or under
20 holdings of 12½ acres or under
 7 holdings of 20   acres or under
14 holdings of 50   acres or under
 9 holdings of more than 50 acres but less than 84.

The extent to which the 'small commoner' was dependent on the use of the open Forest in the nineteenth century is made abundantly clear by evidence given before the 1868 and 1875 Select Committees, and again in the twentieth century by evidence given before the New Forest Committee, 1947. The substance of evidence given before the two earlier committees was that the right of common of grazing enabled a commoner to maintain three times as many cattle as he would be able to maintain without the right. Before the 1947 Committee one commoner stated that, 'he could keep three times as many cattle on a holding in the Forest as on fifty acres in the Midlands.'[16]

Mr Esdaile, in evidence before the Committee of 1868, stated that it was felt among the smaller commoners that, '. . . to lose the common rights . . . would be simply ruin; they would not be able to manage their land in the way they do now . . . I have never been able to find a small owner who would be willing to be compensated for the right which he has. . . .'[17] A considerable weight of evidence was given by others in confirmation and it was strongly emphasised that the partition of the Forest and allotment between the interested parties—Crown, or Office of Woods, and commoners—would involve the displacement of the larger proportion of the smaller commoners. It was considered that the allotment of the wastes in severalty, should disafforestation and general enclosure

112

take place, would be negligible compensation to the commoner for his share in the joint enjoyment of the common lands of the Forest as a whole.

Eyre[1] enlarges on the value of the wide range provided by the Forest for stock as follows:

> . . . attention should perhaps be drawn to some elements which make this region a type of what commonable pasture land should be. It combines an extended range with considerable variety of soil and of water supply, and with, perhaps, every variety of shelter and exposure. Any deficiency in one section, especially in running water, is supplied by sufficiency or excess in another; constant change of ground (essential to success in stock-keeping) is ensured. . . .

He notes that, 'the region is characterised by a moderate but widespread prosperity, even in these hard times, and by the low percentage of pauperism . . . and this can be distinctly traced to the judicious exercise of common rights.' The wastes, the open Forest, he says are the, 'cottager's farm', the source of his livelihood and of a modest capital.

The right of common of turbary was allowed in respect of about 1,500 dwellings in the 1858 Register. The MS account book of George Cooper, Jnr, Keeper of Boldrewood and Castlemalwood Walks, for the years 1853–1856 shows an average of 518,000 turves cut annually; that of Harry Cooper, Keeper of Eyeworth and Bramblehill Walks, for the years 1864–1871 shows an average of 233,570 turves cut annually. A single turbary right averaged about 4,000 turves. Eyre elaborates:

> . . . and with its necessary complement of a few faggots or a little stump wood, keeps a cottager in fuel through the winter. The value of such a right is estimated roughly at ten shillings to one pound annually, but as is the case with all common rights, the indirect value is very great and very difficult to define; when combined with a right of fuel-wood each right greatly enhances the value of the other.

Estover rights were satisfied by the cutting and assignment of a specified number of cords of wood by Forest officials. The policy of the Office of Woods had always been to reduce the numbers of such rights by purchasing them from the holders, in order to check the exploitation of the Forest timber. Eyre gives a total annual assignment of 376 cords, consisting of seven 'large' rights totalling 94 cords, and a large number of 'small' rights of a few cords each.

Lascelles stated that the annual assignment was further reduced from 370 cords in 1880 to 240 cords in 1915.[18] The assignment has since been reduced even further.

The importance of turbary and estover rights dwindled with increasing labour costs and the opening-up of the Forest by roads and railways in the late nineteenth and present centuries. It is doubtful whether either right could be considered an integral part of the smallholder's economy by 1915 or 1920, but unfortunately no records have been kept which might demonstrate their decreasing importance. Turves are cut by fewer than a dozen holders of turbary rights in the Forest today.

The exercise of rights of common of marl appears to have lapsed by the late nineteenth century. Keepers' MSS diaries and account books for the 1850s, 1860s and 1870s contain no reference to the right, although the taking of marl was supposed to be by their 'view and allowance'. Trimmer, writing in 1856, drew attention to the potential agricultural importance of the marls of the New Forest, but his whole essay makes it clear that little advantage was at that time taken of them.[19] Spooner, writing in 1871, leaves the impression that the right had not been exercised for some time.[11] Williamson,[20] and Eyre, mention the existence of the right only in passing.

The cutting of bracken for bedding and litter was a widespread and valuable custom in the New Forest during the eighteenth and nineteenth centuries, exercised apparently by immemorial prescription, but not recognised as a right of common, although in certain cases claimed as such in the 1670 *Abstract*. It was not recognised as a right in the 1858 *Register* and according to Eyre, 'fern' was subsequently sold by the Office of Woods 'under conditions generally considered to be prohibitive.' He adds that it was bought 'chiefly from necessity.' It was cut in large quantities until the late 1930s. At present it is cut on a small scale at a nominal fee charged by the Forestry Commission.

The cutting of gorse for fodder appears, too, to have at one time been a widespread practice, although not recognised as a right. Eyre refers to the gathering of 'furze tops' in winter. There seems to be no reference to its deliberate cultivation in the New Forest area, although it was certainly cultivated elsewhere in England during and previous to the nineteenth century.[21] Gilpin mentions the cutting of gorse faggots in the Forest for firing the local pottery kilns,[8] and it would seem that the cutting and carting of 'furze and heath' faggots for the kilns and also for broom making, was a frequent 'sideline' of many cottagers. Jebb, in 1915, clearly regarded the local potteries as providing an important subsidiary employment for many cottagers.[15]

The exercise of the rights of turbary, estovers and marl, and the customs of bracken and gorse cutting may be regarded as reducing or even eliminating heating costs and reducing overhead costs of manuring and stock keeping on the holding. The rights of grazing and pannage fulfilled an even more important function in that they reduced both overhead costs of stock keeping and capital expenditure on land. They remain important today.

The New Forest commoner dependent or partly dependent on his rights of common in the nineteenth and early twentieth centuries belonged to a class of producer which did not normally keep formal accounts. Most of the occupiers of the smaller holdings had two or three sources of income, inextricably intermixed, revolving round, but not necessarily wholly dependent upon, their common rights. The direct financial advantages of the rights are, therefore, difficult to isolate and assess at any given period. Eyre[1] attempted to do so for the 1870s from his special knowledge.

The value of the right of common of mast he describes as varying with the quality of the mast year and with the capital available to the commoner for buying in 'early and cheap as many pigs as he can hope to keep' until the commencement of the pannage season. He estimates that at the end of a moderately good pannage season, 'they return bettered to the value of about 10s to 20s a-head, and fit for immediate sale.' In a good mast year '£5 thus laid out may be doubled in three months . . . cottagers have been known to make £20 a year by their pigs.'

It is clear from Eyre's study that overhead costs were most reduced in the case of ponies, which required the minimum of labour and superintendence. He gives the price of yearling fillies as between £4 10s 0d and £6 and the total cost of running them on the Forest, including marking fees, as 5s 5d per annum. 'The fillies . . .' he says, 'run with the mares, and in their fourth year breed a good colt. Brood mares are much valued and are rarely sold; a very good one will fetch £15.' He gives the average annual profit on a troop of five ponies as £20.[1]

He takes the cost of a heifer as between £2 and £4, and describes them as 'nearly as self-maintaining as pony stock, until they have

115

their calf . . . in the spring they may be sold with calf at side for
£10 to £14 each.'²

It is tempting to quote at length from Eyre's admirable study,
but it is proposed here to confine further detail to a passage citing
the accounts of an exceptional smallholder who kept them, and to
a short summarising passage:

> . . . it is possible to give the actual profits of a twelvemonth's
> stock-keeping on a little place of six acres, with cottage, cowpen
> and pigstye. . . .

The stock kept on this holding were three cows, a heifer and a
weanling calf; twenty-four pigs were bought in for the pannage
season and subsequently sold. The accounts include the labour bill
for all rough work, haymaking and cleaning and emptying the pen
and styes. The profits 'on the cow kind—made by the sale of
butter, new milk at 4d per quart, skim-milk (to oblige) at 1d a
quart—amounted to £39 18s 6d.' The profits on the pigs amounted
to £21 13s 3d, making a net profit of £61 13s 3d. He adds
that the maximum profit made by this holding in any year was
£77 5s 11d, and the minimum, £59. It will be noted that there
is no reference to ponies. Eyre sums up as follows:

> . . . the profits of his holding will compare with those of a farm
> in an enclosed country of about thrice the size and of about twice
> the rent. The cow provides the weekly, the pig a quarterly, and the
> heifer or pony an annual income, which can be re-invested at a
> good or even high rate of interest.

Jebb, writing a little more than twenty years later, gives a similar,
but less detailed picture, although he enlarges on the most economi-
cal size for a Forest holding. 'Ordinary cottage holdings' he says
'average about six acres. On these the men earn extra wages by
carting, etc.' Twelve acres were locally considered to be sufficient
for an entire living. 'Many Forest men consider this the maximum
size that can be profitably worked' without hired help. 'The size
of Forest holdings is important . . . there is a certain acreage which
is specially adapted to the local requirements . . . regulated by
the amount of stock the wife and family can manage while the
husband is out at work' in the case of cottage-holdings, and 'the
amount of land a man can cultivate himself with his family without
hired help' in that of the smallholdings proper. The average smallholding he describes as 'mostly pasture, for hay', with a strip or so

devoted to roots, cabbage or potatoes. On larger holdings—ie of twenty acres or more—about one-quarter would normally be down to arable. The chief feature of Forest holdings, however, was the large head of stock which the use of the commons allowed to be maintained. He gives an example of a holding of twenty acres, 'typical of many others' which maintained seven milch cows, four heifers and three yearlings, one horse and four brood sows. Four acres were down to roots and oats and the rest to hay.

IV

Fluctuations in the numbers of commonable animals depastured on the Forest are likely to be related mainly to movements in livestock product prices. A study of the nineteenth and twentieth-century material confirms that the commoners as a body do react positively to price movements, that is, increase the head of stock on the Forest as product prices rise, and reduce it as they fall.

A detailed record of the numbers of stock depastured on the Forest is available only for the period from the later 1870s to the present day, the only gap being for the years from 1893 to 1910.[22] Earlier records are estimates, rather than census, but it is possible to trace the general pattern of fluctuation from the early eighteenth century. In the first half of the century some depressive factors were clearly at work—perhaps attempts to enforce the winter heyning and fence month, perhaps the national cattle plagues of 1714 and the 1740s and 1750s. For the second half of the century there are indications of rising cattle and pony numbers, a trend mirrored by the import of large numbers of dairy stock into the area from Guernsey, through the port of Southampton, after 1769.[23] This upward trend seems to have been checked in the 1820s and 1830s. Evidence tendered to the Select Committee on the Woods, Forests and Land Revenues of the Crown in 1848 suggest that this may not only be attributed to external influences, but also to partly successful attempts by the Office of Woods to enforce an Act of 1819 which provided for the removal of stock from the New Forest in winter.

The observations of Trimmer in 1856,[19] Williamson in 1861,[20] Spooner in 1871,[11] Eyre in 1883,[1] and numbers recorded in Forest Keepers' MS notebooks for the 1850s and 1860s suggest that in the 50s, 60s and 70s, there was again an upward trend in the

numbers of both dairy stock and ponies depastured on the Forest—
and this despite the enclosure for silviculture of many of the better
grazings. A census of stock numbers carried out in 1875[22] gave
2,903 ponies, 2,220 cattle and 438 sheep; a total of 5,561 head of
stock. The numbers of ponies depastured thereafter rose to a peak
of 3,194 in 1885. By 1893 this had dropped to 2,600; by 1910, after
the gap in documentation, the figure had fallen to about 1,500. The
numbers of cattle fluctuated between 2,098 and 2,893 between 1875
and 1893. The reduction in the numbers of ponies between 1875
and 1910 may have been consequent upon the declining market
for pit ponies which followed the introduction of undesirable features into the blood by crossing with Arabs about this time, and the
cattle numbers are a clear reflection of the maintenance of market
prices for dairy produce during the same period—a period of arable
depression.

The major national agricultural depressions, based on steeper
falls in grain prices than in stock prices, would tend to be to the
Forester's advantage. On the other hand, during periods when
market prices for his products dropped, he could with his relatively
small overheads, retreat into a near-subsistence economy: to what
extent this happened in the nineteenth century and before remains
uncertain. Eyre, in 1881, noted that 'the region is characterised by
a moderate but widespread prosperity, even in these hard times'
—the hard times, in fact, of an agricultural depression in part the
result of a run of bad seasons culminating in the cold, wet, summer
of 1879. The slump in arable product prices and the maintenance
of livestock prices during the Great Depression appears to have
favoured a continued upward swing in livestock numbers which had
begun at least as early as the 1850s and which conforms well
with the hypothesis of a changing emphasis in national agricultural
practice from cereal to livestock production.[24] The smallholding
system in which the use of the commons reduced overheads and
which was essentially concerned with dairy produce and dairy
stock was, too, moderately well insulated against depression. Some
confirmation of this comes in the form of relative values of smallholdings and larger farms, given by Jebb,[15] who notes that by 1907
the average price per acre of larger farms in the district had dropped
by half in twenty years, whilst the value of the smallholdings had
been maintained. When Mr G. E. B. Eyre succeeded to the Bramshaw property in 1887, he apparently experienced considerable

difficulty in letting the larger farms, their value having by that time dropped considerably compared to that of the smaller holdings. He, therefore, sub-divided the larger farms on the estate into small-holdings, and at the same time added somewhat to some of the existing smallholdings, producing a land distribution more likely to be an economic proposition. The capital expenditure was considered to be justified by the rent returns from the smallholdings. Jebb describes him as 'recreating the original conditions of the district' and it would appear that there had been some considerable aggregation of the smaller holdings into larger farms during the profitable years of mixed farming in the 1850s and 1860s.

Before describing the events of the present century, it is convenient to consider the markets found by the New Forest pony—which might be described as a specialised product of the district—and to note, briefly, the unsatisfactory changes to which the breed was subject late in the nineteenth century. Brief reference has already been made to the introduction of Arab blood. Descriptions of the Forest pony prior to the widespread use of Arab stallions refer to a stocky animal of eleven or twelve hands, hardy and well able to over-winter on the Forest unattended. Wise, in 1863 for example, described the Forest pony as 'strong and hardy, living on nothing in the winter but the furze. . . .'[25] When broken they were, as one writer put it, 'capable of enduring great labour'[26] and had, until around the mid-nineteenth century enjoyed a ready market as pack ponies. More recently, the collieries had taken large numbers. Williamson, Spooner and others, writing in the 1850s and 1860s, however, commented that the breed was 'degenerating' through lack of care in the choice of stallions and advocated the use of Arabs to 'improve' it. Probably these writers were influenced by the late Victorian enthusiasm for 'improvement' and the markets which taller, slenderer animals might find as saddle horses. At all events, Arab stallions were used in the 1870s and 1880s and again in the early years of the present century. The visual results were generally an increase in height and a tendency to throw a spindly, slenderer animal. More important, a temperamental strain was introduced and also the breed lost much of its hardiness and ability to live off the open Forest through the winter: it was no longer functional in its semi-natural environment. The market for small, quiet colliery ponies dropped away, and only the better looking animals found a market as saddle horses. Light road trans-

119

port continued to take them, however, until the innovation of the motor car after the 1914–18 war. Thereafter trade slumped, and by the mid-1930s outlets could be found only by a minority of large dealers making a wholesale trade at low prices and narrow profit margins. Many a commoner will talk today of buying or selling a foal for three or four shillings or a mare for a pound. The war of 1939–45 saw a new outlet in the horse-flesh trade, and after 1942 market prices started to rise, a trend which has continued since with the growing demand for riding ponies.

The figures given by the *Report of the New Forest Committee*, 1947, show that the total number of stock on the Forest during the period 1910–1914 averaged 3,595 head annually. In 1915 it stood at 3,200 and in 1916 at 3,130. Mounting market prices, mainly for dairy produce, are reflected in a corresponding rise in stock numbers—mainly cattle—to a peak of 4,550 in 1920. Thereafter there is a steady decline, following falling prices, until at the outbreak of war in 1939 there were only 1,757 animals on the Forest, of which about 1,000 were cattle—an all-time low. A particularly serious blow to the small commoner between the wars was the loss of his farmhouse butter trade in the face of wholesale importation from Australia and New Zealand, on top of which the importation of Danish bacon began to crush his pig trade.

The national trend to liquid milk production appears to have been followed by a large proportion of the commoners. Kenchington, commenting on the effects of the inter-war period on the smaller commoners, noted that 'Cheap corn and cake well suited the grazier, stockman, pigman and poultryman side of the forester's agriculture. . . .'[14] The low overheads made possible by the use of the commons, enabled the small commoner as a class to 'get by', the profits from the family holding, such as they were, being supplemented by work in the growing light industry zone of Southampton.

In 1940 the stock figure stood at 1,479—571 ponies and 908 cattle. Thereafter, with rising market prices for heifers and dairy produce —traditionally one of the commoners' main lines of production— and the new trade in horseflesh, the numbers of stock on the Forest rose steadily. In 1946 it stood at 3,082 cattle and 775 ponies. In 1963 the total number of ponies on the Forest was in excess of 2,000 and the number of cattle on the Forest in the summer was around 3,000. The upward trend in numbers has continued since.

The period 1944–1952 saw the first deliberate efforts to improve the Forest grazings. During the inter-war period, with only small numbers of stock on the Forest, the grazings had suffered a deterioration to scrub and, with the drive by the War Agricultural Executive Committee to encourage the rearing of dairy stock, it was apparent that some reclamation was necessary. Accordingly, between 1944 and 1948 some 1,000 acres were cropped and finally seeded down,[27] most of the sites having remained in fairly good condition since, although a reversion to indigenous grass species is generally apparent. Three further areas were reclaimed and re-seeded by the Verderers in 1959 under the provisions of the New Forest Act, 1949.

Whilst the numbers of cattle and ponies depastured on the Forest in recent years compares favourably with those of the 1880s, the actual number of commoners exercising their grazing rights is now considerably smaller. The cottager with his tiny holding and a few cows and heifers on the Forest has by and large disappeared. Many such holdings have become desirable residences for the retired and for the commuter to nearby urban areas, whilst others have been absorbed into rather larger units. Particularly since the 1940s, there has been a general trend towards the aggregation of holdings into larger units. The size of most agricultural holdings in the Forest area (excluding the inherently large farms in the area), however, remains less than fifty acres and a large number are a good deal smaller. Many of these holdings today have a central 'core' of meadows, with one or two other fields at a distance from the holding proper. In the event of the death or retirement of the owner the holding may be passed on intact, the outlying fields sold off, or the farm broken up between a number of others. The process of aggregation is a gradual one.

The figures for the numbers of cattle turned out during the past decade or so mask also a trend away from dairy stock to stores. A very small minority of commoners with the necessary capital have commenced turning out several hundred head of stores to calve on the Forest, a practice which has met with a certain amount of local criticism on the grounds that common rights were never meant to be interpreted as a licence for large scale ranching. The trend, however, has been followed by many smaller commoners and it seems likely to continue. It is too early to assess its ecological effects, but since the large herds are kept on the open Forest throughout the year with the aid of supplementary feed, it may ultimately lead to a stocking density which will have significant effects on the vegetation.

References

1 Quoted by G. E. B. Eyre, *The New Forest, its Common Rights and Cottage Stock-Keepers*, Lyndhurst, 1883.

2 see C. R. Tubbs, 'The development of the smallholding and cottage stock-keeping economy of the New Forest', *Agric Hist Rev*, XIII, 1965, from which much of the data in this chapter is derived.

3 *An Abstract of Claims in the New Forest*, published for the Office of Woods, 1854.

4 *New Forest Register of Decisions on Claims to Forest Rights*, (Commissioners acting under Act of 17 and 18 Vict, c 9), 1858.

5 Quoted from MSS copied from the original in the nineteenth century (in possession of the author).

6 W. H. Pearsall, *Mountains and Moorlands*, London, 1950.

7 Public Record Office, E/178.

8 Rev William Gilpin, *Remarks on Forest Scenery*, Vol II, 1791.

9 Figures from MS in possession of Clerk to the Verderers of the New Forest.

10 Select Committee on the New Forest, 1868, *Minutes of Evidence*, question 807. A letter from the Deputy Surveyor to the Chief Commissioner, dated 31 December 1853 and produced in evidence before both the 1868 and 1875 Committees, explicitly advises this course.

11 W. C. Spooner, 'On the agricultural capabilities of the New Forest', *J Royal Agric Soc England*, 2nd ser, Vol 7, VIII, 1871.

12 It is doubtful whether either the winter heyning or fence month had been successfully enforced for centuries—many holders of common rights specifically claimed exemption from both at seventeenth-century Forest Court proceedings. An Act of 1819, providing for the exclusion of stock from the New Forest during winter (but apparently never effectively implemented) confirms that in the absence of the Justice Seat, existing powers were by then insufficient to enforce the winter heyning.

13 Select Committee on the New Forest, 1875, *Minutes of Evidence*, question 1648.

14 F. E. Kenchington, *The Commoners' New Forest*, London, 1944.

15 L. Jebb, *Smallholdings*, London, 1907.

16 *Report of the New Forest Committee*, Cmnd 7245, 1947.

17 *Minutes of Evidence*, question 1648.

18 Hon. G. W. Lascelles, *Thirty-five Years in the New Forest*, London, 1915.

19 Joshua Trimmer, 'On the agricultural relations of the western tertiary district of Hampshire and the agricultural importance of the marls of the New Forest', *J Royal Agric Soc, England*, VIII, 1856.
20 John Williamson, 'The farming of Hampshire, *J. Royal Agric Soc, England*, XXII, 1861.
21 see eg Thomas Page, 'On the culture of furze', *Annals of Agric*, XI, 1788; Sandham Elly, 'On the cultivation and preparation of gorse as food for cattle', *J Royal Agric Soc, England*, 1st ser, VI, 1846.
22 Sources: MSS material mostly in possession of the Verderers of the New Forest; *Report of the New Forest Committee*, 1947
23 Southampton Record Office, SC 5/86-99.
24 E. L. Jones, 'The changing basis of English agricultural prosperity 1853-73, *Agric Hist Rev*, X, 1962.
25 J. R. Wise, *The New Forest, its History and Scenery*, London, 1863.
26 James Duncan, 'Notices of the New Forest, Hampshire', *Quart J Agric*, X, 1840.
27 D. R. Browning, 'The New Forest Pastoral Development Scheme', *Agriculture*, LVIII, 1951.

SEVEN

Recent Ecological History — I

THE general trend away from the primary woodland and towards heathland on more acid soils has been examined in an earlier chapter. The progressive depletion of the woodland in historic times may be discerned in Europe as a whole, the woodland retreating, either before the expanding area of cultivated land, or before the intensification of grazing and browsing by domestic stock, coupled with deliberate clearance. At the same time as the total area of woodland became smaller, wood remained an essential requirement of the expanding human communities. The conflict of needs reputedly reached a critical stage in England sometime during the sixteenth or seventeenth centuries, when such areas as the New Forest, whose legal status did not permit widespread reclamation and where much woodland remained, became important as potential reservoirs of timber. Anxiety for the timber in turn focused attention on the factors inhibiting woodland conservation.

The major biotic forces in the New Forest during and since medieval times have been the domestic stock depastured on the common grazings, and the deer, the preservation of which was originally the prime object of the Crown in the Forest and which were maintained in large numbers until the nineteenth century. Clearly, large numbers of grazing and browsing animals must inhibit the perpetuation of the woodland through natural regeneration, and operate towards the gradual reduction in the total woodland area. The various other forms of exploitation practised over the centuries, such as the cutting of bracken and turf and the deliberate felling of timber without making provision for its replenishment, together with the deliberate and accidental firing of the heaths, would contribute to the physical reduction in the woodland area and to the initiation of those processes of soil development associated with the formation of heathland.

Page 125: Unenclosed woodland, Redshoot Wood (NGR SU18/08). The foreground oak is probably of late seventeenth-century or early eighteenth-century origin, whilst there is profuse late nineteenth-century regeneration. The holly understory is low and heavily suppressed by browsing

Page 126 : A profusion of dead and dying timber is an important ecological feature of the unenclosed woodland. Berry Wood (NGR SU21/05)

Apart from the extensive silvicultural Inclosures established in the Forest since the Act of 1698, a considerable area of deciduous woodland—some 8,000 acres has survived. This has all the superficial appearance of 'natural' woodland—natural, that is, to the extent of not having been planted. This in itself is noteworthy in view of the demands on timber resources since Tudor times and the browsing and grazing to which the Forest has been subject, and any investigation of the recent ecological history of the Forest must necessarily focus closely on the history of the woods. Thus, the present chapter examines the relationship between their age structure, species composition, and extent, and the biotic and anthropogenic factors influencing regeneration. This in turn forms a basis from which to explore the earlier history of woodland depletion and changes in species composition.

Much of the work on the present woodland age structure and species composition was carried out jointly with G. F. Peterken. This, together with a good deal of the material relating to the medieval and seventeenth century history of the woods has been published elsewhere.[1] The theme in this and the succeeding chapter, therefore, centres around the conclusions of these studies and avoids protracted descriptions of methodology.

I

The unenclosed woodlands of the Forest are largely of beech and oak with an understory of holly. The greater proportion of the woods exhibit a diverse age structure, although a consistent feature is the occurrence of an age group of biologically mature trees, which on certain sites—for example parts of Mark Ash Wood (su245073) and Bratley Wood (su228083)—are dominant to the exclusion of succeeding generations. Holly also occurs throughout the Forest, either as almost pure stands, which often assume a roughly circular shape and are known locally as 'holms' or 'hats' or as the dominant in areas of mixed woods of holly, whitebeam, rowan, oak and beech, the latter two species—though more usually oak—often forming a central 'core' to the wood. These latter woodlands are most evident in the northern sector of the Forest, where they are often characteristic of the sides of the relatively steep sided valleys. A further feature of the unenclosed woodlands is their impoverished ground flora—presumably the result of a long history of grazing by deer and commonable animals.

From this very general description it is necessary to turn to more detailed observation. Studies of tree size and branch structure in 1963–4 showed that the majority of the unenclosed woodlands consisted of two, and often three, fairly distinct generations. The oldest —designated as the A-generation—consisted of beech and oak (most often *Quercus robur* but on some sites *Q. petraea*), the trees frequently having widely spread branches beneath which there was an understory of holly. Most of these older hollies, a large proportion of the beech, and on some sites the oaks, have been pollarded, the hollies apparently repeatedly. A-generation yew occurs on some sites. This A-generation may be regarded as species-poor, which is something of a contrast with the remaining two generations.

The species composition of the B-generation, which arose in gaps in the canopy of the A-generation, and around the woodland margins, is biased on any one site in favour of the dominant species in the A-generation, but birch is common and on various sites either ash (*Fraxinus excelsior*), sycamore (*Acer pseudoplatanus*), chestnut (*Castanea sativa*), hawthorn or scots pine has appeared. The youngest generation, C, is also similarly species-variable, and represents the further colonisation of gaps in the canopy, the invasion of small clearings and some expansion—in a few cases some considerable expansion—of the outer margins of the woodland.

The paucity of species in the A-generation is at least partly explained by its age, which exceeds the life span of most species likely to colonise these acid soils other than oak, beech, holly or yew. Although it is broadly true that the species composition of a generation is partly dependent on that of the previous generation on the site, some conspicuous changes have taken place within limited areas. In parts of Redshoot Wood (SU190085), where the A- and B-generations are predominantly of *Q. Petraea*, ash is the main constituent of the C-generation. In part of Matley Wood (SU334078), in which the A- and B-generations are mainly of *Q. robur*, the C-generation is largely of sycamore. The intrusion of species such as sycamore and ash into areas of the beech-oak-holly community may on some sites, but not all, be traced to the establishment of the mother-trees as 'ornamentals' in the second half of the nineteenth century.

It is also possible to discern more widespread and consistent changes. In the A-generation beech is predominant over oak in the canopy of the greater part of the unenclosed woodlands. In most woods this position has been reversed in the B-generation and it is general in the C-generation. Light demanding species, such as birch and scots pine, are abundant in the B-generation but, in most cases, with a more complete canopy beneath which to become established, they tend to be confined to the woodland margins and clearings in the C-generation. In areas where the A- and B-generations have together established a more or less complete canopy, the C-generation is most often entirely of shade-tolerant holly; holly is universally abundant in all three of the generations distinguished. Over an estimated fifteen per cent of the unenclosed woodlands, the canopy of the A-generation remained dense enough to preclude establishment of the B- and C-generations—for example in part of Mark Ash Wood (SU245074) and the greater part of Bratley Wood (SU228083).

The 'holms' or 'hats' may be fitted into this generation structure. In the greater number of instances, areas of unshaded holly, frequently containing small numbers of oaks whose canopies are starting to expand as the trees overtop the holly, represent the B-generation or B-C-generations. In other cases—a good example is Dark Hat (SU232159)—the holms clearly belong to the A-generation.

The distinction between the B- and C-generations is not always clear, and in some areas the two combined would appear to represent a prolonged and more or less continuous period of regeneration. For example, at Rushpole Wood (SU306097), and other sites on the Barton Clays on the east side of the Forest, a combined B- and C-generation, mainly of oak with a proportion of birch, has arisen, both in clearings and glades, and in small gaps in the canopy of an A-generation dominated by beech.

A very rough estimation of the relative ages of the three generations is possible by observation in the field. The A-generation, and especially the over mature beech and oak, is clearly of great age. The widespread distribution of old pollard oak and beech suggests that it pre-dates the prohibition of the practice in 1698, although there is of course no certainty that illegal pollarding did not continue after that date. The B- and C-generations are, equally clearly, mainly the result of regeneration within the past hundred years or so. It is evident from observation alone that over the greater part of the unenclosed woodlands there is a considerable gap in time between the establishment of the A-generation and the commencement of regeneration of the B and C-generations. To establish the absolute age of the generations, however, it was necessary to count the growth rings at the base of trees selected as representative of the three generations. Sampling and counting methods have been described elsewhere.[2] Some 189 ring counts were carried out in 1963 and 1964 (141 in the initial work with G. F. Peterken in 1963 and a further forty-eight by myself in 1964), of which ninety-eight referred to the A-generation, the age of which will be apparent from the following table.

Relative Ages of A-Generation Trees

Beech and oak were sampled in roughly equal proportions but only eight hollies were sampled; these were carefully selected as representative in size of A-generation holly understory. The oldest was 254 years.

Age-Group	Date of Origin	No of Samples
181–200 years	AD 1763–1782	5
200–250 years	AD 1713–1763	40
250–300 years	AD 1663–1713	39
300–347 years	AD 1616–1663	14

It will be seen that the regeneration of the A-generation occupied mainly the second half of the seventeenth and the first half of the eighteenth century. In fact, the period of most active regeneration was almost certainly the latter half of the seventeenth century, because the above analysis takes no account of the rotten state of the stems of very many of the oldest trees—including many pollards —which made ring counts impracticable. There was, therefore, a bias in favour of sampling the younger trees. Nevertheless, it would seem certain that a good deal of regeneration took place during the first half of the eighteenth century.

The older trees in the A-generation canopy are predominantly beech but in the younger age-groups the proportions of oak and beech seem to be roughly the same. Almost all the pollards sampled for ring counts were more than 250 years old which suggests that in fact the provision of the 1698 Act forbidding pollarding was observed fairly closely. Most of the pollards were beech and it was possible in many woods to divide the A-generation into an older, pollard beech and a younger, unpollarded oak-and-beech category. Such a sub-division could be observed particularly clearly in Ridley Wood (SU203060). The A-generation trees sampled had invariably produced exceptionally wide growth rings in their youth, suggesting that they grew up in unshaded conditions, most likely on the sites of open, derelict or felled woodland. The branch structure of the trees confirms this impression. In sum, the evidence points to the A-generation having developed in unshaded conditions mainly during the second half of the seventeenth and the first half of the eighteenth centuries, in well defined woods, some of which are today monospecific and most of which had a scattered understory of holly.

Generation B arose between 1858 and 1923, but mainly during the period 1860–1900, but regeneration has continued sporadically to the present day with a period of especially active and widespread regeneration, represented by the C-generation, corresponding roughly in age with the Second World War. The distinction between the B- and C-generations is a somewhat arbitrary one, adopted more for convenience of thought and presentation than for strict accuracy. The distinction between the two generations is least clear on unshaded sites. Omitting for the moment the frequent fusion of the B- and C-generations, the main periods of active woodland regeneration in the New Forest since at least the middle of the seventeenth century can be discerned as follows:

Generation	Age	Period of Origin
A	200–300 years	AD 1663–1763
B	40–105 years	AD 1858–1923
C	up to 25 years	AD since 1938

The last period of regeneration now appears to be drawing to a close.

II

There is ample evidence to show that in most of the woodland areas of the Forest regeneration is at present prevented mainly by the grazing and browsing of deer, ponies and cattle.[3] Sheep may have played a part in the control of regeneration in medieval times, but during the period covered by the life of the oldest trees now standing—the A-generation—they seem not to have been important in the local economy. Pigs are more likely to have been a modifying influence. The numbers turned out annually since the early nineteenth century have been subject to frequent short-term fluctuations, associated both with price movements and the quality of the mast, but occasionally, in the nineteenth century, there were as many as 5,000 on the Forest. The most recent peak figure was 1,778 in 1962. Their activities, however, are confined mainly to the short pannage season and, moreover, like the small rodents their attentions are confined to the seed and very small seedlings. The other possible factor influencing regeneration, the rabbit population, was never large in the New Forest. Indeed, the rabbit was not abundant in Britain before the explosion of its population in the second half of the nineteenth century[4] and was before that scarce enough in the Forest to be conserved by the keepers as a source of income.[5]

Perhaps the most convincing demonstration of the combined effect of deer, ponies and cattle on woodland regeneration is provided by two experimental enclosures of less than a quarter of an acre each, laid out beneath an open beech canopy in Mark Ash Wood in 1949. In the seventeen years during which herbivores (but not, incidentally, small rodents) have been excluded, prolific regeneration has taken place, mainly of beech but with some oak and rowan, and the enclosures provide a striking contrast with similar but unfenced sites nearby. Clearly the herbivore population can exert a great influence on woodland regeneration and it should thus be possible to establish a correlation between the periodicity of regeneration (as reflected in the present age structure of the woods) and fluctuations in the number of herbivores.

Fluctuations in the numbers of commonable stock turned out on the Forest have been outlined in chapter six. As regards the deer, the earliest census figure is for 1670, when the Regarders gave a return of 7,593 fallow deer and 375 red deer[6] but between that date and 1789 there are only general indications of the size of the population such as may be gleaned from the writings of Gilpin[7] and other contemporaries. The Government Report of 1789, however, gives the average number of fallow deer present annually as 5,900, although it does not indicate over what period. The Report also shows that in two Walks of the Forest alone, no less than 500 deer died during the severe winter of 1787–8, and in enumerating the reasons for the degeneration of the woodlands it says that, 'Ist . . . the Forest is so much overstocked with deer that many die yearely, of want, in the winter.' Bad winters seem to have taken a heavy toll of fallow deer in many Royal Forests since medieval times—the price of overstocking through artificial feeding, though usually dismissed as the 'murrain'. Precisely how accurate the early deer census figures were is difficult to assess. Modern census are known invariably to be under-estimates, but from at least the seventeenth century in the New Forest, in common with other Forests, the deer were largely maintained in winter with hay and by cutting browse and the concentrations of deer on to sites where feed was provided—most often conveniently close to the keepers' lodges and often in browse pens—probably facilitated more accurate counts than latterday census. G. E. B. Eyre described vividly the feeding of the fallow deer in the evenings at Bramble-hill Lodge in the 1840s and says that at that time and before the deer were 'harboured' close to the keepers' lodges.[8]

The numbers of fallow deer (*Dama dama*) in the New Forest seem to have been maintained at roughly the same level as in 1789 until the decade or so immediately before the Deer Removal Act. From 1839 to 1848, however, numbers were reduced, apparently at the instigation of the Office of Woods, from 5,321 at the former date to 3,114 at the latter.[9]

Some estimates of the fallow deer population in the early nineteenth century give a population of between 7,000 and 8,000 head, which is surprisingly close to the census figure for 1670 and might well be taken as a tentative maximum population level which the Forest could carry. Kenchington[10] suggested that the total population may well have fluctuated according to weather cycles between 8,–9,000 and 13,–14,000 head, but this seems highly unlikely. There is no doubt, however, that the population was built up by artificial feeding to a level far beyond that which the ground could carry during the occasional hard winter. It seems likely that Kenchington's lower figure, which coincides with other maximum estimates of the population and with the census figure for 1670, was nearer the limit set on the size of the population by the available food supply, both natural and fed, beyond which severe winters restricted further increases. It is most unfortunate that between 1670 and 1789 there are no precise census figures, for this period spans most of that in which the A-generation of the unenclosed woodlands came into being.

In 1851 the New Forest Deer Removal Act provided for the 'removal' of the deer within three years of the passing of the Act, but the practical problems of ensuring the 'removal' of upwards of three or four thousand deer from so large an area within the space of three years appears to have been glossed over by those who drafted the Bill. Gun, net, snare and hound, decimated but did not exterminate the deer. Lascelles called the attempted extermination a 'jehad', a free-for-all, poacher and Crown official alike contributing. There are no means of estimating the number of deer remaining after the years of persecution, but it was estimated at the time that during the two years following the Act some 6,000 deer were slain 'officially' and an unknown number 'unofficially'. Wise, writing in 1863[11] and describing the 'wild and unfrequented' part of the Forest near Fritham, noted that, 'here a stray deer will bound across the road; and sometimes a small herd of as many as six or seven are browsing on the ivy . . . startled at the slightest sound and trooping off down the glades'. Lascelles recorded the gradual increase of the deer late in the century and for 1900 gave a figure of 200 head.[12] The population has since risen progressively and may now exceed 2,000.

Neither the red (*Cervus elapsus*) nor roe deer (*Capreolus capreolus*) population was of any size during the period concerned here. The figure of 375 for 1670 coincides with the number known to have been imported from France by Charles II in the same year, and it would seem that if not actually extinct, the species was by then at a very low ebb. It has scarcely held its own since. In 1794 Gilpin wrote that, 'the breed of Stags is now generally diminished; tho within living memory they were . . . numerous.'[7] Numbers given in mid-nineteenth century keepers' MS notebooks and diaries suggest that by then the total stock was less than 100 head and may have been only half that figure. At the end of the century only twenty remained,[12] and at present the stock stands around thirty.

The roe seems to have become rare in England by the thirteenth century and was probably extinct by the end of the fourteenth. The roe population in England today is the product of nineteenth- and twentieth-century introductions. In the New Forest roe made their appearance—or reappearance—from about 1870,[12] and the stock has since increased steadily to somewhere around 300 head at the present time.

The sum of knowledge relating to deer, pony and cattle numbers since the eighteenth century is expressed graphically in figure 3. The graph in figure 4 shows the actual population converted to feeding units/acre, a conversion necessitated by a number of variables, chief of which is that deer, ponies and cattle are not equally destructive to vegetation. Moreover, cattle have mostly been removed from the open forest during those periods of winter when keep is shortest—which are also the times when browsing effects are most marked. The conversions adopted were: pony=five feeding units; deer=three feeding units; cattle=one feeding unit. It was necessary to present these figures as units/acre rather than as total feeding units to take account of known variations in the area of unenclosed lands during the period concerned. The basis of conversion to feeding units is necessarily somewhat arbitrary, but the curves of the two graphs are not greatly different and it is not felt that any major error has been introduced into the resulting picture.

Comparison between the graph representing the changing intensity of grazing/browsing pressure (figure 4) and the periods of regeneration in the unenclosed woodlands show certain clear correlations, the most obvious of which is the commencement of regeneration—the B-generation—following the Deer Removal Act in the 1850s and 1860s. Regeneration of the C-generation similarly coincides with a marked decline in grazing/browsing pressure— with a period in fact when stock and deer numbers were at an all time low—in the late 1930s and early 1940s. The end of the intermediate B-generation coincides with the increase in grazing/browsing pressure towards the end of the First World War. Between 1750 and 1850, when pressure was consistently high, very little regeneration seems to have taken place, although some sampling bias involved in selecting trees for ring counts may have exaggerated this. There are, however, two anomalies in the general relationship. First, regeneration proceeded at an index figure of 0·3 units/acre in the 1880s but ceased at a similar index figure around 1920. Second, although there is inconclusive evidence for the size of the herbivore population during the period when the A-generation arose, the single deer census for 1670 does suggest that it was substantial for

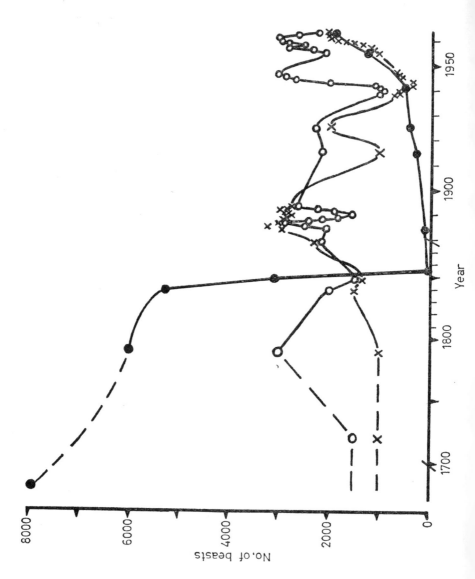

FIGURE 3. *Herbivore Populations in the New Forest since c 1670*

at least part of the time. The possible origins of the A-generation emerge from a consideration of the medieval and seventeenth-century history of the woodlands, and are discussed in chapter eight.

The first anomaly is more readily explained. Investigation of the rate of growth of B-generation hollies, by means of growth ring counts at successive heights, showed that the period of rapid height growth ceased between 1910 and 1920. Seedlings established after 1910 were heavily suppressed, so it may be inferred that the canopy closed during those ten years. On sites where the B-generation holly had developed as a scatter of trees with an incomplete canopy, regeneration was found to have continued throughout the 1920s and 1930s. This and other evidence suggested that the B-generation largely ceased because the canopy itself prevented further regeneration.

If the closing of the B-generation canopy itself inhibited further regeneration, it remains necessary to explain why the outer margins of the woods did not continue to expand and why new areas of scrub and emergent woodland did not come into being on open, unshaded heathland sites. The evidence here points to the development of heath burning practices on an unprecedented scale in the past hundred years, which severely restricted the spread of woodland. Indeed, numerous areas of B, and sometimes C-generation holly scrub, often associated with hawthorn, rowan, oak and other species, were completely destroyed by fire. Good examples of this may be seen at Ringwoodford Bottom (su263106); Lucas Castle (su250105); Acres Down (su274088); Dogwood Bottom (su218065); Fritham Plain (su135224); and near Longwater Lawn (su333083). On many such sites, holly has since regenerated from the base of the burnt stems, although visibly held in check by browsing. The B-generation origin of most of the sites is confirmed by their absence from the nineteenth century Ordnance Surveys. It is of some interest to consider in more detail the documented history of heath burning in the New Forest in relation to the spread on to the open ground of what is usually generically termed 'scrub' in the local literature.

III

Apart from the age structure of the woods themselves, there is good documentary evidence for the regeneration of the B- and C-generations. Evidence given before the Select Committee of the House of Commons in 1875 as to the deterioration of the grazings into scrub reflect the ecological changes taking place. The Office of Woods had claimed that, with the deer gone, there would be more feed for the commoners' animals. Witnesses, however, claimed that in the absence of the deer, scrub and self-sown trees were now over-running the open Forest at an alarming rate. The ponies and cattle alone, it was alleged, were unable to keep the vegetation in check. A good deal of the protestation at this time was no doubt exaggeration prompted by the general grievance against the Office of Woods, but there can be no doubt that it had some basis of fact. G. E. B. Eyre, whose statements usually seem accurate enough, claimed that the grazings, and especially the 'lawns' of sweet grasses, had suffered by encroaching scrub. Many of the lawns had been clearings in the unenclosed woodland areas and it seems likely that much of the 'scrub' comprised the B-generation holly and oak which has colonised so many of these glades and clearings since the mid-nineteenth century.

A further source of dissension was the spread of self-sown scots pine seeding on to the heathland from the now mature stands planted in the Inclosures early in the century. The species was reputedly first introduced into the New Forest in 1776, when two experimental clumps were planted at Ocknell and Boldrewood, but colonisation of the open Forest does not seem to have been remarked upon until the second half of the following century. Eyre drew attention to its spread in the following passage:

> The fact will have struck many of you in visiting our district that the Scotch Fir is rapidly over growing our waste lands. You are aware that the self-sown natural timber is the property of the lord of the soil, but will not perhaps be aware how fatal this is to pasture of any kind, or to what extent the self-sowing of the Scotch Fir is a recognised engine of local encroachment.[13]

Eyre concludes by condemning the Office of Woods for encouraging the spread of scots pine on the open Forest and goes so far as to hint that cones were deliberately broadcast. The herbivore population alone will not check scots pine—it is but rarely browsed—and there seems to have been some confusion in the minds of the commoners between the spread of scrub through a slackening in the browsing pressure and the spread of scots pine through a quite different cause.

The spread of scrub and self-sown trees appears to have coincided also with a deterioration in the drainage of the open Forest, occasioned largely by the volume of water now leaving the new Inclosures. The Office of Woods had no clearly defined responsibility for scrub clearance or drainage on the open Forest and was, moreover, understandably reluctant to carry out such uneconomic work. On the other hand, the Verderers had no powers to touch the soil of the Forest. The situation proved a recurrent source of friction between the Crown and the Verderers until the 1930s and not until the New Forest Act 1949 was the responsibility for keeping the grazings clear and the drains maintained, formally assigned to the Forestry Commission.

It is significant that the first reference to the controlled burning of the Forest heaths by Crown officials occurs in March 1870,[14] about the period when the commoners' agitation as to the spread of scrub and self-sown trees was beginning to take on a particularly bitter note. No doubt, like later controlled burning, it was carried out on the better-the-devil-you-know principle—uncontrolled, illegal firing of the open Forest could cause considerable damage, not least in the plantations.

References to heath fires before 1870 are scattered throughout the literature but without exception they refer to fires engendered by the commoners for the purpose—according to Gilpin—'of making pasturage more plentiful', and to the efforts of the Crown to prevent recurrences. The Swainmote and Eyre rolls of the seventeenth century and before not infrequently record presentments as to the illegal firing of the heaths. In 1785, following a particularly bad fire, a reward of as much as £40 was offered for evidence leading to the conviction of those responsible.[7]

After the 1870s, limited controlled burning of the heaths by Crown officials seems to have become a more or less regular feature, although there were recurrent complaints that insufficient burning was done. In the 1920s and 1930s and, indeed until the present highly efficient fire control system of the Forestry Commission was developed, extensive uncontrolled firing of the heaths became a regular feature of every spring and summer. For this there is not only a good deal of written evidence, but the verbal assurances of present day commoners.

Among the written evidence, that of Heywood Sumner is especially interesting because he records the burning of specific areas of

B-generation holly scrub which had developed on the heaths. In 1931 for example, he wrote: 'I plod up to the top of the hill in order to see how Fritham Plain has recovered from the heath fires of recent years, when many fine outlying hollys were burnt here. . . .'[15] In another case he records the partial destruction of holly holms recorded on the map of 1789: 'Mogshade Hill used to be covered with beautiful old thickets of holly trees, now, alas, badly burned by a recent (1918) fire. . . .'[16] The holms on Mogshade Hill have now virtually disappeared. 'Blackjacks', the charred stems and stumps of holly and gorse, were widely collected for fuel wood during the 1920s and 1930s. Sumner records that the charred holly stems were sold by local collectors who, 'supply local demand for firewood', and that, 'Many loads of charred holly wood have kept my home fires burning for the last three years.'[15] The implication is that the holly holms and scrub on the open Forest were at that time subject to considerable inroads from fire. Sumner also incidentally recorded profuse regeneration of holly in many of the more open woods of the Forest early in the present century.[15]

Another writer, C. C. Dallas, one of the shooting licencees, expands on the burning of the open Forest in the 1920s:

> Another thing which has had a disastrous effect on the Forest from the shooters' point of view is the excessive burning that has been going on during the last few years, and now, (1926) more covert than ever is being burnt. The commoners demand this burning to improve the feed for their cattle and ponies, and I believe the Crown fear that unless their wishes are complied with, there will be a risk of fires in the young plantations. . . . Not only is the Forest burnt excessively by the Crown servants, but many incendiary fires take place which, during the dry weather of the spring can be seen burning day and night. There will soon be no covert left. We are informed that in future 1,600 acres would be burnt every year.[17]

It would in sum seem that the expansion of the actual area of scrub and woodland received a severe check in the 1920s and 1930s. During the war years of 1939–45 a good deal of the heathland was also burnt over regularly to reduce the fire hazard from stray incendiaries intended for Southampton. Subsequently the New Forest Act 1949 provided that the Forestry Commission should be responsible for ensuring that, 'the grazings shall be kept sufficiently clear of coarse herbage, scrub and self-sown trees.' This has since been achieved by the controlled burning of between 1,500 and 3,000 acres annually, together with a certain amount of machine cutting on sites where it would be dangerous to burn. Heath burning is confined by the Heather and Grass Burning (England and Wales) Regulations (Statutory Instrument 386, 1949) to the period between 1 November and 31 March and in practice burning takes place in the Forest mainly during March, the only time during the permitted period when the vegetation has been found to fire effectively.

Some indication of the extent to which scots pine has been eradicated from the open Forest may be gained by comparing surveys carried out in 1937, 1944 and 1963, although it seems likely that the acreage figures given in the earlier two years are exaggerated. In 1937 scots pine occupied 11,000 acres of the open Forest; in 1944, 4,000 acres; and in 1963, 1,700 acres.[18]

IV

The age structure studies of the unenclosed woodlands show that they consist of two main elements: the mature A-generation, which arose during the second half of the seventeenth and first half of the eighteenth centuries; and the younger B- and C-generations which have arisen during the past hundred years. The periodicity, extent and nature of regeneration since the middle of the eighteenth century may be related to fluctuations in the population of herbivores in the Forest, to characteristics developed in the woods themselves and to the incidence of heath burning. The A-generation is considered further in the next chapter.

This picture of the unenclosed 'Ancient and Ornamental' woodlands of the Forest conflicts strangely with the opinion generally held until recently, that they were largely, if not entirely, composed of stands of over mature and even aged timber with little natural regeneration to replace the old trees as they fell. The Report of the New Forest Committee, 1947, remarked that, 'Trees of the younger age classes appear very infrequently.' The Committee 'visited some of the woods and found the process of disintegration very conspicuous' and, in common with other observers before them, concluded that in the absence of any protection from animals, the woods were unable to perpetuate themselves. It was unfortunate that the Committee chose to visit just those woods where the preponderance of old trees was most conspicuous, rather than a more representative cross section. Following recommendations from the Committee, the subsequent New Forest Act of 1949 made provisions for the active management of the unenclosed woodlands, and during the succeeding ten or fifteen years some 900 acres were enclosed in blocks of ten to twenty acres, partially felled and either replanted or encouraged to regenerate naturally. The establishment of a young crop, however, proved difficult in the face of browsing by deer and the invasion of noxious weeds; moreover, the opening up of the old canopy resulted in the exposure and rapid death of much of the adjoining old timber. The technique was clearly neither successful nor, in the light of recent research into the structure of the woods, was it generally necessary, and more subtle treatment has now been adopted based mainly on the encouragement of regeneration in small enclosures under existing gaps in the woodland canopy. At the present time grazing and browsing by herbivores would seem to be approaching the level beyond which regeneration outside of specially fenced sites will be virtually precluded, and it is thus important that the present policy is actively pursued if the concept of a true uneven-aged woodland is to be the guiding light of management.

References

1   C. R. Tubbs, 'Early encoppicements in the New Forest', *Forestry*, XXXVII, 1964; and G. F. Peterken and C. R. Tubbs, 'Woodland regeneration in the New Forest, Hampshire, since 1650', *J App Ecol*, 2, 1965.
2   Peterken and Tubbs, *loc cit.*
3   see esp G. F. Peterken, 'Mortality of holly (*Ilex aquifolium*) seedlings in relation to natural regeneration in the New Forest', *J Ecol*, 54, 1966.
4   G. E. N. Barrett-Hamilton and M. A. C. Hinton, *A History of British Mammals*, London, 1920–21.
5   see eg *Fifth Report of Commissioners to enquire into the woods, Forests and land Revenues of the Crown*, 1789.
6   Public Record Office, E/178.
7   Rev William Gilpin, *Remarks on Forest Scenery*, II, London, 1791.
8   G. E. B. Eyre, 'The New Forest: a sketch', *Fortnightly Review*, 1 April 1871.
9   *Report of the Select Committee on the Woods, Forests and Land Revenues of the Crown*, 1848.
10   F. E. Kenchington, *The Commoners' New Forest*, London, 1944.
11   J. R. Wise, *The New Forest, its history and scenery*, London, 1863.

Page 143: The edge of Highland Water Inclosure, enclosed 1868 (NGR SU24/09). This stand of Corsican pine was planted in 1921

Page 144: (above) Forest edge smallholdings, Frogham (NGR SU17/13); (below) Recreation on the open Forest, Denny Wood (NGR SU33/06)

12 *Victoria History of Hampshire*, Vol II, London, 1900.
13 G. E. B. Eyre, *The New Forest, its common rights and cottage stock keepers*, Lyndhurst, 1883.
14 MS Diary of Harry Cooper, Keeper of Eyeworth and Castle-malwood walks; in possession of Forestry Commission, The Queen's House, Lyndhurst.
15 Heywood Sumner, *Local Papers*, London, 1931.
16 Heywood Sumner, *Guide to the New Forest*, Ringwood, 1923.
17 C. C. Dallas, *New Forest Shooting, Past and Present*, Lymington, 1927.
18 The figures for 1937 and 1944 are given in the *Report of the New Forest Committee*, 1947, Cmnd 7245. That for 1963 is derived from a survey by the Forestry Commission.

EIGHT

Recent Ecological History — II

IT has been shown that the oldest generation of trees in the unenclosed woodlands of the Forest—the A-generation—arose between about AD 1650 and 1750 in well defined woods which, in the main, consist of roughly even aged, often monospecific, stands in which the trees are widely spaced and below which the surviving contemporary understory is of holly. It would seem that the woods arose under more or less open conditions, suggesting that they represent a period of regeneration following one of widespread woodland exploitation. Their origins are thus best considered further within the context of a study of the medieval and seventeenth-century history of the Forest woodlands.

Forest Law, which protected the vert as well as the venison, must have checked the process of woodland depletion in medieval times, but the evidence suggests that the survival of the woodlands depended also on a policy of aiding regeneration by enclosure. Silvicultural enclosure was practised in the New Forest at least as early as the mid-fifteenth century, and almost certainly from a much earlier date[1] but the management practices adopted proved in the long run to be ineffectual for large scale timber conservation and a critical point in diminishing supplies of timber for shipbuilding and other major constructional works seems to have been reached by around the middle of the seventeenth century. The latter half of the century saw renewed attempts to perpetuate the woods, culminating in recourse to Parliament in 1698. By the closing decades of the eighteenth century, the potential timber supplies appear again to have become a matter of acute anxiety. This pattern, with local modifications, applied at a national level. The study of early silviculture in the New Forest has not only thrown a little light on the origins of the A-generation of trees, but also demonstrates the progressive depletion of the woodland cover in medieval times and,

146

indeed, wherever the woodland remained unenclosed, into the nineteenth century.

I

Medieval and seventeenth-century silviculture in England consisted of enclosing a site which contained mother trees and relying on natural regeneration, supplemented if necessary by sowing, for a crop. The plans accompanying a survey of 'coppices', as the enclosures were known, in the New Forest in 1609, made by John Norden,[2] shows three methods of enclosure: a fence surmounting a bank with an outside ditch; a fence alone, apparently of pales; and a quickset hedge alone. Only the first method seems to have been entirely effective in excluding the deer. Since the area occupied by a group of mother trees rarely conformed to a regular pattern the shapes of the coppices were themselves irregular and wherever their banks and ditches are traceable on the ground today their alignment is in complete contrast to the rigid boundaries of the present day statutory Inclosures.

Under the Forest Law as it was understood by the fifteenth and sixteenth centuries the Crown, as well as others, was precluded from making enclosures, at any rate of a permanent nature. By definition, however, encoppicement in Forests was a process both of enclosure and of throwing open again after a specific interval of years, during which the crop became established and beyond the reach of stock and deer. The Act of 22. Edward IV, *c* 5–7, 1483, recited the enclosure of land in Royal Forests for a period of three years as accepted practice and extended the period to seven years. The management of the Crown woodlands was put on a systematic basis in the Act of 33. Henry VIII, *c* 39, 1542, which provided for the appointment of a Surveyor or Master of the King's Woods. The King's Surveyor was to 'cause to be surveyed . . . all the wood and underwood . . . in the King's Forests, Chaces . . . (etc) and shall have full power . . . to make sale or sales thereof . . . forsying always that the said wood shall be fenced from time to time as need be reqyre for the increase thereof.' The profits from the woods were to be paid into the Treasury and the Surveyor was to render annual accounts.

The Statute of Woods, 35. Henry VIII, *c* 17, 1544, went much further and laid down what amounted to a working plan for coppice management in Forests. It provided that in coppices cleared at or under twenty-four years' growth, twelve standards were to be left to every acre, each of which must be of twelve inch diameter at three feet from the ground before they could be felled. If over twenty-four years' growth, twelve standards were to be left to every acre, to remain for at least twenty years before they could be felled. Coppices in which underwood of fourteen years' growth or less had been cleared were to be enclosed for four years after clearing; if over fourteen years' growth but under twenty-four years', they were to be enclosed for six years after clearing; and if cleared after twenty-four years' growth they were to be enclosed for seven years. A further Act of 1588 extended the period during which coppices could be enclosed in Forests to one of nine years.

Woodlands in Forests were the responsibility of a specific Forest officer, known in the New Forest by the fifteenth century as the Woodward. It was the practice, however, to lease the underwood in coppices to a tenant, the Crown reserving all rights to the timber trees. The lease of Catshill, Brodstone and South Bentley coppices in the New Forest to Augustine Hill in 1595 demonstrates the system. The three coppices, totalling 110 acres, were leased in consideration of the sum of £9 5s 4d and an annual rent of £5, all 'great trees' and 'trees fit for timber' being reserved to the Crown. The lessee was to make not more than two cuttings of the underwood during his tenancy and after each cutting was to enclose the coppices with 'ditches and hedges' and ensure that neither deer nor stock entered them, for the period required by the law.[3] Coppices were thus managed on a system similar to that later known as 'coppice-with-standards', the standards being claimed by the Crown whilst the coppice was cut by a tenant. The Crown—in theory—benefited in two ways: it received a rent for the underwood; and protection for the timber crop. In the New Forest the crop which the lessee might realise included hazel, holly, thorn, alder, willow and defective timber trees, the first two species being those most often mentioned in sixteenth- and seventeenth-century documents relating to coppices. Pollarding, though generally prohibited in leases, was clearly regular practice and references to 'lop-able' oaks suggest that it may sometimes have been accepted as such.

Whilst it is by no means easy to prove, it is probable that most of the woodland in the New Forest had been subject to periodic encoppicement during the fifteenth and sixteenth centuries: certainly the profusion of coppice banks traceable in the Forest today suggests that this was so, though many may pre-date the fifteenth century. In the latter part of the sixteenth century the state of the Forest woodlands formed the subject of Articles of Enquiry addressed to the Regarders by the Exchequer.[4] The Regarder's returns confirm that encoppicement was then and had formerly been widespread practice in the Forest. It becomes clear from the returns, however, that the system was subject to increasing abuse as the century progressed. These, together with similar but less regular returns of the seventeenth century, suggest that the increasing neglect of the coppices arose because in the late sixteenth and in the seventeenth centuries underwood was no longer an economic proposition. At the same time the conservation of timber—the Regarder's main concern—was dependent in part on the periodic enclosure and regeneration of the coppices. Their returns are full of references to coppices, enclosed by the Woodward, degenerating into convenient stock pounds and paddocks. Enclosure banks were broken down repeatedly and there are frequent references to deer damage. 'John Stockman and his keepers do continually put into the coppices within our office both horses, colts and swine and when we offer to impound them they say they will answer the same.'; 'Stockley Coppice, by the deer and by the putting in of calves and horse beasts into the said coppice by Richd Okeden of Royden . . . is greatly hurt and spoiled' are typical returns. Many of the coppices were apparently rented by members of the local squirearchy, often holding honorific Forest offices such as Gentleman Keeper, who were themselves considerable graziers and who, after perhaps realising one crop from the coppices, used them as paddocks for their stock. There is also clear evidence of an obstuctionist attitude towards enclosure on the part of officers of the deer forest and commoners alike. The position is further complicated by the fact that the Regarders themselves seem sometimes to have been the tenants of coppices and responsible for the very depredations which they were required to prevent.

A witness before an Inquisition held at Brockenhurst by the Lord Warden at the request of the Exchequer on 7 April 1610, summed up the position:

> Edward Willoughby one of the Rangers . . . saith that upon his knowledge for want of maintaining the fences about His Majesty's coppices according to the Statute he verily thinketh most part of the coppices be utterly spoiled to the loss of His Majesty

about £100 yearly, which should have been made unto His Majesty . . . had they been preserved by the Woodwards and such as have charge of them.[5]

The report of a similar Inquisition taken later in the same year strikes a distinctly helpless note:

> We think it fit and very necessary that woods should be increased and preserved within the said Forest and that the doing thereof shall bind posterity . . . to a thankful memory of the authors of the same . . . but for the making of any new coppices we cannot find how it will be available to His Majesty, for some of us do know that the like hath been attempted before in the late Queen's time, but nothing has ensued but expense of money and spoil of timber trees and the intended coppices never well finished nor at all preserved or continued.[5]

There were fundamental economic reasons for the neglect of the woodlands. It has often been assumed that the dual strain of industrial fuel consumption and the shipbuilding industry was largely responsible for draining timber resources in England, and particularly in southern England, nearest the shipyards, in the fifteenth, sixteenth and seventeenth centuries. It is now clear that this is a somewhat sweeping view; that although anxiety for ship timber had been expressed since the fifteenth century the actual tonnage of shipping built was really comparatively small before the seventeenth century; and that by the early seventeenth century the demand for underwood had slackened rather than increased. Coppice was primarily intended for industrial fuel. Yet by the early seventeenth century, if not much earlier, many markets had been lost to coal. Coppice only remained profitable where it was within economically transportable distance of industrial plant which still used it, such as ironworks and glassworks. Hammersley produced evidence to show that during the late sixteenth and early seventeenth centuries the income from coppices on the Crown lands in England was small and that the coppices were difficult to let except in a few localities. Of 40–50,000 acres of coppices surveyed between 1604 and 1612, no more than 16,000 acres were let at the latter date, despite strenuous efforts to improve the Royal revenues.[6]

At this period, the New Forest area would seem to have had no industrial consumer, though a little later in the second or third decade of the century an ironworks was established at Sowley. The salt industry of the Hampshire coast had almost certainly gone over to coal at an early date. The only other likely industrial consumers would have been potteries, and although kilns certainly existed in and around the Forest, they appear to have been small and scattered units. Perhaps the best testimony to the absence of adequate local industrial markets is that of the surveyor who in 1608 suggested the introduction of ironworks, glassworks and charcoal hearths into the New Forest to exploit the unused woods.[7] Furthermore, most local inhabitants had rights of estovers, which would largely have precluded domestic sales. The exercise of the rights would themselves, incidentally, have contributed to the general deterioration of the woodlands.

With regard to shipbuilding timber—the stems and limbs of mature oak, much of it necessarily of odd shapes and sizes—markets were strictly limited by the proximity of shipyards, the cost of long distance haulage being prohibitive. The nearby port and yard of Southampton, however, had faded into temporary obscurity early in the sixteenth century, though a small tonnage of merchant shipping continued to be constructed both here and at nearby Red-bridge and also at Lymington. Portsmouth, important as a naval station and yard from early in the fifteenth century until the 1520s, built no ships between 1509, when the *Mary Rose* and *Peter Pomegranate* were launched, and 1650, when the frigate *Portsmouth* went down the way.[8]

Despite a trend towards woodland depletion through neglect, pastoral exploitation and the depredations of the deer, a considerable area of woodland remained in the early seventeenth century, much if not most of it owing its survival ultimately to intermittent encoppicement. The New Forest was included in the surveys of the Crown woods carried out between 1604 and 1612. The Forest survey was reported upon in 1608[7] and gave a total of 123,927 'Timber Trees', or mature trees fit for felling, and enough standing 'Fyerwood and Decayed Trees' to yield 118,072 loads. Calculating on a basis of approximately one and a half loads per tree (the equation used in similar calculations in the Government report of 1789) the actual number of silviculturally over-mature trees was around 79,000—a remarkably high proportion of the standing crop. The crop was described as, 'for the most part oake, and some small quantetyes of Beech and Ash.' The local markets were specified as, 'first to the Countrye, next to the Coopers, for Barrell and Clap-boardes, and lastlye to the Shipwrights of Redbridge, Southton and

Lymington.' The survey made no reference to younger generations of trees and the surveyors passed a general remark that, 'all the said trees are very old and in great Decaye.' From this and from the sheer quantity of mature and over-mature trees it is probable that there was a strong imbalance in the age-structure of the woods in favour of old timber. This is much as one would expect from the consistent tale of deer and stock damage over preceding decades which emerges from the returns of the Regarders.

In addition to their figures for the standing timber, the surveyors of 1608 recorded that there were 1,304 acres of coppice in the Forest and ninety-two acres of 'Aldermoores . . . which may presently be felled.' Norden's survey of the following year[2] refers to fourteen former encoppicements totalling 741 acres which, from his descriptions, had mostly been virtually stripped, both of their underwood and timber trees.

II

The first real demands on the Forest woodlands for navy timber did not come until about the middle of the seventeenth century or shortly after. Various suggestions were made for the re-establishment of Portsmouth as a naval yard in the second and third decades of the century and in 1627, Buckingham in fact had estimates prepared for the construction of a dock. His death deferred the matter, but shortly after, in the 1630s, Portsmouth was again used as an anchorage for ships preparing for service. An objection to the establishment of a more permanent station was the alleged prevalence of the wood boring worm *Toredo navalis.* On the other hand it was pointed out that it frequently took as much time and trouble to negotiate the tricky passage from Portsmouth to the Thames as it did to make the passage from Portsmouth to the Mediterranean and finally, just before the outbreak of the Civil War in 1642, five frigates were ordered to be laid down there. The first of these to be completed, the *Portsmouth,* was launched in 1650. Between 1653 and 1656 the yard at Portsmouth constructed 4,085 tons of naval shipping and Southampton a further 255 tons.

In 1649, at the beginning of the Interregnum, the Royal Navy had about 21,000 tons of shipping. Between then and 1685 this had increased to 103,558 tons. By 1702 it stood at 159,017 tons. Geographically the Hampshire coast was eminently suitable for the construction and servicing of a rapidly expanding navy, and indeed Portsmouth, Southampton, Bursledon and, after 1698, Bucklers Hard on the Beaulieu River, shared a new prosperity. In the seven years between 1691 and 1698, for example, the four yards between them built 17,452 tons of naval shipping. The growth of the Hampshire industry, however, was slow compared to that of the yards at Woolwich, Deptford, Bristol and Plymouth.[9] The main factor constricting growth appears to have been the difficulty experienced by the middle of the century of obtaining sufficient suitable timber within economically transportable distances of the yards.

In the interval between the 1608 timber survey and the 1660s, the practice of encoppicement seems to have been abandoned in the New Forest. By the latter date, the woodlands had certainly been severely depleted of their timber. According to the account given in the Government report of 1789, the greater part of the woods were felled or destroyed during the troubled years of the reign of Charles I and the Civil War and Commonwealth. By the time of the Restoration, 'the greatest part of the Trees had been felled, the Fences of the ancient Coppices destroyed, and the Deer and Cattle every where admitted.' It is probable that this account may be modified somewhat. Considerable destruction there may have been in the confusion of contemporary political conflict, but the lack of ship timber in the 1660s is likely also to have been the result of the deterioration of the mature timber recorded in the survey of 1608 and the lack of adequate regeneration to replace it, occasioned by neglect of the coppices and inhibitory grazing and browsing of the deer and commonable stock. At all events, the resources of mature timber in the Forest in the 1660s were slight and the renewed demand for it gave rise to fresh silvicultural activity. Returns of the Regarders for 1670 and 1673[10] show that there was then widespread re-enclosure of coppices. The earlier return refers in addition to 100 acres of land at Homehill (Holmhill, later Holmhill Inclosure, su260085) which had recently been enclosed, 'for the growth of wood' at the orders of the Exchequer. The return of 1673 records the enclosure of a further 300 acres at Aldridgehill (later Aldridgehill Inclosure, su275033) and Holidays Hill (Holidays Hill Inclosure, su265075) 'for a nursery and supply of timber.'

These 400 acres appear not to have been managed on the usual coppice system, but seem to have been the first oak plantations made and managed in severalty by the Crown. That large scale, systematic enclosure and planting and the single control of Crown Officers was necessary for successful timber production, was ultimately recognised in the Act of 1698—though, as it turned out, the Act was ineffectually implemented. Concurrent with enclosure there was evidently a determined effort during the second half of the century to check the abuses of the Forest which had led to the depletion of its timber—the common practice of the Keepers of exploiting the woods under the guise of providing browse for the deer; the running of stock on the Forest during the winter; and overstocking with deer.

The attention bestowed on the Forest woodlands during the second half of the seventeenth century clearly succeeded in initiating a period of active regeneration. This is evident, for example, from the return of the Regarders for 1670, in which fifty-three demesne woods of the Crown are listed—evidently those sites known to the Regarders which the Crown had in the past been accustomed to enclose as coppices, though the list is by no means exhaustive of former coppice sites. Whether they were all enclosed in 1670 is doubtful from the return, though some evidently were and others were recorded as being encoppiced in the return of 1673. The nature of the crop is not specified, but the general condition of the wood is described briefly. Fifteen woods are referred to as, 'decaying' and thirty-eight as 'prosperous' or 'very prosperous'.

A more general confirmation of the regeneration phase which commenced in the latter part of the seventeenth century comes from a timber survey carried out in 1707.[11] This gave 12,476 sound oak which could be felled for the navy (compared with 123,927 a hundred years previously), of which the surveyors considered that 300 could be felled annually for a period of forty years. 'there being so many young trees which are not of sufficient Bigness to be useful to His Majesty's navy now,' that the Forest would be at least as well stocked at the end of forty years as in 1707. The survey also refers to a 'considerable number' of large beeches which might be felled at the rate of 100 per year for forty years without detriment to the Forest crop; and a large number of old oaks 'from the limbs of which might be picked some useful parts.' A further timber survey of 1764 gave 19,836 oak fit for the navy, none containing less than 70 cu ft, and records that this represented between one-quarter and one-fifth of the potential navy timber in the Forest, the remainder having not yet sufficiently matured for felling. Another survey of 1783 recorded 12,447 oaks fit for the navy, but a further 72,990 of less than 30 cu ft. The few statutory Inclosures which had been made in the eighteenth century had been ill cared for and comparatively little of this timber could have arisen from deliberate planting resulting from the Act of 1698.

The three timber surveys record the results of a regeneration phase which would seem to have lasted well into the eighteenth century. From the 1789 report it is evident that this phase drew to a close towards the middle of the century, owing (according to the report) to a relaxation in the administration and management of the Forest, and a deterioration in the control exercised over Forest privileges and the numbers of the deer: a return, in fact, to pre-1660 conditions. In sum, the documentary evidence confirms that the existing A-generation of trees in the unenclosed woodlands arose as a result of deliberate management policies in the second half of the seventeenth and early part of the eighteenth centuries. As the age structure studies suggest, it is probable that much of the regeneration took place in the 1650s or 1660s in unshaded conditions on sites largely cleared of their former tree cover. It is unfortunate that the documentary sources do not provide any specific numerical information about the numbers of deer and stock during the critical period.

It is of considerable interest that the 1650–1750 regeneration phase in the New Forest had its counterparts in other Royal Forests. The seventeen *Reports of Commissioners to Enquire into the Woods, Forests and Land Revenues of the Crown*, 1787–93, include the testimonies of expert witnesses as to the age and condition of the woodlands in many of the Forests. Thus in Alice Holt:

> The trees now standing are mostly oak, some beech, and a few ash; and I judge them to be nearly all of the same age . . . most of them appear to me to be of the same standing, which I suppose to be about 115 or 120 year's growth; and I cannot discover the traces of either banks or ditches . . . or any appearance whatever of . . . Inclosures.

It can be inferred from this passage that the 1,942 acres of woodland in Alice Holt in 1789 (the date of the testimony) arose as a more or less even aged stand in the 1660s and 1670s on ground which had been almost completely cleared of its timber. In Bere Forest—closest of all the Royal Forests to Portsmouth and the one exploited earliest and most intensively for navy timber—the position was not dissimilar. The produce of the Forest in the late eighteenth century had arisen, 'principally from a stock of timber nursed up and protected during the latter part of the last century,' again without benefit of enclosure. In the Forests farthest removed from shipyards, where there was the least incentive to conserve timber supplies, the 1650–1750 regeneration phase was absent. Thus, in Sherwood, the timber recorded in the 1604–12 surveys had been felled and nothing remained except within recent enclosures. The reports are consistent in attributing the destruction of the timber standing in 1604–12 to the Civil War and Commonwealth periods, and the subsequent regeneration in Forests close to the yards to deliberate policies of enforcing the winter heyning; preventing the cutting of thorn, underwood and fern, which provided a nursery for the trees in their early years; and discouraging the practice of overstocking with deer. The failure of the woods to regenerate after around the middle of the eighteenth century, if not earlier, is attributed to a deterioration in management arising from the 'relaxation and neglect in the officers of the department of the Surveyor-General.'

III

The first precise record of the distribution of the Forest woodlands is the map which accompanied the Government Report of 1789. Made by Messrs Richardson, King and A. and W. Driver, and published at a scale of 4 in to the mile, it is remarkably accurate considering the survey techniques then in use. It provides a satisfyingly clear picture of the Forest before the advent of large scale afforestation. Isaac Taylor's map of Hampshire, published thirty-two years earlier, shows the woodland distributed in much the same general areas as in 1789, but the scale is small—1 in to the mile—and there was clearly some formalisation in denoting woodland. The first Ordnance Survey, published in 1811, at a one-inch scale, similarly shows insufficient detail; the surveyor's drawings, made at a scale of three inches to the mile in 1797, seem to have relied very largely on the Survey by Richardson, King and the Drivers. The distribution of both unenclosed woodland and statutory Inclosures in 1789 are reproduced in figure 5. For comparison, figure 6 shows their distribution in 1968. (See fold-ins at back.)

The total area of unenclosed woodland in 1789 has been calculated as roughly 13,500 acres. From the density of tree symbols, however, much of it was in a fairly open condition and from the recurrence of 'holm' and 'hat' place names a significant proportion was probably composed of the holly-dominated woods so character-istic of the Forest. In a general way the woods occupied much the same tracts as today. Comparison of figures 5 and 6 shows that the extensive blocks of woodland—much of them statutory Inclosure—today occupying zones across the centre and along the north-east side of the Forest were then a mosaic of woodland, glades and fairly extensive clearings, with belts of timber following the courses of the streams. Where the pattern of change has not been obscured by the blanket of nineteenth-century Inclosures, the most striking change has been the expansion of the woodland margins—seen on the ground to be of B- and C-generation age—to absorb much of the open ground between and among the woods. At the same time there has locally been some retraction of woodland edges. In the north and west of the Forest the woodland in 1789 was confined largely to the wide, U-shaped valleys, though in places it extended up on to the plateaux between them. The valleys of the Linford Brook and Latchmore Brook carried extensive tracts of timber but in general it was more open and scattered, and may largely have been holms mainly of holly.

Where the woodland areas have remained unenclosed since the eighteenth century there has, in many places, been a retreat of the A-generation timber, whilst in others there has been a considerable expansion of the woodland edges representing the success of the B- and C-generations since the 1850s and 1860s. In the South-west the general picture which emerges from figures 5 and 6 is of a retraction of the woods wherever they have remained unenclosed, the expansion phase of the past hundred years having failed to compensate for this in terms of total woodland area. A further general feature emerging from a comparison of figures 5 and 6 is the widespread disappearance of smaller, more isolated woods and of areas of scattered woodland which formerly were spread across the heaths. This is especially apparent in the south-east of the Forest, where in 1789 open woodlands (from the symbols possibly largely holly holms) occupied an extensive tract of what is now open heathland.

Of the 13,500 acres of woodland unenclosed in 1789, approxi-mately 5,500 acres were subsequently absorbed into the nineteenth-

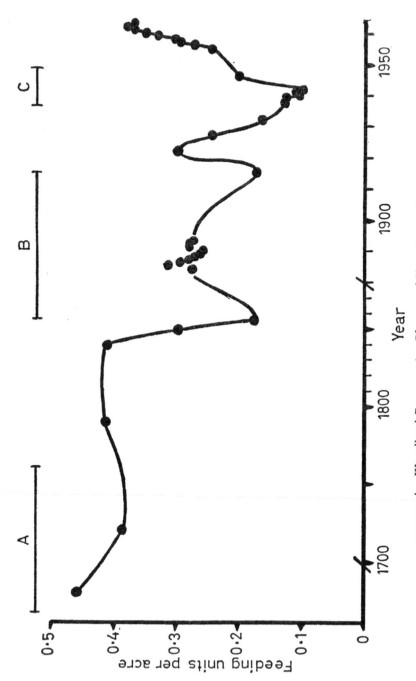

FIGURE 4. *Woodland Regeneration Phases and Variations in Browsing
Pressure in the New Forest since c 1670*

century Inclosures. The balance of 8,000 acres is a similar area to that of the unenclosed woods today, but straightforward comparisons of area mask, first, the contraction of the woodlands, mainly during the first half of the nineteenth century; and second, their expansion during the past hundred years. Expansion and retraction have not always taken place on the same sites, so that the distribution of the woods today is different in detail from that of 1789. That much of the contraction phase took place before around the middle of the nineteenth century is confirmed by comparison between the 1789 map and the late nineteenth century Ordnance Survey. Some isolated holms have disappeared more recently and wherever their destruction has been recorded, it has been caused by heath fires—the holms on Mogshade Hill (su2410), of which Sumner wrote, is an example, and there are others, many of them within the reach of local memory. The expansion phase of the past hundred years may be attributed to the relaxation of grazing and browsing pressure. This phase was marked particularly by the 'infilling' of glades and clearings, but was not entirely confined to it: colonisation of heather moor and acid grassland has been widespread, although many sites, again, bear evidence of fire damage.

What vegetation has succeeded woodland on sites from which it has gone since 1789? Where the parent material of the soil is clay, loam or sand, the site almost invariably now carries bristle bent grassland, often with bracken and gorse and frequently with a scatter of old hollies and hawthorns. The soil usually exhibits little visual leaching and might be termed a slightly degraded brown earth. In at least one instance, however, where Denny Wood (su3305) has contracted since 1789, the site of former woodland now carries heather and the soil profile exhibits marked leaching. It is noteworthy that the soil here is derived from the base-deficient Barton Sands.

In instances where the woodland of 1789 has retreated from sites on the gravels, the soil today often exhibits an incipient podzol profile, with heather, usually plus rather stunted bracken, as the dominant vegetation. An interesting example of such a site is at Hampton Ridge (su145204). Here, on plateau gravel with a good deal of clay in the lower soil horizons, a formerly quite extensive wood has been reduced since 1789 to a group of about thirty oaks and a thin scatter of holly representing the former understory. When investigated in 1964 the soil under the oak canopy exhibited no signs of leaching and the humus was clearly a mull. Twenty yards beyond the limit of the present woodland edge, but well within the area indicated as woodland both on the 1789 map and the first OS of 1811, a soil pit showed an incipient podzol under heather and bracken with bristle bent locally abundant. Beyond the 1789 woodland edge heather was dominant on a marked humus-iron podzol.

These observations suggest that, as one might expect, succession to heather moor seems to have been most rapid on the poorer parent materials, on which an intervening acid grassland phase was of an ephermeral nature if it ever existed at all.

How does the woodland area in 1789 compare with what may be inferred of its extent in earlier centuries? Using the timber survey of 1783, the 13,500 acres of woodland in 1789 probably carried little more than 12,000 mature oak and 73,000 smaller trees; whilst the timber survey of 1608 gave 123,927 mature oak, besides the estimated 79,000 over mature trees. Much would depend on the stocking density, but assuming there to have been extensive areas of holms and open or scattered woodland (as seems likely), and remembering that coppice management implied a comparatively low density of standards, it is probable that the woodland area at the beginning of the seventeenth century was considerably in excess of that at the end of the eighteenth. There are other indications of the former extent of woodland in the wide distribution of banks and ditches with the alignment characteristic of en-coppicements, mainly in the southern half of the Forest (roughly south of the A31 trunk road), on sites which were in 1789, and are today, heathland. Most of the coppices specifically mentioned in the seventeenth-century record (including the 1670 list of fifty-three sites) can be identified with the 1789 woodland, and it is likely that many of these coppice banks represent pre-seventeenth-century woodland. Many, indeed, may be of early medieval origin and it is perhaps significant that most have now succeeded to heather, whether on gravels or other parent material.

V

Soil-pollen analyses suggest that the main changes in the tree and shrub flora of the New Forest in historic times have been the gradual disappearance of hazel and the increasing abundance of holly in the shrub layer; and the intrusion of beech into the oak dominated canopy. It is useful to consider in this chapter whether the documentary evidence can throw any light on the recency of these changes.

Since the Iron Age, hazel has been drastically reduced on soils such as those of the Forest: in modern soil surfaces it is most often represented by only about two per cent of the total pollen preserved. Some idea of the time scale involved in its reduction to this low value may be obtained by comparison with the amounts of hazel pollen preserved in soil surfaces buried beneath medieval and earlier earthworks. For example, in the soil surface buried beneath the bank of Lyndhurst Old Park, which dates from the end of the thirteenth century, hazel formed six per cent of the total pollen, whilst in the surface beneath a Bronze Age barrow near Burley it formed fifteen per cent.[12] In many Bronze Age surfaces it may comprise as much as twenty to thirty per cent of the total pollen.

In the unenclosed woodlands of the Forest today, hazel occurs only infrequently—a few stools scattered here and there. This, however, is often in marked contrast to privately owned woodlands in the area, most of which are hazel coppice and oak standards except where they have been converted to conifers in recent years. Almost all this woodland is the result of deliberate planting during the late eighteenth and nineteenth centuries, designed to supply the growing markets for such produce as hurdles and cooping wood. The disappearance of hazel from the Forest woodlands may to some extent have been associated with a general decalcification of the soils, but it is more likely to have been the result of long continued browsing. Hazel is browsed readily by stock and is today absent from most woodlands in this country where animals are allowed freedom of access.

The persistence of hazel into medieval times and later in the New Forest is indicated by the recurrent mention of the species as the underwood in coppices, although it is probable that it had to be encouraged by planting. It is significant that of the fourteen derelict or potential coppices described by Norden in 1609, hazel is mentioned in only two cases. Its distribution in medieval times probably depended on the success and extent of encoppicements, that is, on protection against browsing. The deterioration of the coppice system in the sixteenth and seventeenth centuries no doubt signalled its final withdrawal.

Holly, in contrast to hazel, is highly resistant to elimination by browsing. Indeed, the late Professor Pearsall claimed that there was a distinct correlation between an abundance of holly and a history of pony grazing. At what period the species achieved abundance in the New Forest it is not possible to determine from the written evidence. Certainly 'holm' was common in the fifteenth and sixteenth centuries and probably before.

A useful indication of the relative abundance of oak and beech in the Forest at the close of the medieval period may be found in a survey of 1563, which lists 143 parcels of woodland on which stood timber trees and gives a brief description of the crop which each carried. The descriptions may be analysed as follows:

Description of crop	*Number of parcels*
oak	61
dominantly oak, some beech	23
dominantly beech, some oak	9
beech	21
oak and holm	19
crop not stated	10

The general dominance of oak early in the seventeenth century is reflected in the statement of the surveyors of 1608 who noted that, 'All the said trees are for the most part oak, and some small quantetayes of beech and ash.' The timber surveys of 1707 and 1764 give more precise figures for the numbers of mature beech compared to oak. In 1707 there were some 4,000 mature beech, compared with 12,746 mature oak; and in 1764, 7,104 beech compared with around 20,000 oak. The present dominance of beech over the greater area of the unenclosed woodland must have been brought about by the success of beech regeneration during the period when the present A-generation of trees arose. No doubt too, the preferential removal of oak for the shipyards in the eighteenth and nineteenth centuries has contributed to this.

Towards the end of the eighteenth century Gilpin dwelt at length on the felling of the Forest oaks for the navy. Of Denny Wood, for example, he writes thus:

> It has once been a noble scene, but is now stripped of its principle honours, and consists chiefly of beech. . . . Everywhere

we saw noble *stools* as they call them, the stumps of such trees as have been cut down; and we could form an idea of their grandeur by the respectful space they have formerly occupied.[14]

He refers to other similar areas which had been stripped of their sound oak as, 'These ravaged parts of the Forest.' By the end of the eighteenth century the purveyor of wood for the navy was reduced to seeking even scattered and isolated trees out on the open heaths. In 1801–2 Commissioners sat to enquire into encroachments on the Forest and to decide on cases where there was a dispute as to whether certain of the heaths were Crown land or manorial waste. A recurrent feature of the evidence for the Crown is the assertion of witnesses that, 'oak for the navy' had been cut by Crown officials on the disputed heathlands.[15] Examples are Ogden's Purlieu, much of the heathland around Burley and Holbury Purlieu, all of which are treeless today, apart from scots pine. The removal of oaks from the unenclosed Forest continued well into the eighteenth century. It was finally prevented by the 1877 New Forest Act, which made provision for the 'preservation' of the unenclosed woodlands. Descriptions of the woods in the nineteenth century by contemporary writers—for example Eyre[16] and Lascelles,[17] to choose two of the more reliable—suggest that the unenclosed woods were dominated by beech by the middle of the century.

The documentary evidence tends to support the indications of soil-pollen analyses, referred to in chapter three, that beech has only comparatively recently become important in the Forest. Except on the heavier clays, beech is generally dominant in the A-generation of the unenclosed woods today. In the B- and C-generations, however, oak is clearly the more abundant species and it is probable that here one is seeing the commencement of a reversion to oak dominance.

The degrading effect of beech woodland on soils derived from especially base-poor parent material is well known. A widespread feature of the soil profile under beechwoods on sands and gravels in the New Forest is the occurrence of a 'micropodzol', a bleached layer and dark brown enriched layer at the top of the mineral soil, that is, in the top 2-3 in of the profile. This is presumably an indication that the acid beech litter has encouraged limited podzolisation. The soils under many areas of beechwood on plateau gravels exhibit a more normal, though often incipient podzol profile and, although it is not possible to establish an absolute correlation (though pollen analysis might help) the degraded condition of the soil may be the result of a long period of beech dominance. It may thus be that the intrusion of beech into the oak dominant woodland has left behind it a legacy of soil impoverishment.

References

1　An early reference for a comparable area, the Forest of Dean, is for AD 1237 (C. E. Hart, *in litt*).
2　Public Records Office L.R. 2/303/1-15.
3　Patent Roll, 37, Eliz I.
4　Public Record Office, E/179.
5　Copy of original, dated 1875, in possession of the author.
6　G. Hammersley, 'The Crown Woods and their exploitation in the sixteenth and seventeenth centuries', *Bull Inst Hist Res*, 30, 1957.
7　Public Record Office, S.P. 14/42.
8　*Victoria County History of Hampshire*, V, 1912.
9　*Victoria County History of Hampshire*, V, 1912; *Reports of Commissioners to Enquire into the Woods, Forests and Land Revenues of the Crown*, 1789–93;
　　M. Oppenheim, *A History of the Administration of the Royal Navy, 1509–1660*, London, 1896.
10　Copies of originals, dated 1875, in possession of the author.
11　Reproduced as Appendix 32 of the *Fifth Report of Commissioners. . . .*, 1789.
12　G. W. Dimbleby, *The Development of British Heathlands and their Soils*, Oxford Forestry Memoir No. 23, Oxford, 1962.
13　Public Record Office, L.R.R.O. 5/39. Survey of woods in Forests south of Trent in the name of Roger Taverner, the Queen's Surveyor.
14　Rev William Gilpin, *Remarks on Forest Scenery*, II, 1791.
15　*Return made by Commissioners . . . as to Encroachment, etc in the . . . Forest, 1801–2*, London, 1853.
16　G. E. B. Eyre, 'The New Forest: a sketch', *Fortnightly Review*, 1 April 1871.
17　G. W. Lascelles, *Thirty-Five Years in the New Forest*, London, 1915.

NINE

The Statutory Inclosures

THE statutory silvicultural Inclosures probably exhibit a greater diversity of species and age classes of timber than any other large commercial forest in Britain. They include the relicts of crops planted at a variety of periods since the early eighteenth century. Partial felling and replanting of the early hardwood Inclosures, and the planting of a variety of conifer species as well as hardwoods after the Act of 1851 has resulted, moreover, in great diversity within comparatively small areas, the more so because the need to have due regard for amenity, stipulated by the New Forest Act 1877, has since led to a patchwork system of forestry in which clear fellings of more than a few acres have for the most part been avoided.

Conifer afforestation has by no means been the dominating feature of more recent silvicultural management. Extensive areas of coniferous woodland, mainly scots pine, were first established following the Act of 1851 and there has since been a good deal of conversion from hardwoods to conifers. Fear that such conversion would continue until the hardwood areas had been completely supplanted, however, led to a good deal of agitation in the 1920s and 1930s, the eventual upshot of which was that the Forestry Commission gave an assurance that they would maintain at least forty per cent of the Inclosures under hardwoods. More recently the policy has become modified to one of maintaining fifty per cent of the total area of woodland (both enclosed and unenclosed) under hardwoods, thus reducing the area of the Inclosures which will in the foreseeable future carry hardwoods, to a little over thirty per cent.

Of the twenty-three silvicultural Inclosures made in the eighteenth century under the Act of 1698 and comprising some 3,296 acres, most appear to have occupied sites which had formerly been at least partly wooded. Some, such as Ocknell, South Bentley and

165

North Bentley, were re-enclosures of former coppices. In the cases of North and South Bentley Inclosures the boundaries actually conformed to those of the earlier coppices, as their irregular shapes, contrasting with the regular patterns of most statutory Inclosures, to this day bear witness. At least three of the Inclosures made were on sites which probably carried little or no woodland at the time of enclosure—Prior's Acre, Etherise and Long Beech. Despite the depredations to which the early Inclosures were subject in the eighteenth century—two, it will be remembered, had been converted to rabbit warrens and most had suffered depletion of their timber by 1789—and subsequent felling and replanting, a good deal of the original crop has survived. Most of this is distributed in small fragments among extensive tracts of more recent enclosures into which many of the early ones were absorbed. The big beeches of Woodfidley, planted early in the eighteenth century, for example, still form a well-known feature of the skyline as one looks from the open heathlands west across the central woodland area, although most of the original planting has since been converted to conifers.

Five large blocks remain. These include the greater part of Raven's Nest Inclosure, part of Sloden Old, Ocknell Inclosure and Long Beech Inclosure, which have not been re-enclosed since the eighteenth century. The remaining site, Burley Old Inclosure, was re-enclosed in the nineteenth century, but remained untouched until it was recently part felled and replanted. To some extent these woods resemble the Ancient and Ornamental woodlands, although their age structure is somewhat different, depending as it does on the success which the original planting obtained in producing an even aged stand whose canopy subsequently precluded the regeneration of succeeding age classes, and to their history of enclosure against stock.

The first statutory Inclosures were of beech and oak and some at least were sown, not planted. Spits of ground were turned up at intervals of a yard and three acorns sown in each spit. Following sowing, the ground was broadcast with hawes, holly berries, sloes and yew berries so that protection would be afforded the young oak crop until it was past danger from browsing. Thus, Sloden Old Inclosure, sown in 1775 and crowning the ridge between the Dockens Water and Latchmore Brook valleys in the north of the Forest, is today a mixed wood of oak, holly, hawthorn and yew.

In parts the yew forms a closed canopy—the only site in the Forest where it does so, although the species is a normal component of the Forest 'holms'. A large number of the trees are now dead or dying, a phenomenon for which no really satisfactory explanation has so far been advanced. A ring count made in 1963 from the butt of a yew felled during the process of improving the gravel track through part of the wood confirmed the age of the stand. The canopy formed by the original planting remained closed until comparatively recently, effectively preventing the widespread establishment of younger age classes; and in recent years, during which both oak and yew have suffered from die-back, regeneration has been prevented by intense grazing and browsing, although there has been some expansion of the margins of the wood.

Raven's Nest and Long Beech Inclosures, planted in 1775, are of even-aged sessile oak and beech respectively. Both have a dense understory of holly. Both are currently being partially re-enclosed and felled.

Ocknell Inclosure and Burley Old Inclosure are beech-oak woods with understories of holly. The beech dominates the canopy on both sites. In age-structure they closely resemble the unenclosed Ancient and Ornamental woodlands, comprising a well spaced A-generation of mature trees, in between which a B-generation became established in the second half of the nineteenth century, coinciding both with the reduction in herbivore populations at the time and the re-enclosure of Burley Old. The combined canopy of these two generations has since precluded regeneration. There is documentary evidence to show that Ocknell was encoppiced in the late seventeenth century and judging from the massive size of the A-generation beeches, both here and in Burley Old Inclosure, it seems likely that the oldest trees pre-date the enclosure of the sites in the eighteenth century. Unfortunately no ring counts by which this could be confirmed have been carried out.

The first plantations in the Inclosures made between 1808 and 1848, pursuant to the Act of 1808, were mainly of pedunculate oak, although scots pine shelter belts were widely used and some areas of chestnut were planted. In the later plantations, chiefly those made between 1830 and 1848, scots pine and in some places larch, were used as nurses to the oak crop. A programme of heavy thinning, necessary to obtain the big, spreading crowns which would carry the 'crooks' and 'knees' required by the naval shipwrights, was carried out until late in the century. The earlier oak plantations of the eighteenth century appear never to have been thinned until the 1880s. Lascelles records that their timber was particularly sound until that time, following which there was a deterioration with every thinning. A major inducement to thin heavily in the nineteenth century, in addition to the requirements of the shipyards, was the high price obtained for tanbark, which was largely stripped under contract on the ground. This market continued to prompt repeated thinnings long after the market for shipbuilding timber had been lost with the advent of the ironclad.

The original purpose of much of the oak plantations may never have been realised, but it was these which bore the brunt of the heavy fellings necessary during the 1914–18 war, when the Forest contributed a little more than a quarter of a million tons of timber to the war effort. Few of the plantations of the first half of the nineteenth century remain standing today, although they are well represented by Amberwood, Islands Thorns and Backley Inclosures, the last also containing one of the few blocks of mature chestnut in the Forest.

The planting programme which followed the Deer Removal Act of 1851 was on the grand scale. By comparison the Crown had hitherto been merely toying with silviculture. Now, between 1851 and 1874, some 12,000 acres were enclosed and planted—nor was the crop now restricted to oak for the shipyards. 'Instead of the varied intermixture of moor and wood and the groups of oak, beech and holly scattered over the open spaces between the pervious woods, monotonous plantations of Scotch Fir are gradually overspreading the soil and obliterating its undulations', wrote G. E. B. Eyre in 1871.[1] The Hon G. W. Lascelles, who took office as Deputy Surveyor in 1880, himself observed with apparent regret that much of the 'old Forest' had gone for ever, the scattered woodland consolidated into the large compact blocks of the new plantations. Enclosure, he says 'went far to exhaust the oak-growing soil of the Forest . . . and quickly they came to the bad heath lands, which could only carry Scotch Fir.'[2] Such scots pine plantations as those of Milkham, Slufters, Highland Water and Parkhill Inclosures, established on the 'bad heath lands', were to provide a good deal of the Forest's contribution to the national timber output during the war of 1939–45.

Conifer planting was by no means confined to scots pine after the 1851 Act. Corsican pine, for example, was used in Knightwood Inclosure and Weymouth pine in Dames Slough Inclosure. A number of Douglas fir stands were established, including the well-known stand of Boldrewood Grounds. Norway and Sitka spruce were later used widely. The introduction of this range of species may be regarded as a significant step towards the diversification of the woodland environment. The felling and subsequent regeneration of these conifer plantations, mainly during and after the two world wars, involving the opening up of the canopy and the creation of open and half-shade conditions over large areas of the woods, has since brought about further diversification.

In a number of cases the 1851–75 enclosures were of pre-existing deciduous woodland. Here the object seems to have been to regenerate the existing wood by merely excluding stock. The age-structure of what remains of the original stand in Denny Inclosure clearly reflects a period of active regeneration after its enclosure in the late 1860s. The exclusion of commonable stock and the removal of the deer seems to have succeeded in closing the canopy of a previously degenerate wood without any further deliberate management: Lascelles says that not even windfallen and moribund trees were removed. The re-enclosure of Burley Old Inclosure appears to have been a comparable case.

The period of active enclosure came to an end in 1875, and two years later the Act of 1877 closely defined the area which the Crown might manage silviculturally. Thereafter there followed a period during which management operations were almost entirely confined to carrying out thinnings. Inclosure fences in many cases fell into decay and by the first decade of the present century much re-enclosure and replanting was required. By 1913 a programme of re-enclosure commenced, but almost immediately the 1914–18 war intervened and the emphasis necessarily passed to felling rather than planting. Well over 2,000 acres were felled, and over large areas of the woods the potential crop rotation was completely upset. These clear fellings were subsequently to prove a considerable problem. Fences were damaged and stock over-ran many of the Inclosures. The commoners, it has been alleged, objected strongly to the removal of their animals from them and much difficulty was supposedly experienced in re-stocking the woodlands.

The fellings necessary during the 1939–45 war, when the Forest provided some 400,000 tons of timber, were carried out with a careful eye, both to the future regeneration of the woods and to causing the least damage to the Forest scenery. Under the direction of Mr D. W. Young, the Deputy Surveyor, clear fellings were in the main avoided and the timber removed in groups. Where possible the Inclosures were replenished by natural regeneration. The first deliberate attempts to regenerate the Forest Inclosures naturally appear to have been made following the heavy wartime fellings of the 1914–18 war: natural regeneration of oak at Salisbury Trench and Aldridgehill Inclosures had then proved highly successful and similar methods were now adopted after the fellings of 1939–45, for example, in Roe, Holly Hatch and Broomy Inclosures. In the latter two, oak regeneration proved very poor, owing mainly to a dense growth of bracken. In Roe Inclosure it was rather more successful. In Shave Green and South Oakley Inclosures wartime fellings were followed by complete restocking of both hardwoods and conifers by natural regeneration.

In most of the extensive scots pine plantations, where extensive felling has taken place during and since 1939–45, either belts or an even scatter of mother trees were left to replenish the timber crop by natural regeneration and the results have on the whole been most impressive from a silvicultural point of view. The policy of the Forestry Commission subsequent to the 1939–45 fellings has continued to be one of group felling and replenishment where possible by natural regeneration, so that there is a constant flux in the amount of open ground and half-shade conditions, which together with the wide range of tree species grown and the high proportion of hardwoods to which the Commission has committed itself, ensures great ecological diversity.

The provision of the New Forest Act 1949, whereby the Forestry Commission might, with the consent of the Verderers, enclose up to a further 5,000 acres of the open Forest, has led to the first direct afforestation of heathland for nearly one hundred years. In July 1958 the Verderers gave their consent to the enclosure of approximately 2,000 of the possible maximum of 5,000 acres, the sites of the new Inclosures—known for convenience as 'Verderers' Inclosures'—being chosen in consultation with the Verderers and after the views of the various local societies and of the Nature Conservancy had been heard in open Court.

The siting of the new Inclosures was chosen with some care

and largely with a view to utilising areas of the more degraded soils carrying heather, which were least likely to make a significant contribution to the value of the Forest grazings as a whole. A number were distributed along the Forest perambulation adjacent to the expanding industrial zone on the west side of Southampton Water, partly as a 'screen' from development and partly to assist the sealing off of the Forest against animals straying on to main roads and into gardens outside the Forest. The remainder of the Inclosures were sited at various points where they were least likely to obstruct or divert the passage of stock from Forest edge holdings to the grazings. The new Inclosures have for the most part been assigned to conifer production, but hardwoods have also been widely used in order to satisfy the requirements of amenity, even though the degraded soils are on the whole not suited to satisfactory growth of hardwoods. Reseeded strips round the periphery of the Inclosures serve both as grazing areas and firebreaks.

It is problematical whether the Forestry Commission will receive the consent of the Verderers to the enclosure of the remainder of the maximum of 5,000 acres. At the time of writing opposition to any further enclosure of the open Forest is strong among the commoners and it must be confessed that it is difficult to reconcile further enclosure with the other recognised functions of the Forest as a wildlife reservoir and recreational 'lung'.

References
1 G. E. B. Eyre, 'The New Forest: a Sketch', *Fortnightly Review*, 1 April 1871.
2 Hon G. W. Lascelles, *Thirty-Five Years in the New Forest*, London, 1915.

TEN

Grassland, Bog and Heath

THIS chapter is mainly concerned with the ecological characteristics of the heathlands (using the term in its strict sense to mean those areas over which heather is dominant), grasslands and valley bogs of the open Forest. From the ecological standpoint a classification of the main plant communities can most usefully be related to a descending scale of nutritive values. This has been attempted in table III, although it should be borne in mind that the sequence adopted in the table is open to modification in the light of more chemical and protein analyses of Forest soils and vegetation than are at present available. The sequence in the table will in part reflect stages in the succession from woodland to heathland and its associated soil deterioration; in part the texture of the parent material, which locally may influence the extent of such a succession; and in part the topography, which may give rise to water receiving areas where either bog and wet heath will have developed hand in hand with peat formation, or fertile 'lawns' have formed on deposits of alluvium. 'Flush' effects are also apparent on many valley slopes and are often marked by the persistence of acid grassland on what is otherwise a tract of heathland. One important vegetation type is the result of the recent and direct intervention of man—the re-seeded areas.

I

Although it is possible to classify the grasslands of the Forest in considerable detail according to criteria such as productivity, soil base status, and soil moisture regime, it is sufficient here to confine description to the broad categories distinguished in table III—the bent/fescue 'lawns'; the re-seeded areas; and the acid grass-

172

TABLE III

Classification of New Forest Vegetation (excluding statutory Inclosures)

Vegetation type and approximate total area	Parent Material (texture)	Soils
Deciduous woodland, c 8,000 acres	Mainly on clays (c 5,000 acres); partly on sands and loams (c 2,500 acres); locally on gravels (c 500 acres)	Brown forest soil, commonly gleyed; podzol profiles frequent on gravels, especially under beech
Agrostis tenuis/*Festuca ovina* grassland—'Lawns', c 800–900 acres	(a) on clays in close association with deciduous woodland (b) on deposits of alluvium in valleys	Brown earth, gleyed in subsoil
Re-seeded areas (now mainly dominated by *A. tenuis*/*F. ovina*), c 1,200 acres	Variety of sites but best results achieved on free draining sands, loams and gravels	Brown earth
Valley bog and wet heath, c 7,000 acres	Developed mainly on impermeable subsoil usually of transported material which has infilled valleys	Peat, maximum recorded depth c 20 ft. Depths 4–5 ft common. Wet heath normally on shallow peat over humus-gley podzol or peaty gley
Agrostis setacea/*Molinia caerulea* with associated *Pteridium* and *Ulex europaeus*—acid grassland, c 11,000 acres	Clays, loams, more restricted distribution on sands and gravels	Brown earth, locally gleyed in subsoil; often visibly degrading
Calluna vulgaris, c 18,000 acres (a) associated with *Molinia* and *Erica tetralix* (b) associated with *Erica cinerea* and *Ulex minor*	(a) on materials with high clay fraction in subsoil (b) mainly on sands, sandy loams and gravels	(a) humus-gley podzol (b) humus-iron podzol
Pinus sylvestris, c 1,700 acres	On similar material and soils to *Calluna* communities. Result of colonisation of *Calluna* heath within past century.	

lands dominated by bristle bent (*Agrostis setacea*) and purple moor grass (*Molinia caerulea*).

Bent/fescue grassland, dominated by fine bent (*Agrostis tenuis*) and sheep's fescue (*Festuca ovina*) is in the New Forest confined mainly to comparatively base-rich alluvial soils occurring in valley bottoms; to woodland glades, clearings and margins where it is associated with the less acid clays; and to village greens and road-side verges.

The inherent fertility of the streamside lawns may be satisfactorily explained as a flush effect, the valleys receiving the products of leaching on the higher ground. They are for the most part flooded in winter and some remain wet for the greater part of the year. As a general measure of fertility these valley sites will frequently give a pH reading of 7.0. The upper horizons of the soil are especially rich in phosphate and nitrogen and are far from being acutely deficient in calcium. These 'lawns', as they are known in the Forest, occupy only a small part of the total area of the open Forest—between 8–900 acres—but their inherent site fertility makes them of considerable significance to the grazier. In an experiment carried out in 1964, Mr H. C. Scowen of Rothamsted Experimental Station, showed that the yield of grass from one such site—a small streamside lawn in the valley of the Dockens Water—was considerably greater than that from a nearby re-seeded area. Expressed in cwt dry matter per acre the yield from four 'cuts' taken in May, July, August and October, from plots caged against grazing, gave 49·7 cwt/acre for the streamside lawn and only 24·5 cwt/acre for the re-seeded area.

A characteristic of New Forest grasslands is the small number of plant species which are represented in the sward. On the bent/fescue lawns the two dominants often occur to the virtual exclusion of other species. On streamside sites associated species are practically confined to the following thirteen:

wild white clover (*Trifolium ripens*), ribwort plantain (*Plantego lanceolata*), creeping buttercup (*Rununculus ripens*), annual poa (*Poa annua*), sweet vernal grass (*Anthroxanthrum odoratum*), perrenial rye-grass (*Lollium perenne*), Yorkshire fog (*Holcus lanatus*), heath-grass (*Sieglingia ducumbens*), moor mat-grass (*Nardus stricta*), moor rush (*Juncus squarrosa*), oval sedge (*Carex ovalis*), carnation sedge (*Carex panicea*), common sedge (*Carex nigra*).

The representation of heath-grass, carnation sedge and common sedge would appear to depend on the frequency with which a site is subject to waterlogging. On the wettest sites, heath-grass may occasionally achieve dominance. Moor mat-grass and moor rush, too, are associated with impeded drainage, although both occur also in dry lawns, often as a peripheral belt or zone, and may here possibly be an effect of intensive grazing. Wild white clover and Yorkshire fog are essentially characteristic of lawns but rarely flooded, and here they may sometimes occur in great abundance. The small, isolated patches of perennial rye-grass which appear on many lawns probably originate from seed brought on to the site in the dung of animals recently turned out on the Forest from enclosed holdings.

In the woodland lawns species diversity tends to increase with the proximity of the tree canopy, when woodland grasses such as tufted hair grass (*Deschampsia caespitosa*) and creeping soft-grass (*Holcus mollis*) appear; and, as on streamside sites, with the degree of waterlogging.

The woodland lawns, like the greater part of the unenclosed woodlands with which they are associated, are distributed on the less acid clays, mainly those of the Headon and Barton series. Though the persistence of comparatively fertile grasslands here may be associated with inherent qualities of the parent materials, it is also tempting to postulate that site fertility may be maintained by a nutrient cycle in which the base reserves of the woodlands are tapped through the browsing and grazing of herbivores and passed to the grasslands in the dung of the animals. Certainly the maintenance of the lawns would seem partly at least to be associated with very intensive grazing. Many former lawns have been colonised by cross-leaved heath (*Erica tetralix*), heather and purple moor grass and it is asserted locally that this commenced during the inter-war period, when the numbers of herbivores were minimal.

The woodland lawns are demonstrably only a fraction of their former total extent. The map of 1789 shows many 'lawn' place names which have since been lost to the successive enclosures of land for silviculture, or to the expansion of the woodland margins during the past hundred years. At the same time, new lawns are currently forming in places where the woodland is mature and even-aged and where the trees are now dying without younger generations to replace them. Many of these sites, however, are on materials such as sands and gravels, prone to rapid soil degradation and it is likely that the bent/fescue grassland will succeed to more acid tolerant vegetation.

Away from valley floors and woodlands, bent/fescue grassland is virtually confined in the Forest to roadside verges, village greens, and to the periphery of a number of ponds situated on the plateau gravels. These ponds probably have man-made origins and apparently receive their water from a water table perched on a clay lens in the subsoil. Their surrounding lawns probably owe their origins to intensive dunging by livestock going to drink and to their function as 'shades', or places where cattle and ponies congregate to escape fly-irritation during hot weather.

The strips of bent/fescue grassland which occur along the verges of practically every road and lane in the Forest are clearly artefacts but it is less easy to determine precisely how they have arisen. The explanation most often offered is that the material used in road surfacing, much of which finds its way to the verges and which in the Forest is derived mainly from gravels, is comparatively base enriched: certainly the pH of verge soils may be as high as 6·5. At all events, the verges form a considerable attraction to stock and the commoner pays dearly for the grazing they provide in the shape of animals lost in accidents with motor vehicles.

Roadside lawns may be relatively extensive where there is ready access for motor vehicles on to the adjoining heath. Both fine bent and sheep's fescue appear in the Forest to be favoured by heavy trampling and soil compaction. Dunging by animals attracted by the possibility of tit-bits, to say nothing of the not inconsiderable detritus left by the holiday-maker must also contribute to the base status of the soil. Similarly the persistence of bent/fescue grassland in the form of greens adjacent to Forest villages may be partly associated with similar factors, although the constant dunging by livestock congregating near holdings (and especially cattle between milkings) may be the most significant single factor. Clearly, however, the ecology of features such as the roadside verge lawns and village greens, is open to closer examination.

II

The cropping and re-seeding of a substantial area of the open Forest between 1941 and 1959 represents the first deliberate attempt to improve the agricultural productivity of the open Forest. From the grazier's point of view, the years prior to the 1939–45 war witnessed a considerable deterioration in the condition of the Forest grazings, a deterioration which had probably been going on more or less progressively since the late nineteenth century, but which had accelerated rapidly between the wars. By 1940 it was feared that deterioration had gone too far for natural improvement to keep pace with the prospective rise in the numbers of stock on the Forest, and some deliberate improvement was considered necessary. Thus the New Forest Pastoral Development Scheme was born, under the auspices of the County War Agricultural Executive Committee. Interference with the soil of the Forest was strictly speaking illegal, but under the exigencies of wartime the agreement of the Verderers, Forestry Commission and commoners was obtained and work commenced in 1941.

The first experimental leys at Ober Heath (su285040), Longcross Plain (su241150) and Long Bottom (su185140) were ploughed with prairie busters, treated with half a ton of lime and a small dressing of phosphate per acre and re-seeded with barn sweepings from seed merchants. This somewhat unconventional treatment might have been more successful had the sites been enclosed against grazing whilst the ley became established. As it was, the improvement achieved was of a somewhat ephemeral nature. Clearly more permanent improvement could only be achieved by enclosure and the policy subsequently adopted was to reclaim, enclose, crop for three or four years, re-seed and control graze for a further year before finally pulling down the fences. Between 1944 and 1952 about 900 acres in fifteen localities were treated thus, although at two sites cropping was abandoned after the first year or two, owing to drainage problems.

The selection of the sites is of some interest. Most would appear formerly to have been occupied by bristle bent grassland, with gorse and bracken. Browning, in his account of the scheme[1] records that the old saying:

> Under bracken lies gold,
> Under gorse lies silver,
> Under heather lies lead.

was a useful guide to the quality of the soil and that, 'It can be taken that land on which there is little bracken or gorse is unsuitable for this scheme of operations; even this land could be improved, but to attempt to grow crops profitable enough to pay for the fencing and reseeding is folly.' The sites chosen were all in the southern half of the Forest and mostly on loams and sands. All showed moderate to severe phosphate and potash deficiencies and an acute shortage of lime. Heavy applications of ground chalk and lime were applied, the available phosphate deficiency thus accentuated being guarded against mainly by super-phosphate dressings.

The seeds mixtures used in the final re-seeding varied considerably from site to site. Coxfoot S.143 and S.26; rye-grass S.101 and S.23; and timothy S.48, comprised the bulk of the seeds mixtures, but they also variously included clovers, crested dogstail, red fescue S.59 and meadow fescue S.53. The wartime airfields at Stoney Cross (su245125), Holmsley (sz217990) and Hatchet Moor (su350010) were also re-seeded at this time, almost entirely with rye-grass. Today the re-seeded areas have largely succeeded to indigenous grasses. Fine bent and sheep's fescue dominate their swards, although on the freer-draining soils the rye-grass has remained abundant and on most sites white clover, Yorkshire fog and crested dogstail are well represented. In the main, extraordinarily little recolonisation by bristle bent, bracken and gorse has taken place. Although analyses carried out by the National Agricultural Advisory Service in 1959 showed that mineral deficiencies were probably too acute for most conventional agricultural leys pH values remained between 5·9 and 6·8—still considerably higher than one would anticipate in soils carrying bristle bent grassland.

The experience of the New Forest Pastoral Development Scheme showed that if agricultural leys are to be established on the open Forest, then rye-grass is likely to persist longest and that the free-draining sites are the best subjects for such work, even though they may initially be the most base-deficient. Phosphate deficiency emerged as the main inhibitory factor in establishing meadow grasses and clovers and nitrogen status appeared to be critical in the maintenance of the leys. Lime deficiency seemed to be of less significance.

Loss in soil fertility since re-seeding has been accompanied by the establishment of fine bent and sheep's fescue grassland at the expense of the ley species. The indications at present are that the site fertility of the re-seeded areas is rather lower than that of the natural lawns, although it is clearly higher than that of the bristle bent/purple moor grass community. Presumably, in the absence of further fertilising, a reversion to the pre-treatment vegetation is likely ultimately to take place. It may be useful here to compare the recently cropped and re-seeded areas with other sites on the open Forest in agricultural use at earlier periods, for example the numerous small abandoned encroachments on the Forest edge, many of which were probably last in use in the early nineteenth century.[2] If these were ever down to meadow grasses (and this is most likely) they have long since succeeded to bristle bent/purple moor grass, often with a vigorous growth of bracken and gorse. A much more recently abandoned site, which had been in occupation since at latest 1775, is Ashley Lodge (su201147), abandoned in 1944 when it became part of a bombing range. After 170 years or more of manuring (and probably marling), some of the paddocks still carry a fair rye-grass ley in places, although the sward is for the most part dominated by fine bent, with sheep's fescue and annual poa locally abundant; one paddock has completely gone over to bristle bent and carries patches of bracken and gorse.

It is finally relevant to record the most recent re-seeding work, carried out on behalf of the Verderers. Limited re-seeding became legal after the New Forest Act 1949, and in 1959 three sites were enclosed, rotovated, dressed and re-seeded direct. The results, on fairly well drained gravels and using a seeds mixture of 16 lb rye-grass S.23 and $1\frac{1}{2}$ lb white clover per acre, have been as reasonable as might be expected without regular subsequent attention. It would perhaps be fair comment that if further improvement of the grazings is desirable it would be better to improve within the limitations of the environment and aim, not at a rye-grass ley likely to revert within a comparatively short space of time, but at more indigenous grasses which will persist longer in the absence of successive dressings of fertilizer.

III

Bog and wet heath occupy a total area of something of the order of 7,000 acres of the unenclosed Forest and are characterised by accumulations of organic material—peat—in valleys and basins. The most extensive of the bogs occur in the southern half of the area, where contour is gentlest and water receiving areas tend to be wide and shallow with comparatively slow stream movement. The commencement of peat formation appears to have been associated with two main factors—the presence of impermeable material of transported origin in the valleys; and the receipt of drainage and run-off water from the surrounding area. Subsequent development has depended largely on the shape of the valley and the volume of water entering it. With the onset of significant peat accumulation, the valley bogs will have become increasingly water-retentive, which will have further assisted the peat forming process. Where valley drainage has remained unimpeded, often because the transported material which infilled the valley was permeable, accumulations of humose, iron-rich alluvium have given rise to the valley lawns.

No systematic investigation of the peat deposits in New Forest valley bogs has been attempted, but it is known that depths of up to 5 ft are common, and a depth of about 20 ft has been recorded from Cranesmoor bog (SU195029). From pollen analyses of the Cranesmoor peats Siegrief[3] concluded that peat rapidly infilled a wide shallow basin during Boreal and Pre-Boreal times. There was no evidence of deposits more recent than the late Boreal or early Atlantic, though Seagrief clearly recognised that the upper layers of the peat might have been removed in recent times and the later pollen record thus destroyed. In fact, on air photographs Cranesmoor, and indeed all the more extensive valley bogs of the Forest, exhibit signs of systematic disturbance. These take the form of parallel lines across the bogs at close and more or less regular distances which, when examined on the ground appear to be slight ridges left between excavations, presumably for the peat. The period during which excavation took place is unknown. From the remark in the Government report of 1789 that 'those who make a trade of cutting peat and turf, for sale, are becoming so daring as to threaten the burning of the Forest if they are interrupted'[4] it would seem likely that many excavations are fairly recent. Others may have been medieval or earlier. At all events they have effectively truncated the peat (and pollen) profile. Pollen analyses from sites carefully chosen as being the least disturbed by man are badly needed, both for an elucidation of the more recent history of peat accumulation and to provide a post Atlantic pollen record which may be compared with the results of soil-pollen analysis.

An essential ecological feature of the valley bogs is that they receive some of the products of leaching on the higher ground and they are thus in general likely to be comparatively base-enriched, the degree of enrichment depending largely on the base status of the materials from which they receive soil water. Soil water derived from the Headon Beds or Barton Clays may be decidedly base-rich, as in the central water courses on Denny Bog (SU347053), Matley Bog (SU335073) or Holmsley Bog (SU240002), whilst that derived from sands and gravels may be neutral or acid in reaction, as at the heads of Backley Bottom (SU223085), Harvest Slade Bottom (SU216070) or Buckherd Bottom (SU214083). In a comparative study of a number of valley bogs in the Forest, Newbould[5] distinguished three main plant communities, the distribution of each of which appears to be determined mainly by the base status and distribution of the water flow through the bog.

Where the central water flow of a bog is alkaline in reaction the vegetation forms a distinctive lateral zonation. The water course itself will usually be flanked by alder carr with tussocks of the sedge *Carex paniculata*. In the middle or lower reaches of such a bog the water course tends to become canalised into a definite stream, which has often cut down through the peat into the underlying material. Flanking the central carr, where the soil water tends to be intermediate in reaction and slow-moving, occur communities in which purple moor grass is consistently present, sometimes to the virtual exclusion of other species, but which variously include as main components: bog myrtle (*Myrica gale*), bog-rush (*Schoenus nigricans*), reed (*Phragmites communis*), bog-bean (*Menyanthes trifoliata*) and marsh cinquefoil (*Potentilla palustris*).

On drier sites, particularly where the central stream has bitten into the subsoil and increased lateral drainage, bog myrtle may form a distinctive zone alongside the carr, whilst the reed/bog-bean/marsh cinquefoil assemblage occurs on the wetter parts. These communities finally give way to an outer bog-zone dominated by *Sphagnum* mosses, through which there is a diffuse seepage of base-poor water. Purple moor grass is prominent in this outer zone, whilst a wide range of species, including cross-leaved heath, bog asphodel (*Narthecium ossifragum*), sundew (*Drosera spp.*), white beaked sedge (*Rhynchospora alba*) and cotton grass (*Eriophorum augustifolium*), occur in both this and the flushed communities.

The *Sphagnum*-rich zone will in turn be flanked by wet heath. The wet heath community includes heather, cross-leaved heath, purple moor grass, lichens and various species of *Sphagnum* moss, and is characterised by very shallow peat formation. Associated species include sundew, brown-beaked sedge (*Rhynchospora fusca*), butterwort (*Pinguicula lusitanica*), and deer-grass (*Scirpus cespitosus*), whilst the club-moss *Lycopodium inundatum* is virtually confined to this vegetation type.

Bogs receiving neutral or base-poor water lack the central zone of heavily flushed vegetation—the alder carr—though willow-birch carr may develop locally, whilst on other sites, the *Sphagnum* dominated vegetation may extend over most of the bog. Modifications to the idealised zonation also arise where the water flow through the bog is split. Newbould showed that at Cranesmoor bog, for example, there were two main lines of flushed vegetation marginal to the bog, and that the *Sphagnum*-rich community had developed in the shielded area between them. As he points out, it is a short step from this situation to a typical raised bog, though further development in this direction is presumably precluded by low rainfall.

IV

Acid grassland composed of bristle bent and purple moor grass occupies a considerable area of the New Forest—roughly 11,000 acres. It is the more surprising, therefore, that it seems never to have received more than a passing mention in the literature. The bristle bent is a grass which is in this country confined to base-poor soils in the south and west. The purple moor grass was described by Professor Pearsall as, 'one of half a dozen or so moorland plants which cover an enormous area of country.' In the New Forest it is a prominent component of valley bog, wet heath and dry heath, as well as of acid grassland.

Its status appears mainly to be related to drainage, and where it occurs in association with the bristle bent, the latter is the dominant on more porous soils, purple moor grass becoming progressively better represented with increasing soil moisture. Except where it is shaded-out by bracken or gorse, the bristle bent/purple moor grass sward forms a dense mat on the soil surface to the virtual exclusion of other species of grass: the heath-grass (*Sieglingia ducumbens*) is practically the only other grass species occurring with any frequency. The only really common flowering plants are tormentil (*Potentilla erecta*), heath milkwort (*Polygala serpyllifolia*), heath spotted orchid (*Dactylorchis maculata*), heath dog violet (*Viola canina*) and petty whin (*Genista anglica*).

Bracken is widespread, especially on the better drained and deeper soils, and where it is particularly dense it has shaded-out much of the grass, leaving little cover on the soil surface apart from its own litter and rendering the area useless as grazing for stock. Gorse, too, is widespread on the acid grasslands, distributed mainly in well defined concentrations, known in the Forest as 'brakes'. The plant assemblage of bristle bent and purple moor grass, bracken and gorse is characteristic of the range of soil types which may be embraced by the term 'brown earth'. It is at the same time associated with the more or less recent loss of a woodland cover.

At the upper end of the scale of potential fertility there are clay soils giving a pH reading of as high as 5·5 in the upper 6 in of the soil profile, though usually poor in phosphate. At the lower end there are soils derived from coarser material, severely deficient in potash and phosphate, acutely deficient in lime and giving pH readings as low as 3·7; pH values from the upper horizons of soils carrying acid grassland normally, however, fall within the range 4·5–5·4. Earthworm—and mole—activity is evident in the less acid soils. Indeed, the presence of earthworms may be taken as a fair measure of fertility since they do not normally appear to tolerate soils with a pH lower than about 5·0.

Acid grassland extends over large areas of the lower terraces in the south of the Forest and here the soil may be derived from the superficial gravel deposits (often containing a high clay fraction), a mixture of gravel and loam of transported origin, or the Headon and Barton solid formations. Here, bristle bent/purple moor grass, bracken and gorse are often an indicator of extensive areas of comparatively fertile soils which, but for the legal status of the Forest, would no doubt have been reclaimed long ago. On terraces elsewhere in the Forest this vegetation is usually an indication of 'pockets' of brown earth soils distributed on what is otherwise degraded heathland. In places these pockets may be quite extensive, as in the plateau gravels on Rockford Common (SU1708), Ibsley Common (SU1710), Hyde Common (SU1712), and Godshill Ridge (SU1815) down the west side of the Forest overlooking the Avon valley. Off the terraces, acid grassland is widely distributed, although notably absent from extensive tracts where acutely impoverished sands of the Barton and Bracklesham series are exposed. Topographically acid grassland is a recurring feature of the slopes of valleys and basins, where its persistence may in part perhaps be attributed to flushing. This is most apparent in the extreme north of the Forest where wide, deep valleys run westward into the Avon between high plateaux. Podzol soil profiles and heath dominant vegetation are characteristic of the gravel capped plateau, whilst on valley slopes acid grassland associated with gorse brakes and scattered holms of holly become widespread, giving way in the valley bottoms to purple moor grass bog or sometimes to a mosaic of lawn and thorn thicket. Scattered holly, hawthorn, oak and yew occur widely on the bristle bent/purple moor grass grasslands and serve to emphasise that much of the area now occupied by this vegetation type was probably wooded in comparatively recent times.

The ecological status of the acid grasslands of the New Forest is precarious. Soil profiles often exhibit iron movement and in many, especially in sands and gravels, there are definite signs of the onset of podzolisation—a clear, though very immature bleached zone with a visible deposition layer below. Profiles such as this occur today, for example, in the plateau gravels of Rockford Common under vegetation dominated by bristle bent and bracken. More extreme forms, exhibiting the clear characteristics of a humus-iron or humus-gley podzol, occur under bristle bent and purple moor grass, for example in Howen Bottom (SU2315), on Ocknell Plain (SU225115) and Broomy Plain (SU2010) and on Holmsley Ridge (SU215014). All these sites exhibited a patchy distribution of heather when the soils were examined in 1965. There would thus seem to be evidence that the direction of change over much of the grassland is likely to be towards the heather/podzol association. At the same time, there are clear indications that under the right conditions a reversion to woodland is equally possible. Much of the woodland expansion of the past hundred years (see chapters seven and eight) has taken place on acid grassland, and here gorse may have played an important part in shielding regenerating holly and oak. At least four factors are involved in controlling the succession from grassland to woodland: intensive grazing; periodic burning; the dense mat often formed on the soil surface by the grass sward, which may preclude the establishment of seedlings; and proximity to a seed source. At the present time intensive grazing would seem to be the main factor in restricting woodland establishment, whilst burning (particularly of the areas of gorse) is clearly also important.

As was mentioned in chapter seven, heath burning proved a restricting factor earlier in this century and, indeed, many areas of active holly and oak regeneration on the grassland were destroyed or severely damaged. The significance of the grass mat in preventing regeneration is difficult to evaluate, but both this and distance from seed sources may well be of only secondary or local importance. Holly—manifestly the most successful initial tree colonist—appears to have a capacity for establishing itself in the densest sward and is at the same time likely to be spread avificially, so that distance from the nearest woodland is comparatively unimportant.

V

Vegetation in which heather, or ling (*Calluna vularis*) is dominant extends over an estimated area of approximately 18,000 acres of the open Forest and is essentially associated with degraded soils of the podzol type. Heather dominated communities may be conveniently subdivided into two categories, the distinction between them arising from subsoil drainage. Where profile drainage is unimpeded a humus-iron podzol is usual and the plants associated with the heather are dwarf gorse (*Ulex minor*), bell heather (*Erica cinerea*) and purple moor grass. In most cases the deposition zone in the soil profile, the B-horizon, forms a 'soft pan', but 'hard pans' with a higher iron content are widespread. Compaction in the B-horizon alone, however, is not normally sufficient to prevent root penetration if once trees are able to become established. The B-horizon in humus-iron podzols can vary in depth from about 10 in to 3 ft and occasionally more. Where drainage is impeded in the subsoil, the usual soil type is a humus-gley podzol. Here the main species associated with the heather will be cross-leaved heath and purple moor grass. Where drainage is particularly poor, this vegetation type often assumes some of the characteristics of wet heath and species such as the sundews, deer-grass and various species of *Sphagnum* moss (especially *S. compactum*) become widely distributed.

A bleached horizon is common to both humus-iron and humus-gley podzols, the distinction between them becoming visually obvious in the B-horizon. In the humus-gley podzol this invariably occurs at the change in texture where, below the zone of humus deposition, the profile assumes the mottled appearance associated with constant soil water movement. In humus-iron podzols a distinct iron-pan occurs below the humus layer and immediately above the little altered parent material. Humus-gley podzols occur widely in the plateau gravels, which commonly have a high clay fraction in the lower soil horizons. They are also usual over extensive areas of the Forest where a thin spread of transported sand or loam overlies heavier solid formations, as around the junction of the Barton Sands and Barton Clays. The humus-iron podzols are most widely distributed on sands and loams. The two soil types probably occupy an approximately equivalent area of the total of about 18,000 acres of heath moor.

The significant feature of podzolised soils is that the bleached zone in the A-horizon is acutely impoverished of mineral nutrients. The humus-iron podzols are extremely liable to drought in the summer, and by contrast, where a hard pan impedes drainage, to some degree of waterlogging in winter. The humus-gley podzols are more water retentive in summer, but are liable to extreme waterlogging in winter. Taking pH as a measure of acidity, values for the bleached horizon range from around 3·5 to 4·0. Under these conditions heather and the heaths (*Erica spp.*) would seem to be the species best adapted to survival. There are, however, indications that the impoverishment of the podzol soils over much of the Forest is less acute than on heathland areas elsewhere on Tertiary deposits. The Dorset heaths, most remaining areas of which lie on the inherently poor Bagshot Beds, exhibit soil profiles demonstrably more base deficient in the upper horizons and difficulty has frequently been experienced in establishing even acid tolerant conifers on such sites. In the Forest, holly has become established on podzolised soils (both humus-iron and humus-gley podzols) on a wide scatter of sites during the past hundred years, and there are examples of much older woods on similar soils.

The distribution of gorse on the heather lands provides some further indication of their status. On most heathlands dominated by heather, gorse is confined largely to sites which exhibit signs of disturbance—old gravel workings, spoil heaps, boundary banks, barrows, trackways and other features arising from human activity. In his study of the Dorset heaths, Dr N. W. Moore asserted that there, '*U. europaeus* is closely associated with past human activity; it is virtually restricted to boundary banks, old tracks, the sites of old fields and plantations.'[6]

Similarly strong anthropogenic influences on the distribution of gorse have been demonstrated for Ireland,[7] and the Isle of Man,[8] and in an investigation of its distribution at Cap Frehal, Cote-du-Nord, France, Gehu-Franck showed that the species required a higher nutrient level than is usual in podzolised soils, and that it is only able to establish itself on such sites if the soil profile has been modified by disturbance or where, as along trackways, the soil receives regular dunging.[9] A survey of the distribution of the species in the New Forest[10] affirmed the relationship with disturbance features but showed also that there are extensive areas of gorse on heather moor on visually well developed podzols, suggesting that the mineral nutrient status of much of the heather lands of the Forest may be relatively high; a point which can, however, only be confirmed by chemical analyses.

Despite their impoverished soils, there would seem to be no reason why the heather lands of the Forest should not ultimately revert to woodland, given a prolonged relaxation of grazing and burning, and provided adequate seed sources are available. There is abundant evidence for the colonisation of heathland podzols by trees. Such colonisation is visibly apparent today on sites where holly, oak and rowan are still in the comparatively early stages of establishment (see chapter eight) and much earlier reversion of heathland to woodland in the Forest has been demonstrated by the use of soil-pollen analysis—for example by Dimbleby and Gill, who demonstrated the development of oakwood from heathland on two of six woods they investigated by this method.[11] As on the acid grasslands, it is possible that gorse is a precursor to woodland establishment. Certainly gorse is today closely associated with many groves of holly which have arisen in the past century and which have yet to close their canopy, and some further confirmation is available in the shape of frequent birch regeneration among gorse brakes which have remained unburnt for a long period. A more successful colonist of the heathlands today is likely to be scots pine. Woods of self-sown scots pine now occupy approximately 1,700 acres of former heather moor and in the absence of burning the species would undoubtedly very rapidly become widespread.

Fire is undoubtedly the major factor today in perpetuating the heather dominated communities. The heaths are burnt by the Forestry Commission on a rotation, which may vary from six to twelve years from site to site, depending on the varying needs of reducing the hazard to extensive accidental fires by breaking up large tracts of old, fire-prone heather; of providing young growth for stock; and of fulfilling the statutory duty of the Commission to keep the grazings clear of scrub. The burning is planned on a fragmentary basis, on lines not dissimilar to those adopted on a grouse moor, in order to achieve the maximum variation in age classes of the vegetation, which in turn facilitates fire control and ensures that the least damage occurs to the wildlife and amenities.

Burning is carried out almost entirely in March. By early April, a thin cover of purple moor grass will have became established, the burnt sites often forming conspicuous light green patches against the darker heather. By mid-April heather shows signs of regenerating from rootstock and dwarf gorse and bristle bent appear by early May. The heather very often appears to make little headway for a year or two and bristle bent and purple moor grass may achieve dominance for that period or even longer, though it is more likely that the soil surface will largely remain devoid of vegetation. In some instances the grasses do not persist after the first season and the site is left to gradual recolonisation by the heather. One of the main reasons put forward for the burning is that it is followed by fresh young growth which provides feed for the stock depastured on the Forest. It is debatable, however, whether burning in the Forest significantly benefits the commoners' animals. Its main ecological consequence is to maintain the heathlands in what can only be described as a fire-climax. The further development of the heathland is a matter for speculation.

VI

It is perhaps useful to conclude this chapter with some very brief assessment of the merits of the different vegetation types from the standpoint of the grazier. On the face of it the lawns and re-seeded areas are likely to provide the most valuable grazings. The sward, however, is never allowed to make much growth and is grazed hard as soon as the spring bite appears. It is doubtful whether any single animal could graze off more than a few pounds during the course of a day. Thus, although these areas must fulfil an important role in providing mineral nutrients essential to growth, which are largely lacking elsewhere, they are clearly only one of a number of food sources, each of which plays a role which is complementary to the others.

Observation of the behaviour of Forest ponies strongly suggests that the bulk of their food is purple moor grass and that this is grazed (mainly at night) in the valley bottoms and on the acid grasslands. On the latter areas, purple moor grass is grazed preferentially throughout the summer and only after October or early November is attention paid to the less palatable bristle bent. Food sources, the importance of which should not be underestimated, are gorse and holly. Both are eaten in large quantities by the ponies and in winter many groups of animals virtually live among—and off—the gorse brakes and holly holms. The nutritive value of gorse has long been recognised. During the eighteenth and nineteenth centuries, and probably before, it was cultivated as a fodder crop in England and quite sophisticated machinery was developed for crushing it before feeding to stock.[12] The practice seems to have found its way into England from France and, indeed, it has been suggested that gorse was in fact introduced into England as a fodder crop. G. E. B. Eyre refers to cottagers collecting the tender gorse tops for winter feed for stock on the holdings in the Forest in the late nineteenth century.[13] Young holly growth is often severely suppressed as a result of browsing and mature trees characteristically exhibit a 'browse line' at the maximum height the animals are able to reach, below which successful lateral growth has been precluded.

The unenclosed hardwoods of the Forest offer a further range of food sources apart from their holly understory. Bilberry (*Vaccinium myrtillus*), which occurs throughout the woodlands, is characteristically browsed down to a level mat across the woodland floor. Ivy is also subject to intensive browsing, not to mention sapling trees of practically any hardwood species.

From even a superficial assessment it is apparent that the Forest offers a wide variety of food sources, the extensive use of some of which may balance the intensive use of others. A clear implication for management of the open Forest is that whilst it is important to retain the natural lawns and useful to extend the re-seeded areas, it is equally important to conserve the remaining natural vegetation types and to resist any temptation, for example, to 'improve' the valley bogs (the main source of pony feed, by bulk) by drainage. The range of food sources available is also clearly greater than in most other areas where commonable stock are depastured in numbers throughout the year (for example, the West Country moorlands). An abundance of shelter and water, and a generally mild climate—the last rendering the herbage available to the animals for the greater part of the winter—are further factors which render the area, in the words of G. E. B. Eyre, 'a type of what commonable pasture land should be.'

References

1 D. R. Browning, 'The New Forest Pastoral Development Scheme', *Agriculture*, LVIII, 1951.
2 E. L. Jones and C. R. Tubbs, 'Vegetation of sites of previous cultivation', *Nature*, 198, 1963.
3 S. C. Seagrief, 'Pollen diagrams from Southern England: Cranes Moor, Hampshire', *New Phytol*, 59, 1960.
4 *Fifth Report of Commissioners to Enquire into the Woods, Forests and Land Revenues of the Crown*, 1789.
5 P. J. Newbould, 'The ecology of Cranesmoor, a New Forest valley bog. I. The Present vegetation', *J Ecol*, 48, 1960.
6 N. W. Moore, 'The heaths of Dorset and their Conservation', *J Ecol*, 50, 1962.
7 A. T. Lucas, *Furze: A Survey of its Uses in Ireland*, National Museum of Ireland, 1960.
8 I. M. Killip, 'The use of gorse in the Isle of Man', *J Manx Museum*, VI, 1962–3.
9 J. Gehu-Franck, 'Donees nouvelles sur l'ecologie d'Ulex europaeus L. Relations avec substratum dans une land semi-naturelle', *Bull Soc Bot Nord France*, XIV, 1961.
10 C. R. Tubbs and E. L. Jones, 'The distribution of gorse (Ulex europaeus L.) in the New Forest in relation to former land use', *Proc Hampshire Field Club*, XXIII, 1964.
11 G. W. Dimbleby and J. M. Gill, 'The occurrence of podzols under deciduous woodland in the New Forest', *Forestry*, 28, 1955, 95-106.
12 see, eg Thomas Page, 'The culture of furz', *Annals of Agriculture*, IX, 1788;
J. Anderson, 'of furze . . . as a food for horses and cattle', *Letters and Papers of the Bath & West Society*, V, 1790.
Accounts of gorse crushing machines may be found in the *Journal of the Royal Agricultural Society of England*, 1st series, XII, 1851, pp 635-36; XIII, 1852, p 327; 2nd Series, XV, 1879, pp 694-96; and 3rd series, IX, 1898, p 37.
13 G. E. B. Eyre, *The New Forest, its common rights and cottage stock-keepers*, Lyndhurst, 1883.

ELEVEN

The Larger Vertebrates — Losses and Gains

T O attempt to chart in detail the faunistic changes which have
taken place in so relatively small an area as the New Forest
is to tread on dangerous ground. The record of faunistic
change relating specifically to the Forest district before the nineteenth century is at best fragmentary, and in consequence it is
possible to do little more than infer the directions of change from
the broad trends discernible on a wider scale. The quickening
interest in natural history during the nineteenth and twentieth
centuries is reflected in an increasing volume of publications relating
to or containing references to the bird and mammal life of the
Forest: sufficient to enable one to chart the more recent losses and
gains in the avian and mammalian fauna of the area but, with
some exceptions, inadequate for tracing changes in terms of
numerical status.

In view of the paucity of past records for other classes of our
fauna, the present, tentative attempt to trace the trends of faunistic
change is necessarily confined largely to birds and mammals. The
main intention will be to draw attention to the major causes of
change—or at least, the causes most readily discernible—and to
illustrate their operation with specific examples for which there is
sufficient direct or inferential evidence.

I

In the process of modifying his vegetative environment, man has
inevitably greatly modified its fauna. Sometimes such modification
has been a deliberate act on his part—the extermination of certain
predators for example—whilst it has sometimes been incidental to
the advent of particular land uses—the crossbill for instance could
hardly have bred in England before the introduction of conifers

in the eighteenth century. Despite additions to our fauna arising from the creation of new habitats, man's impact on his environment, in Britain at least, has by and large been accompanied by progressive faunistic depletion. As Macaulay clearly appreciated when he wrote the following passage,[1] this depletion has been considerably accelerated in recent centuries.

(State of England in 1685.)

At Enfield, hardly out of sight of the capital, was a region of five and twenty miles in circumference, which maintained only three houses and scarcely any enclosed fields. Deer . . . wandered there by thousands. It is to be remarked that wild animals of large size were then far more numerous than at present. The last wild boars, indeed, which had been preserved for the royal diversion, and had been allowed to ravage the cultivated land with their tusks, had been slaughtered by the exasperated rustics during the licence of the civil war. The last wolf that has roamed our island had been slain in Scotland a short time before the close of the reign of Charles the Second. But many breeds, now extinct, or rare, both of quadrupeds and birds were still common . . . there were not seldom great massacres of foxes to which the peasantry thronged. . . . The red deer were then as common in Gloucestershire and Hampshire, as they are now among the Grampian hills. . . . The wild bull with his white mane was still to be found wandering in a few of the southern forests. . . . The yellow-breasted martin was still pursued in Cranborne Chase. . . . On all the downs, from the British Channel to Yorkshire, huge bustards strayed in troops of fifty or sixty. . . . Some of these races the progress of cultivation has extirpated. Of others the numbers are so much diminished that men crowd to gaze at a specimen as at a Bengal tiger, or a Polar bear . . . it seems highly probable that a fourth part of England has been, in the course of little more than a century, turned from a wild into a garden.

The processes of faunistic depletion in this country may perhaps be enumerated as follows:

1. The extension of cultivation (and more recently of urban and industrial development), whilst on the one hand producing many new habitats, has involved the destruction of others, the fauna of which has largely been unable to adapt itself to change. This has been accompanied by the deliberate destruction of agricultural pests, whilst the progressive intensification of farming methods (for example the recent use of pesticides) has involved further faunistic depletion.

2. The domestication of wild animals, commencing during

Neolithic times, has been accompanied by the gradual extermination of the wild ancestors. Describing these processes, Zeuner commented that, 'the domesticated stock was becoming standardised, and so different from the wild ancestral species that interbreeding with the wild must have been highly undesirable, for interbreeding would have spoiled the qualities which had been obtained laboriously through selection. For this reason the wild species is likely to have become regarded as an enemy and this . . . stage therefore spells the doom of the wild ancestor.'[2] The wild ancestors of some domestic breeds—for example the tarpan (*Equus caballus*), the wild horse of south-west Europe—survived into medieval and later times and there is written evidence for the destruction of relict populations or their absorption into local domestic breeds.

3. As the human population has increased, so man's demands on wild animal populations for food and hunting and other purposes has increased. In Britain a signpost in faunistic depletion was undoubtedly the development of firearms in the nineteenth century. Until then, to quote A. C. Smith:

> when the sportsman's only weapon was a flint lock gun, and breach loaders and percussion caps had not yet been invented; and when to 'shoot flying' was an art mastered by a select few; our wild birds enjoyed such security and freedom from disturbance as one can hardly realise.[3]

4. With the advent of deliberate preservation of game there arose what can only be described as a 'vermin complex'. Game rearing and preservation in the modern sense in this country was an eighteenth and nineteenth century innovation, but the keepered estate has its origins deeper in history than this. Its beginnings may be seen in the gradually restricted franchise of the chase in Anglo-Saxon times, evolving in medieval England into the designation of forests, the hunting grounds of the Sovereign, and parks, chases and warrens, the hunting grounds of the subjects. The purpose within these game reserves was the preservation mainly of deer and wild pig (*Sus scrofa*) for hunting and for food. Predators of these animals were thus zealously persecuted. There are many records for example, of attempts to exterminate wolves (*Canis lupus*) in Royal Forests in the twelfth and thirteenth centuries and even later. Turbervile[4] makes it clear that by the thirteenth century species such as the fox (*Vulpes vulpes*), wild cat (*Felis silvestris*) and marten (*Martes martes*) were regarded as vermin, to be destroyed wherever

and whenever possible. In the keepered estate of the nineteenth century any predatory animal or bird (and a good many others which bore a superficial resemblance to predators) were the automatic subjects of persecution without trial. The 'vermin complex' had clearly got out of hand. It persists today, despite enlightened thought and legislation.

5. Finally, the collecting mania—the 'glass case complex'—of the nineteenth century played a not inconsiderable part in the depletion of the British fauna. The nineteenth century collector, hiding behind a righteous interest in the pursuit of knowledge, shed crocodile tears as he aimed his gun. Many of the losses sustained by collectors have now been either partly or wholly made good, but modern counterparts of the nineteenth-century collector of bird skins and eggs still operate on a scale that is not always suggestive of a dying outlook.

All these processes are to a lesser or greater extent discernible for the New Forest, but for the purpose of the present argument, the first may justifiably be ignored: the pragmatic considerations which have ensured the retention of such a large tract of unsown vegetation, whilst similar areas elsewhere in Lowland Britain have disappeared before the advance of cultivation and development have been described earlier. Faunistic depletion attributable to the remaining processes, and also to unknown and probably 'natural' causes have been accompanied by faunistic accretion through deliberate introductions and the diversification of parts of the habitat by silviculture during the past two hundred years or so, and it is thus intended in this chapter to survey both the losses and gains.

II

Looking back more than a thousand years, the fauna of a largely uncultivated tract of land such as the New Forest might reasonably be expected to have included a number of predatory mammals in addition to those present today—bears (*Ursus arctos*), wolves, wildcats and martens—besides wild cattle (*Bos taurus*) and pig. The number of species of predatory birds would almost certainly have been greater than it is today.

The larger predatory mammals were clearly undesirable, to say the least, even in a thinly inhabited countryside. The bear had probably been exterminated in England by the tenth century;[5] the wolf suffered a longer history of persecution, and did not finally become extinct in England until the sixteenth century—its last strongholds were probably the Royal Forests of the Peak, Bowland and the Wolds of Yorkshire.[6] The smaller predators, wildcat and marten, probably disappeared from this part of the country not long afterwards.

At what date aurochsen, wild cattle, became extinct in southern England is not clear. Certainly they were not 'to be found wandering in a few of the southern Forests' as late as 1685, as Macaulay says—the last aurochs died in a Polish park in 1627. The early history of the horse in Britain, and of the development of the modern breeds of pony is even more obscure. Indeed, it seems uncertain whether a wild horse was indigenous to this country when domestic breeds were introduced from the Continent in prehistoric —probably Bronze Age—times. Documentary references to 'wild' horses are likely to relate to animals bearing the characteristics of domestication—the long mane and tail for example—which had reverted to a wild state. The *Charta de Foresta*, purporting to date from 1016, but known to be a Norman forgery, mentions both wild horses and cattle as being within Forests, but neither this nor other medieval sources make it quite clear whether wild, ownerless animals or merely free-ranging domestic stock, was referred to. There are some indications, however, that the former was sometimes the case.

In medieval times, a succession of statutes were enacted for the improvement of the stature of horses running on unenclosed lands and the wording of these statutes suggests the presence of wild animals. The Statute for the Drift of the Forest, 1224[7] for example, provides that on such drifts, or round-ups, poor specimens were to be put down; there is no reference to an owner merely being obliged to remove them from the common wastes. As late as 1791 Gilpin wrote: 'A diminutive breed of horses run wild in the New Forest. In general, however, the horse is private property; tho sometimes with difficulty ascertained'.[8] Some subsequent writers—notably Brayley and Britton in 1818[9] and Robert Mudie in 1838[10]—seem to have taken this as a quite definite statement as to the existence of wild, ownerless ponies in the New Forest: no reference is made to Gilpin's observation, but the relevant passages are quite clearly plagiarised from his writing.

There is a little more information in respect of wild pig in the New Forest. Pig appear to have been common in most suitable extensive uncultivated areas of England until the fourteenth century; they survived in Lancashire, Durham, Staffordshire, Windsor Forest, Cranborne Chase (a few miles from the New Forest) and the New Forest and elsewhere, in the sixteenth century. In the New Forest they had probably become extinct by the early decades of the seventeenth century, during which there was at least one re-introduction. Aubrey, writing in 1689, says that Charles I imported wild pig from France into the New Forest and that they increased considerably and become a danger to travellers; and that 'in the civill warres . . . they were destroyed.' Gilpin and others say that Charles II introduced pig from Germany and that they 'propagated greatly in the New Forest'; they were certainly extinct, however, by Gilpin's time. Another introduction was made during the nineteenth century, although I have been unable to trace any details. The last survivor—perhaps the last wild pig loose in Britain— was shot by the Head Keeper around 1905, apparently because it had become an unmitigated nuisance. A foot, made to contain an inkwell and inscribed by the Deputy Surveyor of the day, the Hon Gerald Lascelles, survives to this day.

Such faunistic losses as these were of a general nature in Britain. It might perhaps be expected that the preservation of deer and other game would have resulted in considerably greater faunistic depletion in the New Forest, but on the contrary the status of the area as a Royal Forest clearly extended an umbrella of protection over all but those species considered the most noxious until the collecting era of the nineteenth century, when a war of extermination was waged against many species of birds—and especially the predators. Before then, uncontrolled destruction of predatory animals and birds, such as is so often reflected in churchwardens' accounts in the seventeenth and eighteenth centuries, was precluded on the Crown lands. The keepers, it is true, were supposed to carry out vermin control, but predators of deer were few, the keepers—as has been shown in earlier chapters—were pre-occupied by occupations other than simply keepering, and such vermin control as was carried out seems to have been of a fairly nominal nature. Keepers' manuscript diaries and notebooks of the nineteenth century[11] suggest that in an age of keepered estates it must have formed a 'reservoir' for animals such as badgers (*Meles meles*), and foxes, and birds such as buzzards (*Buteo buteo*) and sparrowhawks (*Accipiter nisus*), despite the depredations of the collector.

III

The collection of birds' eggs and skins was always illegal in the Royal Forest except with specific authority to do so. In medieval times predatory birds were specially protected for hawking purposes. The nineteenth century collector, one of whose main targets was predatory birds, far from being persecuted was actively assisted by the Forest keepers in return, of course, for monetary reward— one of the keepers' perquisites of the day.

By the middle of the nineteenth century ornithology and egg and skin collecting were more or less synonymous. What had begun as the formation of collections in order to extend knowledge had largely been transformed into collecting for collecting's sake, kleptomania in the guise of scientific purpose. The attitude of the mid-century period emerges in the following comments by Wise.

> I am afraid it is too late to protest against the slaughter of our few remaining birds of prey. The eagle and the kite are, to all purpose, extinct, in England, and the peregrine and honey buzzard will soon share their fate. The sight of a large bird now calls out all the raffish guns of a country-side. Ornithologists have, however, themselves to thank. With some honourable exceptions, I know of no one so greedy as a true ornithologist. . . . This, I suppose, must be, from the nature of the study, the case.[12]

Wise, it might be added, seems to have been somewhat less of a kleptomaniac than most, although he and his associates, Farren, Hart, Rake and others, all made their contributions to the destruction of the predators and rarer birds of the New Forest.

The 1850s, 1860s and 1870s saw the maximum persecution of the birds of prey in the Forest by collectors and collector-inspired keepers. By this time a combination of gamekeeping and collecting had severely reduced the populations of predatory birds over much of Britain. Wise unwittingly contributed to their persecution in the New Forest when in 1863 he wrote of the survival there of breeding populations of honey buzzards (*Pernis apivorus*), Montagu's harriers (*Circus pygargus*), common buzzards, hobbys (*Falco subbuteo*) and other species. Thereafter the war of extermination gathered momentum. By the closing decade of the century the honey buzzard had been reduced to at most the odd pair or two in an area which had formerly been the main stronghold of the species in Britain. Montagu's harriers continued to, 'appear annually, and attempt, with more or less success, to rear their young' where once they were fairly numerous.[13] Common buzzards were scarce and rarely allowed to breed successfully. Hobbys were 'becoming scarce'[12] as early as the 1860s, and the last kite's (*Milvus milvus*) eggs had been taken in 1850.[13] In 1880 Lascelles described the raven (*Corvus corax*), which had once been not uncommon, as having disappeared well before that date.[13] These are examples. Time and protection—and more specifically the absence of gamekeeping—have in most cases allowed the losses of the nineteenth century to make good. Some, however—the kite and raven for example—have never reappeared.

The collecting mania of the nineteenth century went altogther too far in depleting the Forest of its birds, and it would probably have gone further had the Hon Gerald Lascelles not been appointed Deputy Surveyor in 1880. On his appointment Lascelles found that the keepers were all hand in glove with a collector or taxidermist. No bird whose skin was likely to make money was allowed any peace. 'Everything in the shape of a bird of prey was, of course, looked on as vermin, killed, and if possible, sold. Had it not been for this laxity, the honey buzzard might have continued to be a far more regular breeder in the Forest than I have found it to be' he wrote.[11] He goes on to describe how kingfishers (*Alcedo atthis*) were shot and found a good market in a bird stuffer's shop in Southampton. To Lascelles the situation was abhorrent, and he seems to have lost no time in re-organising his keeping staff and checking the depredations of the collector. Kelsall and Munn quote Meade-Walpo's description of Lascelles' attempts to protect the honey buzzard, which was one of the principal targets of the collector, thus:

> The principle war of extermination was between the years 1860 and 1870. But in the year 1880 . . . a different state of affairs commenced, and all that could be done was done to preserve the honey buzzard, and the remainder of the interesting inhabitants of the forest; for this particular bird it seems to have been too late. . . .[14]

Lascelles remained Deputy Surveyor until 1915 and pursued his policy of wildlife conservation until he retired. Not only does this seem to have had immediate effects, but it ingrained a tradition of conservation among the Forest keepers which has remained strong to this day, particularly so because appointments as Forest keepers have generally been retained within a relatively small number of families.

Some species which have been lost to the New Forest, or have declined in numbers in the last century or more, for which there are written records, reflect national trends which are not man induced so far as the evidence shows. The disappearance of the wryneck (*Jynx torquilla*) is an example. In the early years of this century it was quite common in the New Forest and was known as the 'rinding bird' because it arrived at the beginning of April when the bark-strippers were at work.[13] There are records which suggest that it was still breeding regularly in the area in the 1920s and 1930s,[15] but today it is recorded only very occasionally. This is the picture from most of the species' former breeding range in Britain, but the reasons for its disappearance are obscure.

The red-backed shrike (*Lanius collurio*) is clearly following the same path. In the past fifty years the breeding range of the species in England has retracted to the south and east and its population has been decimated. In the New Forest, which has long held the largest remaining 'pocket' of breeding shrikes, the population was halved between 1961 and 1966.[16]

Another lost species is the black grouse (*Lyrurus tetrix*). The history of the species in the New Forest and elsewhere in Hampshire, and in the neighbouring counties of Dorset and Surrey during the past two hundred years, is comparatively well documented. When Gilpin was alive it was widespread on the Lowland Heaths, although even then it was clearly on the decline. In 1791 Gilpin wrote about black game in the New Forest thus:

> It scorns the enclosure and all the dainties of the stubble. The wild forest is his only delight, and there his pleasures lie more in its open than its woody scenes. The bird was formerly found in great abundance in New Forest; but he is now much scarcer, though he has the honour which no other bird can boast, of being protected as royal game. To this day, when the chief justice in eyre grants his warrants to kill game in the Forest, he always exempts the black cock, together with red and fallow deer.[8]

Five years later, the decline of black game in the New Forest was the subject of special legislation which provided for a close season in the Forest from 10 December to 20 August. In 1803, further legislation was enacted, 'for the Better Preservation of Heath Fowl, Commonly called Black Game, in the New Forest,' which extended the close season from 10 December to 1 September, 'because the taking and killing of them as early as the 20th day of August has been found prejudicial to the increase of such fowl.' There are further indications, in keepers' MS diaries and from other sources, that black game continued to decrease steadily in the New Forest throughout the nineteenth century. By the middle of the century the species seems to have ceased to receive the protection against shooting referred to by Gilpin. Black game were also shot by the keepers for the disposal of the Lord Warden, until this post fell in abeyance after the 1851 Deer Removal Act. The indications of keepers' MS diaries are that the numbers shot by the keepers was generally small, eg a total of forty-one for the 1845–6 season, but a considerably greater number seem to have been shot by the sporting licensees. Lascelles gives a total of thirty-three black game shot by two licensees, the brothers Wingrove, between 1876 and 1879 inclusive. At that time there were between forty and fifty licensees shooting the Forest, so the total number of black game killed was probably considerable, and must have hastened the decrease of the species, perhaps significantly so. It still appears to have been present in fairly large numbers in the 1850s and early 1860s, however, for Wise refers to the bird in a way which suggests this. As late as 1880 it must still have been fairly common on Wigley Common, adjacent to the Forest, because it is recorded that the Lord of the Manor was attempting to enclose the common, 'on account of its being the resort of black game'.[17] By 1905, it had, 'not quite died out' in the New Forest[13] although the birds which remained were partly at least of stock introduced by Lascelles. He wrote of them as follows:

> Black game, alas! have now nearly died out in the New Forest, where once they were so plentiful. . . . When first I went there I realised, from what I was able to learn, that their numbers were diminishing rapidly. My first step was to put a stop to shooting them altogether. . . . I also subsequently did all I could to introduce fresh blood. . . .

He goes on to describe three attempts to increase the stock by introductions, none of which seem to have had more than a temporary effect. The effect of the introductions he describes as transitory.

> We had . . . a few additional broods, and then the decrease set in again,

he continues:

> so that, for the last few years, the days when one encounters a black cock or grey hen are few. . . . And I can recollect myself counting 23 blackcocks on a 'curling ground' near Ridley Wood. In those days one never rode about the Forest, especially on its northern side, without encountering at least half a dozen black game.[11]

Black game seem to have become extinct by the 1920s. In the 1930s a further introduction was made, although the details of this attempt seem to be obscure. A letter found inserted in the MS notebook of B. J. Ringrose suggests that the introduction may have been effected in the south-east area of the Forest, whilst local stories are told of black game surviving in the extreme north of the Forest until well after the 1939–45 war. At all events the species has now been extinct in the Forest for a number of years.

Other heathland areas which once held populations of black game, have a similar story to tell—progressively decreasing numbers throughout the latter half of the eighteenth and during the nineteenth and (if they were not extinct already) twentieth centuries, bolstered up from time to time by the introduction of fresh blood. In Wolmer Forest, for example, the species became extinct and was re-introduced at least twice, the first time being as early as Gilbert White's time. They had gone from this and the other heaths of north Hampshire by the 1890s[13]; from Surrey by around 1910–15[18]; and there were only a very few left in Dorset by 1888.[19] Indeed, to judge from the fact that the intrepid Colonel Hawker says that eleven brace was considered 'extraordinary success' for a day's shooting in Dorset in 1859, they had been at a low ebb there for some decades.[20]

The decrease of black game has taken place over a good deal of the country. In the lowland zone they are now extinct (unless there has been a very recent reintroduction somewhere) and in many upland areas—for example Exmoor, Dartmoor and Bodmin Moor—they have similarly disappeared or become significantly reduced in numbers. Various reasons have been suggested. In Lowland

Britain the reduction of suitable habitat by the extension of cultivation during and since the eighteenth century has no doubt played a major role in restricting the species' distribution. In Hampshire, for example, Kelsall records that it became extinct on the enclosure and allotment of Titchfield Common.[21] This would not, however, account for the disappearance of the species from such an extensive surviving tract of habitat as that in the New Forest or for its decline on the West Country moorlands, and clearly other unknown factors are involved.

IV

In the New Forest faunistic depletion in the last two or three hundred years has probably been 'balanced', in terms of numbers of species, by additions resulting from habitat diversification, from deliberate introduction and from 'natural' causes.

The planting of extensive silvicultural inclosures in the Forest since the eighteenth century must clearly have added considerably to its fauna by providing a whole new range of habitats—deciduous and coniferous—associated with commercial woodland—young plantation, thicket, pole crop, and mature stands. In a completely even aged commercial timber crop each of these habitats will have only an ephemeral existence, but in the Forest the varied overall structure of the woodland resulting from the felling and replanting of comparatively small areas at different times, ensures that overall there are always considerable areas of each habitat available.

Few of the faunistic changes associated with the establishment and subsequent management of the silvicultural inclosures have been documented, though it would be fair to conclude, for example, that birds such as crossbill (*Loxia curvirostra*) and siskin (*Carduelis spinus*) have bred in the Forest only since the establishment of conifer plantations, and that the breeding populations of many other open woodland or woodland edge birds have increased with the wider availability of young plantation and thicket stage crops as the first rotation timber has been felled.

Perhaps two species may be considered in a little detail. There are many references to influxes of crossbills into Hampshire, and particularly into the New Forest, during the first half of the nineteenth century, but it is significant that the earliest records of breeding are for the earliest period at which there were fairly substantial areas of mature scots pine in the Forest—the 1850s and 1860s. Wise in 1863, records that the bird was, 'not uncommon' and that 'a few pair' were sometimes present in the Forest during the summer. However, he gives only one positive breeding record, for 1858[12] and it does not seem to have been until early in the present century that the crossbill started to breed regularly in the Forest. Today the breeding population is substantial, although it varies in size a good deal from year to year and whether the species is able to maintain its numbers without augmentation from the periodic 'invasions' seems uncertain.

The plantations, in their younger stages, provide good roe deer country, and silvicultural management has thus encouraged the species here, as elsewhere in England. Roe appear to have become extinct over most of Britain during medieval times. From the scarcity of presentments to the Forest courts in which roe deer are mentioned, Turner[22] considered it rare during the thirteenth century and although it persisted in many areas during the fifteenth century—Cox, for example, gives an instance of Edward II in 1322 paying the large sum of £5 for cord to make nets to catch roe deer in Pickering Forest[6]—it seems to have been extinct in England by at latest the seventeenth century. The present stock are derived from nineteenth and twentieth century introductions from the continent. In the New Forest the first definite record is for 1870, in which year Lascelles records that an old buck was shot by one of the keepers.[23] By the 1880s and 1890s odd roe, usually old bucks worsted in fighting, were turning up fairly frequently, and at the turn of the century a small breeding stock seems to have become established, the origin of the beasts reputedly being Dorset. Their numbers during the present century seem to some extent to have fluctuated with the available area of thicket-age plantation (the most favoured habitat) and the species undoubtedly benefited by the replantings which followed the war-time fellings of 1939–45. Today roe are widespread throughout the Forest and the total population may be in excess of 300 head.

Deliberate introduction has added sika deer (*Sika nippon*), grey squirrel (*Sciurus carolinensis*), little owl (*Athene noctua*), red-legged partridge (*Alectoris ruta*), Lady Amhurst's pheasant, and the European tree frog (*Hyla arborea*), to the Forest fauna, whilst it is of passing interest to note that the Hon Gerald Lascelles attempted to introduce capercaillie (*Tetrao urogallus*) in 1886.

Japanese sika deer were introduced by Lord Montagu on to his estate at Beaulieu in the early years of the present century and from there they subsequently spread into the Forest itself. They have, however, remained confined to an area south of the main London–Dorchester railway line, and have seldom been seen north of it. The present stock is believed to be between forty and fifty, at which level the population appears to have remained more or less constant for a number of years.

The spread of the grey squirrel in Britain, and the corresponding disappearance of the indigenous red squirrel (*Sciurus vulgaris*) is well known. The New Forest seems to have been colonised by the grey squirrel during the 1930s; the last red squirrels disappeared around 1947. The hardwoods and mixed hardwood-conifers of the New Forest inclosures are ideal grey squirrel habitat and the area carries a high population which requires constant control by trapping and shooting.

The spread of the little owl in Britain, following the successful introductions in Northamptonshire in the 1880s and in Kent in the 1870s, has been traced by the late H. F. Witherby,[24] whose map indicating the rate of spread suggests that the species reached the New Forest area at sometime between 1909 and 1918. There is some evidence, however, that the species was breeding in the Forest at an earlier date than this. Wise, as early as 1863, gives some highly unsatisfactory evidence of breeding,[2] but in the late 1870s an introduction into the Forest was made by E. G. B. Meade-Waldo, who had also been responsible for the Kent introduction,[13] and there is some evidence for breeding in the Forest in the 1880s and 1890s. Its distribution today in the Forest area is mainly peripheral to the areas of heathland and woodland, and it is really a bird of enclosed, cultivated land.

The red-legged partridge was first introduced to Britain in the eighteenth century. It seems to have become established in the New Forest during the second half of the nineteenth century after introductions into neighbouring estates, and in some respects has perhaps occupied the niche left by black game. Red-legged partridges never seem to have become particularly abundant on the open Forest, however, and so far as I know there has never been any significant attempt to increase the stock.

The period at which Lady Amhurst's pheasant was turned down in the Forest seems to be obscure; probably it was fairly recently.

Although it can be a secretive species and difficult to find, it is probably fairly numerous and there is certainly a substantial population in parts of the central area of woodland.

The final species in the list of introductions is the European tree frog, a single but numerous colony of which has existed for many years in a small pond on one of the southern heaths. The colony is quite well known locally: the animals are extremely noisy in the spring, and the colony is fairly close to the local pub—closing time on a spring evening is a highly convenient time to hear the evening chorus of croaking. Many elderly people assert that the frogs, 'have always been there' or that they remember them fifty or sixty years ago. Occasionally specimens have been caught and attempts made to colonise other ponds, but without success.

The tree frog colony, strangely enough, seems to have been quite unknown among herpetologists until 1961, when the identity of a specimen was confirmed by Miss A. G. C. Grandison. It is probably the only successful colony in Britain. Various attempts to introduce the species elsewhere are known to have failed, whilst at other sites to which it was introduced and apparently thrived for some years, it cannot now be found. It would be of considerable interest to establish precisely what conditions have been conducive to the persistence of the New Forest colony over such a relatively long period of time, and indeed to know something of the history of the introduction here—it is at present quite obscure.

A number of birds have spread to or have increased markedly as breeding species in the New Forest during the nineteenth and twentieth centuries, such changes in status apparently being unrelated to human influence. Redshank (*Tringa totanus*) and curlew (*Numenius arquata*) are examples. The former species seems to have been quite unknown until Wise discovered it breeding in the Forest in the 1850s or early 1860s.[12] During the latter part of the century it seems to have increased considerably and Kelsall and Munn describe it in 1905 as 'one of the most characteristic birds of the Forest,' nesting commonly in 'marshy meadows and boggy places.[13] If this was really so, then there has probably been some reduction in the size of the breeding population since then: unfortunately no attempt had been made until 1961 to assess the total number of breeding pairs, and there are thus no data for proper comparison.

The curlew, too, first appears to have become established as a breeding species in the Forest—and indeed elsewhere on the Lowland Heaths—in the second half of the nineteenth century. It apparently did not breed in Wise's day, but by 1890 'a pair or two occasionally nested on the wildest heaths of the New Forest';[13] by 1932 'a few pairs' were breeding[25]; in 1927, 1928, 1930, 1931, 1932 and 1934 three or four pairs were recorded as breeding in the north of the Forest[26]; at the present time it is widespread as a breeding species throughout the Forest.

V

In the preceding pages an attempt has been made to categorise and illustrate with examples the processes of faunistic change. It would be interesting to draw up a more comprehensive balance sheet of losses and gains, but the data are inadequate. Written records, even for the present century, are too sparse to provide a picture of the status changes of more than a few species of birds and mammals. Probably the most obvious point emerging from a survey of what is known of the faunistic history of the Forest, however, is that the embargo on fundamental changes in land use, extending over a long period of time, together with the umbrella of protection provided by deer preservation (whether actively pursued or not) has checked the widespread faunistic depletion such as that which has occurred over the greater part of the lowland zone of Britain since the eighteenth century. In this context it may be of interest to compare the Forest with the neighbouring Wessex chalklands.

The successive waves of cultivation which have swept over the chalklands of Wessex and elsewhere, the latest of which now laps the highest ever shoreline, together with game preservation and the persecution of 'vermin', have, since the eighteenth century, decimated their fauna. With a number of exceptions—the fox, preserved for hunting; the badger, which has increased again in recent decades as persecution has slackened; and the smaller predators such as the kestrel, sparrowhawk and stoat—the predators have gone, or retain only a shaky foothold. The great bustard (*Otis tarda*) is extinct. Improved agricultural techniques have eliminated the corncrake (*Crex crex*) within the past half century. Woodlarks

(*Lullula arborea*), stonechats (*Saxicola torquata*), whinchats (*Saxicola rubra*), wheatears (*Oeanthe oeanthe*), tree-pipits (*Anthus trivialis*), red-backed shrikes and many other birds have become scarce as the sheep walk and scrub has gone under the plough. The stone curlew (*Burhinus oedicnemus*) is probably the only characteristic bird species of the chalk which appears to have adapted itself more or less successfully to the changed conditions of arable cultivation.

No such drastic changes in land use and fauna have taken place in the New Forest. It is, indeed, virtually the only large area of Lowland Britain where drastic change has not taken place and, moreover, it receives statutory protection against such change in the future. It cannot necessarily be assumed, however, that the Forest will remain an inviolate wildlife reservoir. The possible effects of what may broadly be termed 'human pressures' on the Forest are a concern of the final chapter, but it seems appropriate to conclude the present one with some reference to the form of human activity most likely to influence the Forest's fauna in the foreseeable future—the use of this large area of unenclosed and beautiful countryside for recreation.

The disturbance arising from recreational use—picnicking, camping, caravanning and so on—is likely to become as great or greater an adverse factor in the future faunistic history of the New Forest as was the collecting of the nineteenth century—and with the virtual certainty of indefinite perpetuation. The effects of intensive recreation uses on wildlife populations may be less obvious than those of collecting, or say reclamation, and they are certainly more difficult to chart. They are likely, however, to be crucial unless adequately controlled. The effects of disturbance are today probably manifest in decreasing populations of several species of birds—for example the lapwing and woodlark—although it is difficult to isolate the recreational factor from others in any individual instance. Recreational use may undoubtedly, however, be regarded as potentially the most potent factor in the future history of the Forest's fauna. It is perhaps some measure of the rapidity with which this potency is increasing that when this chapter was first drafted, in 1963, it was concluded that, 'the overall effects on wildlife have so far probably been of no great significance'. Only a sublime optimist would re-affirm such a statement in 1968.

The Larger Vertebrates—Losses and Gains

References

1 Lord Macaulay, *Works*, edn 1898, pp 326-8.
2 F. E. Zeuner, *A History of Domesticated Animals*, London, 1963.
3 Memoir of Mr John Legg of Market Lavington, an advanced Ornithologist of the 18th century, Wilts Arch & Nat Hist Soc *Magazine*, XXVIII, 1894, p 12.
4 *Noble Art of Venerie or Hunting*, London, 1575.
5 J. E. Harting, *British Mammals Extinct within Historic Times*, London, 1880.
6 J. C. Cox, *The Royal Forests of England*, London, 1905.
7 Quoted eg by John Manwood, *Treatise and Discourse of the Laws of the Forest*, (edn 1615).
8 Rev William Gilpin, *Remarks on Forest Scenery*, II, London, 1791.
9 E. W. Brayley and J. Britton, *Hampshire*, London, 1818.
10 Robert Mudie, *Hampshire*, Winchester, 1838.
11 Hon G. W. Lascelles, *Thirty-Five Years in the New Forest*, London, 1915.
12 J. R. Wise, *The New Forest, its History and Scenery*, London, 1863.
13 J. E. Kelsall and P. W. Munn, *The Birds of Hampshire and the Isle of Wight*, London, 1905.
14 Kelsall and Munn, *op cit*, quoting from *Victoria History of Hampshire*.
15 *Proceedings* Hampshire Field Club & Arch Soc, MS Diary of B. J. Ringrose, a local ornithologist of the 1920s and 1930s.
16 C. R. Tubbs, unpublished data.
17 Lord Eversley, *Forests, Commons and Footpaths*, London, 1910.
18 J. A. S. Bucknill, *The Birds of Surrey*, London, 1900.
19 J. C. Mansell-Pleydell, *The Birds of Dorset*, London, 1888.
20 Col Peter Hawker, *Instructions to Young Sportsmen*, London, 1859.
21 J. E. Kelsall, *Proceedings* Hampshire Field Club & Arch Soc, III, 1889.
22 G. J. Turner, *Select Pleas of the Forest*, Selden Society, London, 1901.
23 Hon G. W. Lascelles, *Victoria History of Hampshire*, I, 1908, p 250.
24 in H. F. Witherby *et al*, *The Handbook of British Birds*, II, edn 1949.
25 *Proceedings* Hampshire Field Club & Arch Soc for 1932.
26 MS Diary and Notes of B. J. Ringrose.

TWELVE

Features of the Modern Fauna

THE most readily discernible factors in the depletion of the
fauna and flora of the Lowland zone of Britain since the
beginning of the eighteenth century have been the progressive
reclamation of its tracts of unsown, or semi-natural, vegetation and
the intensification of agricultural use and techniques. It is tempting
to return to part of the quotation from Macaulay with which the
previous chapter began: 'It seems highly probable that a fourth part
of England has been, in the course of little more than a century,
turned from a wild into a garden.' In the century since that was
written demands on the land for agriculture, silviculture and urban
and industrial development have grown apace. The wild has become
yet smaller.

The heathlands* which are so essential a feature of the New
Forest today, were formerly part of a broad belt which extended
across the Hampshire Basin from Southampton Water nearby, as
far west as Dorchester, broken only by the valleys of the Avon,
Stour and Frome. In a valuable study of the heaths of Dorset and
those of Hampshire west of the Avon, Moore[1] showed that they
had been reduced in area from about 75,000 acres in 1811 to about
25,000 acres in 1960, and that this reduction had been accompanied
by fragmentation into more than one hundred separate parcels.
Urban and industrial expansion, radiating from Bournemouth—
itself built on what was formerly Poole Heath—and other towns,
together with extensive conifer afforestation and reclamation for
agriculture, has left few extensive areas west of the New Forest.
Many of the fragments which remain have become subject to greatly
increased human disturbance, and in some cases to extensive scots
pine colonisation arising from the seed sources provided by the

* The term is here used to include the associated acid grassland,
wet heath and valley bog communities.

209

plantations. Many hundreds of acres of heathland have disappeared since Dr Moore's survey.

These changes are fairly typical of those proceeding elsewhere on heathlands in Lowland Britain. Moore estimated that since the early nineteenth century the heaths of Breckland in East Anglia had been reduced in area by upwards of seventy-five per cent and those of North Hampshire and Surrey by between fifty and seventy-five per cent. The trend is continuing, and it seems likely that within another decade only numbers of isolated fragments of heath will remain in the south and west of England outside the New Forest.

The amount of space any individual species requires in order to survive indefinitely in a given part of its range is in most cases uncertain, but it would be fair to say that the smaller the individual area of habitat and thus the smaller the population, the more vulnerable a species becomes. Moore showed that in Dorset, the smaller and more isolated the area of heath, the smaller the number of species it carried. It is likely that many, if not most, of the remaining fragments of heathland in southern and eastern England outside the New Forest are too small to indefinitely support many of their characteristic animals and plants. The situation will be further aggravated as the reduction and fragmentation of the heaths continues. The New Forest is, therefore, ecologically important as the one area in which the most complete spectrum of heathland fauna stands the best chance of survival. To some extent it may also function as a 'reservoir' from which re-colonisation of smaller, less viable sites may periodically take place.

The unenclosed woodlands of the Forest are of not dissimilar significance. Uneven aged deciduous woodland working on a more or less natural rotation is now of very limited distribution in Lowland Britain. There has been widespread conversion of deciduous woodland to conifers in the present century, and in any case the economic management of hardwoods does not allow for the development of a wide range of age-classes and the retention of the mature, senile and decaying timber which is such a feature of the Forest woods and with which is associated their exceptionally rich invertebrate and bird fauna.

Three other factors are of importance in considering the faunistic variety of the Forest. First it is a fact that the widest range of animal species tends to occur at habitat boundaries—the bird population at a woodland edge, for example, is larger and more varied than in the wood itself. At the same time many species require combinations of habitats—the curlew, for example, requires both dry heath (for nesting) and bog (for feeding) on its breeding grounds. Great diversity of habitat over short distances is a characteristic ecological feature of the Forest: woodland, dry heath, acid grassland, gorse brake, wet heath and valley bog, form a complex pattern within small areas. The result is an abundance of habitat boundaries and combinations of habitats in close proximity which contributes significantly to the overall diversity of the Forest's fauna.

Second, the Crown lands have never been used for large scale game rearing and to this negative factor can be attributed the survival of a large and varied population of predatory birds—a feature now rare in Lowland Britain and indeed over much of the countryside around the Forest. The third factor is also a negative one—the area is little affected by the use of toxic insecticides or by stream pollution.

It is proposed in this chapter to elaborate on some of the more important factors which contribute to the faunistic richness of the Forest, using as 'indicators' or examples individual species or groups of species. If the range of examples exhibits an inbalance in favour of birds, it must be pleaded that it is for bird populations that the most detailed information is usually available, although it must be admitted that to some extent choice is a reflection of personal interest. At the same time it can be argued that since birds tend to be at the upper end of the food chain, they can be taken as useful indications of overall faunistic richness.

I

The hypothesis that the New Forest offers the best chance of survival in Lowland Britain to the most complete spectrum of heathland fauna may be examined by taking a number of 'indicator' species and comparing their status there with that on other remaining heathlands in the Lowland zone. Table IV lists twelve indicator species, between them representing a wide variety of animals from a wide range of heathland habitats. Most, if not all twelve, occur or have occurred in the past in other habitats besides heathland, but it would be fair to say that the heaths have always been their main stronghold in the sense that there populations have always been densest. This is certainly the case today.

All twelve species listed in table IV occur widely in the New Forest, whilst elsewhere their populations have been greatly reduced and fragmented in distribution by the destruction or modification of their habitats. Few, if any, of the remaining heaths outside the Forest now support anything approaching the full spectrum of indicator species.[2] The presence of the full spectrum in the Forest is largely a function of the extent of the heathland area. The smaller and more isolated the heathland fragment, the greater the chances of an animal population being destroyed by local factors such as fire and the smaller the chances of recolonisation from beyond its boundaries. At the same time, its small size will set limits on the total possible population and proportionately increase the chances of destruction through more general factors, such as hard winters. Of the twelve species listed, only the Dartford warbler (*Sylvia undata*) would seem at present to hold an insecure footing in the New Forest and in this case the population is directly controlled by the incidence of severe winters.

A good deal is known about the history of the Dartford warbler in England and it is worth dwelling upon it at some length.[3] The species has a southern and western distribution in Europe, and in southern England is resident at the northern edge of its range. As a breeding species it is in this country essentially associated with gorse (*Ulex europaeus*) areas on dry heath. During the nineteenth century its breeding distribution extended from Suffolk and Kent in the east, to Devon and Cornwall in the west. Since the latter part of the nineteenth century, however, there has been a considerable reduction in the amount of habitat available. Apart from the more or less irregular establishment of small colonies in Sussex, Devon and the Isle of Wight, it has been confined since the early 1930s (and possibly earlier) to the heaths of the New Forest, Dorset, north Hampshire and Surrey. The species is subject to periodic population 'crashes' coinciding with particularly severe winters, and in north Hampshire and Surrey, where the area of habitat and total population was comparatively small, the breeding stock appears to have been wiped out two or three times within the past thirty years. It has not re-established itself there since the severe winter of 1962–63.

Except for recent years, there is little information about the

TABLE IV
Heathland Indicator Species

Species	Group	Heathland Habitat	General Distribution in Lowland Zone
Woodlark, *Lullula arborea*	Bird	Dry heath & acid grassland; scrub, woodland fringes, etc.	Heathland, chalk grassland, 'rough land' generally; usually associated with scrub scattered trees, etc.
Red Backed Shrike, *Lanius collurio*	Bird	Scrub (esp. *Ulex*, *ilex*, etc.) on dry heath; valley bog	Heathland scrub, etc.
Dartford Warbler, *Sylvia undata*	Bird	Dry heath with *Ulex europaeus*	Confined to heathland
Stonechat, *Taxicola torquata*	Bird	Dry heath & acid grassland with *U. europaeus*	Heathland & 'rough land' generally. Almost always associated with *U. europaeus*
Curlew, *Numenius arquata*	Bird	Dry heath & valley bog	Virtually confined to heathland
Nightjar, *Caprimulgus europaeus*	Bird	Dry heath & acid grassland; scrub, woodland fringes, etc.	Unreclaimed land generally; young plantations, cleared woodland, etc.
Sand Lizard, *Lacerta agilis*	Reptile	Dry heath	Virtually confined to heathland
Smooth Snake, *Coronella austriaca*	Reptile	Dry heath, wet heath, valley bog, acid grassland	Heathland & bordering agricultural land & woodland
Silver Studded Blue Butterfly *Plebejus argus*	Insect (Lepidoptera)	Dry heath	Confined to dry heath
Grayling, *Eumenis semele*	Insect (Lepidoptera)	Dry heath & acid grassland	Heathland & chalk grassland
Ceriagrion tenellum	Insect (Odonata)	Valley bog, pools, etc.	Acid bogs & pools
Ischnura pumilio	Insect (Odonata)	Valley bogs, pools, etc.	Less acid bogs, pools, etc.

actual size of the Dartford Warbler breeding population, either in total or for any given area within its range in England. Various sources, however, show that the major population crashes since about 1850 took place during the winters of 1860–61, 1880–81, 1886–87, 1916–17, sometime during the late 1930s or early 1940s, 1946–47, 1961–62 and 1962–63. In all but the last instance each crash seems to have been followed by a fairly rapid build-up in the population over a period of years.

The available figures for the breeding population of Dartford Warblers in the New Forest from 1955 to 1967 are set out in table V. As it might be argued that the numbers actually recorded from 1955 to 1961 reflect an increase in the area of habitat examined each year, rather than a true increase in the population, the table also includes a calculation of the probable total population each year, based on the assumption that areas of suitable habitat not searched will have held populations similar to those that were. The resulting figures are probably rather exaggerated, but they clearly support the impression of a steady increase from 1955 to 1961 and demonstrate the drastic fall in the population after the successive severe winters of 1961–62 and 1962–63. During 1964 and 1965 the population was probably building up again, but it appears to have suffered a further setback in 1966, apparently as a result of a 'freak' snowfall overnight on 13 April and throughout the following day. This would seem to have come very near to eliminating the bird from the area.

In 1961, when the New Forest population was at its peak, there were probably rather more than sixty pairs in Dorset, and between forty and forty-five pairs in north Hampshire and Surrey. Elsewhere there were small isolated colonies in Sussex, the Isle of Wight and possibly Devon. Accepting an exaggeration in the theoretical population figure for the Forest in that year, it is probable that the total breeding population in England was around 450 pairs, of which more than 300 were concentrated in the New Forest.

Following the severe weather early in 1962 reports suggested breeding at only one site on the north Hampshire/Surrey heaths. On the heaths of the Poole Harbour area in Dorset, where the weather was less severe than elsewhere, a larger proportion of the population seems to have survived—possibly as many as around fifteen pairs. In addition a small colony survived in Sussex.

TABLE V

Recorded and estimated breeding populations of Dartford warblers
(Sylvia undata) *in the New Forest, 1955–1967*

Not necessarily the same areas were examined in each year, except in 1961 and 1962. The habitat estimates for 1955–57 were made retrospectively and are thus tentative. Theoretical total populations are based on the assumption that suitable areas not examined will have carried similar populations to those examined. Where the estimated percentage of habitat examined is given between limits, the upper figure has been used in the calculation.

Year	Percentage of total habitat examined	Breeding pairs recorded	Theoretical total population
1955	15–20%	20	80
1956	25–35%	56	160
1957	25–35%	67	192
1958		no data	
1959	c 35%	98	280
1960	45–50%	152	304
1961	c 60%	229	382
1962	c 60%	36	60
1963	c 50%	6	12
1964	not calculated: casual records only	8 (inc prs at all 6 1963 localities)	
1965	four of the eight 1964 localities examined only	5	
1966	c 80% (inc all 1963–65 localities)	2+ (2 localities)	
1967	one of two 1966 localities examined only	3+	

After the winter of 1962–63 it was virtually certain that Dartford warblers were absent from north Hampshire and Surrey. On the Dorset heaths (where, again the weather was less severe), four breeding pairs were recorded, but no widespread searches were made for the species. At the Sussex locality birds were seen but it was uncertain whether any bred. Since 1963 the Dorset breeding population has built up steadily and in 1967 was certainly in excess of twenty pairs, whilst the Sussex colony has risen to around six pairs—compared with three in the New Forest. Although the succession of events which brought the Forest population to such a dangerously low ebb is unlikely to be often repeated, it may well be that because of the consistently mild climate of south Dorset, the heaths there may assume a significance disproportionate to their small size as the ultimate stronghold of the Dartford warbler in the country.

The stonechat breeds in a wide variety of habitats, including heathland, chalk downland, and stabilised coastal shingle, but as with the Dartford warbler a feature common to virtually all breeding territories is a cover, if only a scattered cover, of gorse. Like the Dartford warbler the stonechat has suffered a long term decrease in England and, also like the Dartford, is subject to periodic population crashes associated with hard winters. In a useful paper on the distribution of the stonechat in Britain published in 1965, J. D. Magee[4] considered that the decline of the species since the beginning of the century was attributable to the steady reclamation and development of its habitats and the extensive colonisation by birch and pine of much of the remaining heathland areas, whilst shorter term fluctuations were the result of hard winters, which periodically severely reduced the total population and wiped out the smaller 'pockets' of birds.

Table VI gives recorded and estimated breeding populations of the stonechat in the New Forest from 1957 to 1966, from which it will be seen that numbers reached a peak in 1961, following which there was a sharp fall after the successive cold, hard winters of 1961–62 and 1962–63. By 1966, however, they had again built up to something approaching the 1961 figure.

Magee gives recorded breeding numbers of stonechats in Britain by counties, in 1961, which show that the bulk of the population was concentrated in Cornwall, Devon, Dorset, Hampshire, Surrey, Sussex, Glamorgan and Pembrokeshire. Only the number recorded from Pembrokeshire (264 pairs) equalled (or indeed approached) that recorded for the New Forest (262 pairs) in that year. The evidence suggests that the Forest now carries the largest single concentration of stonechats in the country. Outside this area its breeding distribution is largely fragmentary and becomes more so after each hard winter.

Features of the Modern Fauna

TABLE VI

Recorded and estimated breeding populations of stonechats
(Saxicola torquata) in the New Forest, 1957–1966

The figures for 1957, 1958, 1959 and 1964 are from *The Hampshire Bird Report*; those for the remaining years are derived from surveys carried out by the writer and others. Theoretical total populations were calculated on the basis that suitable areas not examined will have carried populations similar to those that were. Allowing for the tendency to examine the more promising areas, the totals in this column are probably somewhat exaggerated.

Year	Percentage of total habitat examined	Breeding pairs recorded	Theoretical total population
1957	not known	103	—
1958	not known	130	—
1959	not known	143	—
1960	c 50%	66	132
1961	c 65%	262	430
1962	c 60%	50	83
1963	c 50%	29	58
1964	not known	42	—
1965		no data	
1966	c 50%	162	324

The winters of 1961–62 and 1962–63 probably brought the stonechat population in southern and eastern England to an all-time low. Such evidence as there is suggests, for example, that in Dorset, Hampshire, Sussex and Surrey, it was reduced to less than a quarter of its former size. From many areas, especially in north Hampshire, Surrey and between the New Forest and Poole Harbour, the species disappeared altogether. In the four counties it is doubtful whether a total of more than around 100 pairs bred in 1961 and of these probably more than half were concentrated in the New Forest. The recovery of the population, as table VI shows for the New Forest, has since been fairly rapid, although many of the smaller heaths have yet to be recolonised. A final point, which also emerges from table VI, is that the proportion of the population which survives a hard winter is larger than in the Dartford warbler. The stonechat is known to be a partial migrant—that is a proportion of the population emigrates—and it is likely that many birds avoid severe weather further south.

The woodlark was formerly characteristic of the downland sheep walks and heathlands of southern England. Its national distribution extended over most of Wales and the western peninsula and northwards to Lincolnshire. J. F. Parslow has recently shown,[5] however, that the species has undergone a series of population fluctuations throughout its range in England and Wales during the course of the present century. Since the 1950s it has been steadily decreasing and its range retracting southwards. Loss of habitat has clearly been a contributory factor and mortality during the winters of 1961–62 and 1962–63 hastened the trend. Parslow states that only about 100 occupied territories were known in the whole country in 1965, and although this was clearly a minimal figure it suggests that as a breeding species the woodlark could now justifiably be described as rare. The population in the New Forest, however, although noticeably reduced since 1959 (when it was estimated to be between sixty-five and seventy-five pairs) remains comparatively substantial. Thirty-two pairs were recorded in 1967, whilst sixteen territories known to have been occupied in the previous five years were not examined.

The national decline in the breeding population of the red-backed shrike and the southward retraction of its range in England since the nineteenth century has been attributed mainly to an increasing incidence of warmer, wetter, summers with which has been linked a decline in the numbers of the larger flying insects which form the bulk of the species' food. Loss of habitat has probably been of only secondary importance.

The species was formerly widely, though locally distributed, throughout south and central England as far north as Yorkshire. In 1960 a national census gave a total of only 172 pairs, of which sixty-one were in the New Forest, the only other areas where double figures were reached being Surrey (thirteen pairs), Essex (nineteen pairs), Suffolk (thirty-three pairs) and Norfolk (twelve pairs).[6] A further survey in the New Forest in 1961 gave a minimum of sixty-seven pairs.[7] Since 1960 the species has suffered a further general decline and only in the New Forest, Norfolk and Suffolk would the population appear to be maintaining itself in substantial numbers.

Like the preceding four species, the nightjar (*Caprimulgus europaeus*) has apparently declined widely since the late nineteenth century,[8] though few comparative population figures are available to support such an impression. It has undoubtedly become scarcer in the south and east of England during the past two decades and in most individual instances where its disappearance has been recorded, it has been linked with the destruction of habitat. In the New Forest it remains numerous.

The curlew, on the other hand, has increased markedly as a breeding bird throughout the country and in more northerly counties has spread into agricultural habitats which it would not formerly tolerate.[9] The Lowland heaths seem to have been colonised early in this phase of expansion and its colonisation of the Forest has been mentioned in the previous chapter. Reclamation of the heathland in recent decades, together with the spread of birch and pine, however, has ousted it from many areas and it is now absent from most of the smaller fragments of heath in north Hampshire, Surrey and Sussex. It is indeed doubtful whether any at all have bred in north Hampshire since about 1962. The Forest population stands (1966 and 1967) at around fifty pairs.

Both the smooth snake (*Coronella austriaca*) and sand lizard (*Lacerta agilis*) are now practically confined in Britain to the heathlands of the Hampshire Basin and those of the Thames Basin and Weald on the borders of Hampshire, Surrey and Sussex. In Dorset, Moore[1] found that in the short term the sand lizard was able to survive all but the most drastic habitat changes (such as urbanisation), whilst the smooth snake was not entirely confined to the heathland area. The distribution of both species in the Hampshire Basin, west of the New Forest, now however seems very fragmentary, although both species survive on several sites immediately west of the River Avon and again on the Isle of Purbeck. In the Forest itself both seem to have a mainly western and southern distribution—the heaths immediately east of the Avon and those on the lower lying terraces nearer the coast. With the continued reduction of the heathland area elsewhere it may well be that the Forest offers the best chance of ultimate survival.

Of the two species of butterfly, the silver studded blue (*Plebejus argus*) is almost entirely confined to tracts of heather (*Calluna* and *Erica*), mainly in southern England. It is thus particularly vulnerable, not only to the normal processes of heathland destruction but to fire, which can wipe it out on the smaller sites with little chance of recolonisation. Even in the New Forest, where it has always been regarded as especially abundant, its distribution tends to be somewhat patchy and it is absent from several quite extensive areas. From several of the smaller heathland sites west of the Avon it has now disappeared. The Grayling (*Eumenis semele*), which exhibits greater catholicity of habitat would seem to survive on all but the smallest and most isolated heathland sites.

Of all the dragonflies, *Ischnura pumilio* and *Ceriagrion tenellum* number among those which have suffered most from the drainage and reclamation of their habitats. Both are essentially Mediterranean species with a southerly distribution in this country. The tiny damsel fly, *I. pumilio*, formerly found in a scatter of localities in Cornwall, Dorset and Hampshire, now appears to have disappeared from many of them and may even now be confined to a number of sites in the New Forest. *C. tenellum* remains widespread in the heathland area of Dorset and is common on many New Forest bogs and pools, though elsewhere in the country it seems to be becoming of only local occurrence.

II

Diversity of habitat in the New Forest is reflected in the numbers and abundance of vertebrate species represented. Twenty-seven species of land mammals (excluding the extinct red squirrel), eleven out of thirteen species of native bats; five out of six indigenous amphibia (the natterjack, *Bufo calamita* does not seem to have been recorded in the area) and one introduced species (the European tree frog); and all six native reptiles, are known to be present, whilst ninety-eight species of birds are known to breed regularly. For most groups of invertebrates comparatively little information is available, although many orders of insects (for example Odonata, Orthoptera, Coleoptera and Lepidoptera) are known to be particularly well represented and species lists include a large number of rare or locally distributed insects, some of which are thought to be confined to the New Forest in this country—for example the New Forest cicada (*Cicadetta montana*), rediscovered there in 1962, after having been thought extinct for some twenty years.

Although the total number of land mammals recorded is large, some generally common species are restricted in distribution: a reflection of certain general features of the Forest environment. The absence of earthworms from the more acid soils, for example, is reflected in the limited distribution of moles (*Talpa europaea*) and hedgehogs (*Erinaceus europaeus*). They are present on many of the flushed grasslands in the valleys and among the woods, and locally on the more acid *Agrostis setacea/Molinia* grassland, but elsewhere they are absent. The comparatively poor feed offered by much of the heathland is reflected in the limited number of hares (*Lepus europaeus*) and the rather scattered distribution of rabbits (*Oryctolagus cuniculus*). The comparative scarcity of stoats (*Mustula erminea*) and weasels (*Mustula nivalis*) may in turn perhaps be associated with the comparatively thin rabbit population.

Two major habitats within the Forest, each of which covers a considerable area and supports an especially rich and varied fauna are the unenclosed woodlands and the valley bogs. Numerous small ponds, mostly on the sites of old clay or gravel workings or in bomb craters, add considerably to the variety of freshwater habitats.

An outstanding feature—or perhaps it would be better described as the most easily discernible feature—of the unenclosed woodlands is their large populations of breeding birds, including high density populations of certain species which tend to be somewhat locally distributed in Lowland Britain as a whole; in this category would fall redstart (*Pheonicurus pheonicurus*) and wood warbler (*Philloscopus sibilitrix*). A number of other species which are distinctly local in distribution elsewhere are also consistently present, notably hawfinch (*Coccothraustes coccothraustes*) and lesser spotted woodpecker (*Dendrocopus minor*). The populations of woodland species which require holes or crevices in trees for breeding purposes—for example the woodpeckers, nuthatch (*Sitta europaea*) and treecreeper (*Certhia familiaris*) are particularly large, whilst any area of ten acres or more can be expected to carry a total of thirty or more breeding species.

The size and variety of the bird populations of the unenclosed woodlands arise from three main factors: first, the abundant and varied insect life, which is in turn largely associated with an abundance of mature, senile, decaying and fallen timber; second, the availability of nest sites for species which breed in holes and crevices; and third (remembering the assertion that the woodland edge is a generally more favourable habitat than its interior), the

221

frequency of small clearings and the generally somewhat diffuse and open nature of the woodland.

The unenclosed woods are important as a bat as well as bird habitat and here again the proliferation of holes and crevices for roosting is probably the most significant single feature. Of the eleven species of bat recorded from the New Forest, seven depend to some extent or other on old timber for roosting during at least part of the year. Daubenton's bat (*Myotis daubentoni*), Natterer's bat (*Myotis nattereri*), the whiskered bat (*Myotis mystacinus*), the pipistrelle (*Pipistrellus pipistrellus*), noctule (*Nyctalus noctula*), serotine (*Eptesicus serotinus*) and long eared bat (*Plectous auritus*), all use old timber in summer, although some species—for example the pipistrelle—are equally typical of buildings, and in most there is a marked tendency to hibernate in buildings rather than trees. Natterer's, whiskered, pipistrelle, long eared and noctule may, however, be fairly described as typical woodland bats in the New Forest during the summer and they are clearly associated mainly with the old timber of the unenclosed woodlands. The very rare Bechstein's bat (*Myotis bechsteini*), which was first recorded in Britain from the New Forest, appears to be an exclusively woodland species. This is probably one of the rarest European mammals, being nowhere common anywhere within its range. Little is known about its status in the Forest and the most recent record is probably one found in 1950 by S. C. Bisserot.[10]

The Forest water courses with their associated valley bogs, together with the liberal sprinkling of ponds, mostly of an artificial origin, form an important series of habitats and are, like the old timber of the unenclosed woodlands, outstanding for the wide variety, and more particularly the high density of their insect populations. The variety of insect species recorded is impressive even though little more than casual, irregular and fragmentary recording has been carried out for most orders. Perhaps because they are generally relatively large and conspicuous and the total number of species which occur in Britain is relatively small, information is probably most complete for the dragonflies. Of the forty-three British species, at least twenty-five occur in the New Forest, many of them abundantly. Many species of dragonfly are very susceptible to even slight water pollution and an important feature of the Forest streams and water courses is that by and large they are free of pollution from domestic or industrial effluent.

In the absence of quantitative data the high density of insect popula-tions associated with fresh water habitats in the Forest is difficult to demonstrate, but it is readily apparent in the field in the late spring and summer and is clearly reflected in the breeding distribution of the red-backed shrike, a species which is largely dependent on an abundance of the larger insects—and especially dragonflies and beetles—for food: of the sixty-one pairs recorded in the survey of 1961, thirty-two pairs bred in, or adjacent to, valley bogs or along water courses, the nest often being actually in alder carr. Of the remaining twenty-nine pairs, most bred on valley slopes with a scrub cover at points where shelter tended to form a 'sun trap' and where insect life was prolific to the eye.

The valley bogs are also important during the spring and early summer as feeding grounds, and breeding sites for duck and for the wading birds which breed on the Forest—curlew, lapwing (*Vanellus vanellus*), redshank and snipe (*Capella gallinago*). A survey in 1961 gave a total of sixty breeding pairs of redshank, distributed entirely on valley bogs and associated valley lawns; this excluded two sites which in the following year carried fourteen pairs.

Compared with the woodlands and valley bogs, the dry heaths and acid grasslands are faunistically impoverished. This impoverish-ment is most apparent on the extensive areas of *Calluna* dry heath. Here, for example, the skylark (*Alauda arvensis*), meadow pipit (*Anthus pratensis*) and curlew are practically the only species of breeding birds. The curlew population stands at about fifty pairs, but when this is set against the 18,000 acres of dry heath available, the population density is not high. Most species generally accepted as characteristic of dry heath and acid grassland occur where these habitats are diversified by areas of gorse or alternatively a scatter of trees or light scrub. Here the variety of species increases to include the Dartford warbler, stonechat, whinchat, nightjar, linnet (*Acanthis cannabina*) and yellow-hammer (*Emberiza citrinella*), to mention a few examples. In a general measure the variety of breeding bird species and the density of populations increase with the variety of habitat. To return briefly to the Dartford warbler, the species is not so much characteristic of areas of gorse as of the margins of the gorse where it adjoins *Calluna* heath. Like so many other species it is really a bird of habitat boundaries or habitat 'combinations'. In an equally general measure, the variety of breeding birds and population densities tends to increase with each stage in the succession from dry heath to woodland and is probably greatest at woodland edges. Some species, like the tree pipit are essentially associated with woodland edges, and are particularly numerous in the New Forest.

These generalisations appear also to be broadly true of invertebrate populations, which form one of the major food sources for birds. Almost certainly the main source of food on *Calluna* heath and in the gorse areas is spiders, which would appear to be the only invertebrates which occur in real abundance in *Calluna* and which are also abundant in gorse. Spiders probably form the staple food of species such as the Dartford warbler, stonechat and other insectivorous birds, and since they appear to remain active throughout the winter deep in the gorse, they are probably the factor which enables the Dartford warbler to survive the winter in a habitat otherwise poor in food resources. The paucity of food resources on the heathlands not only for insectivorous birds, but also for seed eating species, is reflected in the virtual absence of large flocks of finches, starlings (*Sternus vulgaris*) and most other passerine birds during the winter: a sharp contrast with nearby agricultural land. Practically the only species of birds which occur in large flocks over much of the Forest in the winter months are thrushes. The numerous berry-bearing trees and shrubs—holly, rowan and yew for example—attract large flocks of redwing (*Turdus iliacus*) and fieldfare (*Turdus pilaris*), and even in a poor berry year large roosts of these species are often established in the Forest, the birds coming in at dusk from feeding areas outside.

Despite their characteristic species-paucity, the open heaths are highly important because the fauna they do support is now becoming increasingly more restricted in its distribution as heathland elsewhere becomes reduced and fragmented in area; because they form an integral part of a whole matrix of associated habitats; and because they are sufficiently extensive to form a valuable 'buffer zone' of undeveloped land around the more species-rich habitats, so that the latter tend to be shielded from the effects of overmuch disturbance which would arise where the heaths developed for residential, industrial or agricultural purposes.

III

It is doubtful whether any area of comparable size in the Lowland zone and indeed in much of Upland Britain, has retained a total population of predatory birds comparable to that of the New Forest. It is most likely that this feature has in the long term been due to the umbrella of protection afforded by deer preservation, which did not involve the destruction of predators of this kind; and to the absence of more conventional game-preservation, which certainly did. Moore, for example, showed that the distribution history of the buzzard in Britain since the beginning of the nineteenth century closely mirrored changes in interest in game preservation, and for 1954 demonstrated a close correlation between the main game rearing areas and the absence of buzzards.[11]

Recent declines in other species of avian predators—for example the sparrowhawk, which has now disappeared from much of eastern England—have been correlated in space and time with the agricultural use of toxic chemicals as pesticides. It has been established that predators are subject to contamination through their prey and for some species—including the sparrowhawk—residues have been found in eggs and adult birds in comparatively high concentrations. Recent analyses of the eggs of sparrowhawks, buzzards and kestrels (*Falco tinnunculus*) from the New Forest, however, have revealed only small amounts of organo-chlorine pesticide residues and it is considered unlikely that locally this factor is significant at the present time.[12]

Apart from the Crown lands themselves, where the use of toxic chemicals is practically unknown, the peripheral and intermixed smallholdings are devoted predominantly to livestock husbandry. The average smallholding has little or no arable land and toxic chemicals are thus comparatively little used as seed dressings. The other major source of organo-chlorines in the environment—through its use in sheep dips in the form of dieldrin—is not involved, since the area is not sheep country.

Five species of predatory bird—buzzard, sparrowhawk, kestrel, hobby and tawny owl (*Strix aluco*)—breed in large numbers in the Forest, whilst there is a scattered population of barn owls (*Tyto alba*), associated mainly with the agricultural land. One species—Montagu's harrier—has probably now ceased to breed regularly. In addition, the Forest provides a regular wintering ground for several hen harriers (*Circus cyaneus*) and two or three peregrines (*Falco peregrinus*) and merlins (*Falco columbarius*), whilst since 1959, as elsewhere in southern England, red-footed falcons (*Falco vespertinus*) have become of almost regular occurrence during May and June, usually during or immediately following a period of south-easterly winds.

Table VII gives populations of four of the five commoner species during the period 1962 to 1966, for a study area of 112·5 square miles which included most of the land within the perambulation and embraced also some areas of agricultural land bordering the Forest.[13] For sparrowhawk, hobby and kestrel, the number of pairs actually recorded certainly fell short of the true total population, since it was never possible to examine the whole area for these species in any one year. The population figures for the buzzard represent the true population, although it is always possible that the odd pair was missed. The fifth species, the tawny owl, is very numerous throughout the Forest woodlands, and although no population data are available, it may well outnumber the populations of the other four species added together. Probable total populations are given as estimates in the last column.

At the beginning of the nineteenth century the buzzard was widespread throughout Britain. By the end of the century, persecution had restricted it to west and central Scotland, north-west England, Wales, the south-west peninsula and one isolated outlier—the New Forest.[11] Although the species has since regained much of its lost ground, it has not recolonised much of central and south-east England and the New Forest population remains more or less isolated. Although few actual figures are available for comparison, the population here seems to have remained at much its present level since at least the 1920s. Salient features emerging from a study of the Forest population between 1962 and 1966 were the small size of clutches laid (an average of less than two eggs) and the low output of young (see table VII). Many clutches failed to hatch and others were found broken in the nest. This situation is reminiscent of events after 1954 when myxomatosis decimated the rabbit, the staple diet of the buzzard over much of its range, and equally, has more recently been associated elsewhere in this and other birds of prey with high levels of organo-chlorine contamination. Ten addled eggs analysed for organo-chlorine residues, however revealed amounts too small to permit any correlation between

226

breeding success and contamination from pesticides. Nor was there any evidence from the study to suggest a paucity of food. Prey remains recorded from nests suggested that the bulk of the diet was made up of medium sized animals such as jackdaws (*Corvus minedula*) and jays (*Garrulus glandarius*), small rabbits and other rodents, and the wide variety of other prey recorded (twenty-five different species of animal and bird) demonstrates the buzzard's great versatility as a predator.

TABLE VII

Breeding populations of birds of prey in the New Forest 1962–1966

Year	Minimum no pairs present	Breeding proved*	Number young reared	Estimated true population
Buzzard, *Buteo buteo*				
1962	30	14	18	
1963	34	16	22	
1964	33	16	13	
1965	33	20	25	
1966	33	16	24	
Sparrowhawk, *Accipiter nisus*				
1962	18	11	27	Probably lying
1963	21	8	22	between 30 & 40
1964	21	14	42	pairs annually
1965	14	8	not known	during study
1966	26	13	27 + †	period.
Hobby, *Falco subbuteo*				
1962	16	5	11	Probably some-
1963	14	4	9	times as high as 20
1964	18	—	—	pairs in study area.
Kestrel, *Falco tinnunculus*				
1962	14	2	5	Probably 17-20
1963	15	3	8	pairs annually
1964	12	2	6	during study
1965	13	4	10	period.

* Figures in this column refer both to successful and attempted breeding, proof of breeding being taken as the laying and incubation of eggs.
† Final visits to most nests were not made until after many of the young had dispersed from them and this figure is therefore minimal.

Information about the breeding population of sparrowhawks is less complete than for the buzzard. Limited time precluded a complete examination of all suitable areas in any one year and in fact the figures in table VII represent little more than random checks on suitable localities. It is possible that the highest recorded population of twenty-six pairs in 1966 was as little as half the true number of breeding pairs. This implies a very large population indeed. With the marked decrease in sparrowhawks, especially in eastern England, in the past decade areas such as the Forest may prove of great importance as sources from which ultimate recolonisation may take place.

The average sparrowhawk brood is large compared with most other birds of prey and since the species seems under normal circumstances to be fairly long lived, there must be a considerable dispersal of young birds away from the Forest—the 'replacement factor' of something of the order of one-third again as many young birds as the adult population can hardly be absorbed by the Forest. Analyses of addled eggs from New Forest nests suggest comparatively low levels of organo-chlorine contamination and this is further borne out by the low incidence of infertility and the normality of brood sizes. During the 1962–66 period only one complete clutch laid failed to hatch.

J. F. Parslow has estimated that in recent years the breeding population of the hobby in this country has probably totalled between seventy-five and 100 pairs. In a breakdown of the known population of about eighty-four pairs during 1962–4, he showed that seventy-four were concentrated in Hampshire, Sussex, Surrey, Wiltshire, Dorset and Berkshire. Of these, twenty-five pairs were in Hampshire (including the New Forest).[14] The Forest population, which may sometimes be as high as twenty pairs, therefore, carries a substantial proportion of the total breeding stock. There is certainly no other area of comparable size whose population approaches that of the Forest—and this despite the still frequent outbreaks of egg collecting. Two factors are probably of major significance here: first, the long term protection that the species has received; and second, the abundance of large flying insects, which form the bulk of the species' prey.

The kestrel, like the sparrowhawk, has suffered a wide-spread decline in recent years, particularly in the southern and eastern counties, although there are now indications that numbers are picking up again in many areas. As with the hobby, little more was attempted in the New Forest during the 1962–66 study period than a check on the presence or absence of pairs in as many previously occupied territories as it was possible to examine in the limited time available. Data from the few nests which were found do not suggest any abnormality in either clutch size or fledgling success and analysis of four addled eggs taken from a clutch of five (the fifth egg hatched and the fledgling was reared successfully) in 1965 revealed organo-chlorine residues of only low toxicity.

The only predatory bird which may recently have been lost to the Forest as a breeding species is the Montagu's harrier. Until the early 1950s pairs bred in a number of localities, but since that time there has been a general decline and in 1966 and 1967 it was uncertain whether any bred at all. By 1954 only two of the former breeding areas were occupied. In 1956 there was an increase in the total number of breeding pairs from two to five, but this was a temporary improvement. In the following year only two pairs were again present and at least one of these failed to rear young. In 1958 only a single pair were known to breed and since then successful breeding has become progressively more intermittent. The story follows a national trend, the causes of which, though probably associated partly with excessive disturbance, and loss of habitat, are generally obscure.

References

1 N. W. Moore, 'The heaths of Dorset and their conservation', *J. Ecol*, 50, 1962, pp 369-91.
2 Where no other reference is given for the sources of population data, etc, in this chapter, the information is derived from the writer's own notes.
3 The present account is taken mainly from:
C. R. Tubbs, 'The significance of the New Forest to the status of the Dartford Warbler in England', *Brit Birds*, 56, 1963, pp 41-8.
C. R. Tubbs, 'Numbers of Dartford Warblers in England during 1962–66', *Brit Birds*, 60, 1967, pp 87-9.
4 J. D. Magee, 'The breeding distribution of the stonechat in Britain and the causes of its decline', *Bird Study*, 12, 1965, pp 83-9.
5 J. F. Parslow, 'Changes in status among breeding birds in Britain, and Ireland', *Brit Birds*, 60, 1967, pp 268-71.
6 M. Peakall, 'The past and present status of the Red Backed Shrike in Britain', *Bird Study*, 9, 1962, pp 198-216.
7 J. S. Ash, *in litt*.
8 J. F. Parslow, *loc cit*, pp 261-3.
9 J. F. Parslow, *loc cit*, pp 114-6.
10 M. Blackmore, *in litt*.
11 N. W. Moore, 'The past and present status of the Buzzard in the British Isles', *Brit Birds*, 50, 1957, pp 173-97.

12 Analyses of Forest Buzzard eggs are given in:
C. R. Tubbs, 'Population study of Buzzards in the New Forest during 1962–66', *Brit Birds*, 60, 1967, pp 381-93.
Analyses of sparrowhawk and kestrel eggs were unpublished at the time of writing. They were carried out by the Laboratory of the Government Chemist by arrangement with the Nature Conservancy.

13 The data on buzzard populations in this chapter is from:
C. R. Tubbs, *loc cit*. That for the remaining predators is derived from unpublished surveys by the writer and others.

14 J. F. Parslow, *loc cit*, pp 42-43.

THIRTEEN

The Future

THE ecological structure of the New Forest has from the earliest times been moulded, consciously or unconsciously, by man. In the Royal Forest his activities became focused mainly on pastoral and silvicultural land uses, competing together and together competing with the increasingly archaic but formally adhered to purpose of deer conservation, a purpose not finally discarded until the New Forest Deer Removal Act of 1851. The ecological characteristics of the Forest are directly related to its history of common grazing, silvicultural management and deer conservation. To the biologist, the Forest assumes special importance because the habitats of which it is comprised are now comparatively rare elsewhere in this country. Furthermore, the embargo on drastic change in land use, originally imposed by the Forest Law and perpetuated in more recent legislation, offers the area a future prospect of relative ecological stability.

The traditional conflict of interests between Crown and commoners has largely been resolved in the past century. The succession of enactments since 1877 have sought to achieve a reasonable balance among the uses and activities taking place and have provided the necessary administrative machinery for implementation. These enactments are, in effect, a multiple use plan which is implemented jointly by the Forestry Commission and the Verderers. Each successive Act has brought the management of the Forest into line with changing social and economic conditions.

What has evolved, then, is an ecosystem in which the controlling uses are mainly indigenous and interrelated and operate within the framework of a mutually acceptable and flexible plan. What of the future? In the absence of strong external pressure there is no reason to suppose that the balance of interests would change in the foreseeable future. The increasing popularity of the Forest as a recreation and tourist area, however, imposes just such a pressure.

Public access over the unenclosed Forest has traditionally been unrestricted and its scenic value was recognised and appreciated by tourists a hundred years ago. The real build up of pressure, however, has accompanied increasing motor car ownership in the past two decades. The Forest is readily accessible to large urban populations and is itself laced with minor access routes, both classified roads and Forest tracks.

To the west of the Forest lies the urban zone of Bournemouth, Christchurch and Lymington, with a population in excess of a quarter of a million; to the east lies Southampton and Portsmouth, with a population of around three-quarters of a million. Immediately adjacent to the Forest, on the west (and Forest) side of Southampton Water is an expanding industrial area dominated by the Fawley petrochemical industry and two electricity generating stations. The population of all these residential and industrial areas is increasing, not only from an excess of births over deaths, but from migration from elsewhere for employment or retirement. *The South East Study Report*[1] in 1964 postulated a population increase in the order of three and a half million in south-east England by 1981 and envisaged that a significant proportion of this could be absorbed by the Southampton—Portsmouth area. In 1966, the *South Hampshire Study*[2] suggested that the area might see an increase in population of half a million by the end of the century. It thus seems probable that within two or three decades the Forest will be within a short drive of one of the largest conurbations in Britain. Its role can readily be envisaged as that of a recreational 'lung': a role which must be accepted but carefully controlled if the indigenous interests are not to suffer and the ecological structure of the Forest not to sustain irreparable damage.

The nearby urban areas are today generating considerable demands on the Forest for recreation. At the same time the Forest has achieved a national appeal as a tourist area. It offers ideal settings not only for the day visitor, but for the holidaying camper and caravanner who, for a 7s 6d per night camping permit from the Forestry Commission, may choose his site at will from a large tract of unenclosed countryside. Field sports apart, the nature of recreational demands may be enumerated more specifically as follows:

(a) Day visiting, eg for picnicking or walking.
(b) Camping and caravanning.

(c) 'Formal recreation': there are three golf courses and seventeen cricket and football pitches on the open Forest.

(d) 'Mechanical recreation': this term has been coined to cover motor cycle scrambling and the flying of radio-controlled model aircraft. One motor cycle scramble per annum is allowed by the Forestry Commission and the flying of model aircraft is confined to one site, the wartime airfield on Hatchet Moor.

Although there are intermittent pressures for further golf courses and for further facilities for 'mechanical recreation', it is the phenomenol increase in the use of the Forest by day visitors, campers and caravanners which poses the most difficult problems of management. Fgures kept by the Forestry Commission for the number of permits issued for overnight stays on the Forest provide a useful index of recreational demand. These rose from 83,000 in 1956 to more than 300,000 in 1967. In 1965, weekend surveys carried out by Colin Buchanan & Partners, as part of their South Hampshire Study, gave a total of 58,005 people (including 3,637 who stayed overnight in tents and caravans) visiting the Forest on 29 August. Forward projections suggested that by the year 2000 the Forest might be receiving about 268,000 visitors in one day at the height of the season. The number of campers and caravanners might be as high as 35,000.

The effects of large scale recreational use on the environment are difficult to quantify. Qualitatively, however, they are manifest in the widespread wear and tear of the vegetation fabric of the Forest; the proliferation of vehicle tracks year by year; the occurrence of accidental (and sometimes malicious) fires; an endless variety of acts of vandalism; disturbance to stock and the sterilisation of many of the better grasslands, which are also prone to provide the maximum attraction to visitors; and the deposition of large quantities of litter, despite the widespread distribution of litter bins and the efficient litter collection service run by the Forestry Commission.

Many of the problems which arise can, and have, been alleviated by management. Others—and particularly the damage sustained by the vegetation by motor vehicles—pose more difficult and fundamental problems. Clearly the Forest has a role to fulfil in serving the recreational needs both of local populations and visitors from a distance. At the same time, if the environment is to remain of the high quality which forms much of its attraction as a recreational area, and if the uses which have shaped it are not to become inhibited, then recreational activities need to be brought under much closer control.

Without control, the Forest as we know it today must certainly be destroyed. Control basically means control over vehicular access —tolerated over most of the open Forest though not a right—since, as Colin Buchanan & Partners' survey showed, few people venture where they cannot take a vehicle. With the co-operation of the various local organisations the Forestry Commission has already restricted vehicular access over certain areas of the open Forest, on a more or less experimental basis, but the time has clearly arrived when a comprehensive long term plan is needed both for the control of recreational use and—its corollary—the provision of necessary facilities (toilets, car parks, water standpipes) at selected places. The need for a new evaluation of the contribution the Forest can, and must, make to the national life is widely recognised among the bodies with direct interests in the area—Forestry Commission, Verderers, commoners, Nature Conservancy and Local Authorities—and at the time of writing various studies of recreational use, access, recreational capacity and demand and effects on other user interests, have commenced. These, it is hoped, will form the factual framework within which effective, practical long term management policies may be implemented.

Recreation apart, there are other consequences which may ultimately arise for the Forest from the expansion of the South Hampshire population. The physical development of land in the Forest itself is likely in the foreseeable future to be confined to residential infilling of villages. The increasing popularity of commuting between the Forest and places of work in nearby towns, and the steady trickle of retired people into the area, however, may well result in significant social and ecological change. The conversion of agricultural holdings to residential purposes is no recent feature, but the pace has quickened in recent years. A frequent feature of such conversion is the subsequent failure to exercise the rights of common which attach to the property and in the long term this trend may culminate in the gradual decay of the common rights. The ecological consequences are likely to be the succession of much of the open ground to scrub and the more successful regeneration and expansion of the woodlands. The control of scrub and the maintenance of the open heaths may to some extent be achieved by controlling burning, but the generally more vigorous regeneration

of the vegetation should the commoners' animals be severely reduced in numbers will be inevitable and will not generally be
acceptable from the amenity standpoint. A further consequence of
the decay of common rights and with them the commoners organisations, would be a weakening in the influence and finances of the
Verderers, one of whose functions is the management of matters
relating to rights of common, but who also have a large stake in
the conservation of the Forest environment and its rich fauna and
flora.

A further consequence of industrial and urban growth may be
increased pressure for the exploitation of gravel and sand in the
Forest. The increase in demand for gravel has been phenomenal
throughout the country in the past two decades. *The Report of the
Advisory Committee on Sand and Gravel*, 1950, which advised the
Minister of Housing & Local Government on sand and gravel
resources, estimated that the annual demand for gravel and sand
from land workings within the New Forest Service Area over the
next fifty years would be about 520,000 cu yds. In fact, the annual
average production over the period 1959–63 rose to approximately
twice that quantity and the strain on available resources is considerable. In the not too distant future the possibilities of exploiting
the plateau gravels on the Crown lands of the Forest may be given
consideration. At the present time, it seems doubtful whether the
Forestry Commission would be in a position to condone large scale
exploitation and it is certain that any proposal to do so would
arouse considerable local opposition on grounds of loss to amenity
and the commoners' grazings. It is equally likely, however, that
opposition would ultimately crumble before repeatedly reiterated
economic argument. Already some limited exploitation of the
gravels on some of the manorial wastes within the Forest has taken
place or is in progress, and further extraction is contemplated.

The unique character of the New Forest is the result of gradual
ecological development. Today the Forest faces the possibility of
rapid and radical change, both in its functions and its ecological
structure. Clearly it must be adapted to the new demands made
upon it, and as a first step in planning it must be firmly decided
whether adaptation is or is not to be at the expense of its essential
ecological features. If the answer is that these should be conserved,
then its capacity to absorb new demands must be seen in the light
of an understanding of its past development and present ecology.

The Future

It may well be that economic loss and some restriction on the degree to which new demands can be satisfied will have to be accepted if it is to retain its peculiar character. One thing is certain. It cannot be all things to all men for all time.

References

1 Ministry of Housing and Local Government, *The South East Study, 1961–1981*, London, HMSO, 1964.
2 Colin Buchanan & Partners, *South Hampshire Study. Report on the Feasibility of Major Urban Growth*, London, HMSO, 1966

Acknowledgments

A great many people have contributed in one way or another to this book—by providing factual information or allowing me access to documents and maps, through discussion, and through collaboration in fieldwork and research. I should like in particular to acknowledge my debt to Professor G. W. Dimbleby, Dr E. L. Jones, W. J. Kennedy, J. H. Lavender, J. H. Pallister, A. H. Pasmore, Dr G. F. Peterken, and W. C. Woodhouse. Much of the research upon which chapters 2, 3 and 7 are based was the outcome of collaboration with Geoffrey Dimbleby, George Peterken and Eric Jones. I am further and deeply indebted to the last named for our innumerable and lengthy discussions and for his continuous encouragement in the preparation of this book.

I should also like especially to record my gratitude to W. A. Cadman, who as Deputy Surveyor of the New Forest always so readily made available facilities for research and allowed me to use manuscript material in the possession of the Forestry Commission at Lyndhurst. My thanks go also to the Verderers of the New Forest and their Clerk, who allowed me access to various of their records; Brian Rozzell, who spent much time and trouble in taking the photographs; and Blackwell Scientific Publications for permission to reprint Figures 3 and 4.

Finally I wish to record the encouragement, help and tolerance of my wife, not least in preparing the manuscript and index for publication.

C.R.T.

November 1968
Lyndhurst

Index

Illustrations are indicated by Italic type

Index